AMERICA'S
TEST KITCHEN

"The sum total of exhaustive experimentation . . . anyone interested in gluten-free cookery simply shouldn't be without it."
NIGELLA LAWSON ON *THE HOW CAN IT BE GLUTEN-FREE COOKBOOK*

"This book is a comprehensive, no-nonsense guide . . . a well-thought-out, clearly explained primer for every aspect of home baking."
THE WALL STREET JOURNAL ON *THE COOK'S ILLUSTRATED BAKING BOOK*

"An exceptional resource for novice canners, though preserving veterans will find plenty here to love as well."
LIBRARY JOURNAL (STARRED REVIEW) ON *FOOLPROOF PRESERVING*

"A terrifically accessible and useful guide to grilling in all its forms that sets a new bar for its competitors on the bookshelf. . . . The book is packed with practical advice, simple tips, and approachable recipes."
PUBLISHERS WEEKLY (STARRED REVIEW) ON *MASTER OF THE GRILL*

"The 21st-century *Fannie Farmer Cookbook* or *The Joy of Cooking.* If you had to have one cookbook and that's all you could have, this one would do it."
CBS SAN FRANCISCO ON *THE NEW FAMILY COOKBOOK*

"This book upgrades slow cooking for discriminating, 21st-century palates—that is indeed revolutionary."
THE DALLAS MORNING NEWS ON *SLOW COOKER REVOLUTION*

"The go-to gift book for newlyweds, small families, or empty nesters."
ORLANDO SENTINEL ON *THE COMPLETE COOKING FOR TWO COOKBOOK*

"Some 2,500 photos walk readers through 600 pains-takingly tested recipes, leaving little room for error."
ASSOCIATED PRESS ON *THE AMERICA'S TEST KITCHEN COOKING SCHOOL COOKBOOK*

"A one-volume kitchen seminar, addressing in one smart chapter after another the sometimes surprising whys behind a cook's best practices. . . . You get the myth, the theory, the science, and the proof, all rigorously interrogated as only America's Test Kitchen can do."
NPR ON *THE SCIENCE OF GOOD COOKING*

"Carnivores with an obsession for perfection will likely have found their new bible in this comprehensive collection."
PUBLISHERS WEEKLY (STARRED REVIEW) ON *THE COOK'S ILLUSTRATED MEAT BOOK*

"This encyclopedia of meat cookery would feel completely overwhelming if it weren't so meticu-lously organized and artfully designed. This is *Cook's Illustrated* at its finest."
THE KITCHN ON *THE COOK'S ILLUSTRATED MEAT BOOK*

"Buy this gem for the foodie in your family, and spend the extra money to get yourself a copy too."
THE MISSOURIAN ON *THE BEST OF AMERICA'S TEST KITCHEN 2015*

"The perfect kitchen home companion. . . . The practical side of things is very much on display . . . cook-friendly and kitchen-oriented, illuminating the process of preparing food instead of mystifying it."
THE WALL STREET JOURNAL ON *THE COOK'S ILLUSTRATED COOKBOOK*

"There are pasta books . . . and then there's this pasta book. Flip your carbohydrate dreams upside down and strain them through this sieve of revolutionary, creative, and also traditional recipes."
SAN FRANCISCO BOOK REVIEW ON *PASTA REVOLUTION*

"Further proof that practice makes perfect, if not transcendent. . . . If an intermediate cook follows the directions exactly, the results will be better than takeout or Mom's."
THE NEW YORK TIMES ON *THE NEW BEST RECIPE*

Naturally Sweet

BAKE ALL YOUR FAVORITES WITH 30% TO 50% LESS SUGAR

BY THE EDITORS AT AMERICA'S TEST KITCHEN

Library of Congress Cataloging-in-Publication Data

Names: America's Test Kitchen (Firm).
Title: Naturally sweet : bake all your favorites with
30% to 50% less sugar /
   by the editors at America's Test Kitchen.
Description: Brookline, MA : America's Test
Kitchen, [2016] | Includes index.
Identifiers: LCCN 2016009055 | ISBN
9781940352589
Subjects: LCSH: Desserts. | Baking. | Sugar-free
diet. | LCGFT: Cookbooks.
Classification: LCC TX773 .N34 2016 | DDC
641.86--dc23
LC record available at https://lccn.loc.
gov/2016009055

AMERICA'S TEST KITCHEN
17 Station Street, Brookline, MA 02445

Manufactured in Canada
10 9 8 7 6 5 4 3 2 1

Distributed by Penguin Random House Publisher
Services
Tel: 800–733–3000

Pictured on front cover: Chocolate Layer Cake
(page 124)
Pictured on back cover: Striped Fruit Popsicles
(page 286), Chocolate Chip Cookies (page 76), Blueberry Cheesecake (page 170), Honey Buns (page 66),
Dark Chocolate Pudding (page 258), Fresh Fruit
Tart with Mascarpone and Honey (page 203)

CHIEF CREATIVE OFFICER: Jack Bishop

EDITORIAL DIRECTOR, BOOKS: Elizabeth Carduff

EXECUTIVE EDITOR: Julia Collin Davison

SENIOR EDITORS: Stephanie Pixley and Sara Mayer

ASSOCIATE EDITORS: Leah Colins, Melissa Herrick, Lawman
Johnson, Nicole Konstantinakos, and Russell Selander

TEST COOKS: Tim Chin and Afton Cyrus

EDITORIAL ASSISTANT: Alyssa Langer

DESIGN DIRECTOR: Greg Galvan

ART DIRECTOR: Carole Goodman

ASSOCIATE ART DIRECTOR: Allison Boales

PHOTOGRAPHY DIRECTOR: Julie Cote

SENIOR STAFF PHOTOGRAPHER: Daniel J. van Ackere

STAFF PHOTOGRAPHER: Steve Klise

ASSISTANT PHOTOGRAPHY PRODUCER: Mary Ball

PHOTOGRAPHY: Keller + Keller and Carl Tremblay

FOOD STYLING: Catrine Kelty, Marie Piraino, and Sally Staub

PHOTOSHOOT KITCHEN TEAM:

   SENIOR EDITOR: Chris O'Connor

   TEST COOKS: Daniel Cellucci and Matthew Fairman

   ASSISTANT TEST COOK: Allison Berkey

CHAPTER OPENER NUMBERING: Sophie Greenspan

ILLUSTRATIONS: Jay Layman

PRODUCTION DIRECTOR: Guy Rochford

SENIOR PRODUCTION MANAGER: Jessica Lindheimer Quirk

PRODUCTION MANAGER: Christine Walsh

IMAGING MANAGER: Lauren Robbins

PRODUCTION AND IMAGING SPECIALISTS: Heather Dube,
Sean MacDonald, Dennis Noble, and Jessica Voas

PROJECT MANAGER: Britt Dresser

COPY EDITOR: Cheryl Redmond

PROOFREADER: Elizabeth Wray Emery

INDEXER: Elizabeth Parson

contents

WELCOME TO AMERICA'S TEST KITCHEN

This book has been tested, written, and edited by the folks at America's Test Kitchen, a very real 2,500-square-foot kitchen located just outside of Boston. It is the home of *Cook's Illustrated* magazine and *Cook's Country* magazine and is the Monday-through-Friday destination for more than 60 test cooks, editors, and cookware specialists. Our mission is to test recipes over and over again until we understand how and why they work and until we arrive at the "best" version.

We start the process of testing a recipe with a complete lack of preconceptions, which means that we accept no claim, no technique, and no recipe at face value. We simply assemble as many variations as possible, test a half-dozen of the most promising, and taste the results blind. We then construct our own recipe and continue to test it, varying ingredients, techniques, and cooking times until we reach a consensus. As we like to say in the test kitchen, "We make the mistakes so you don't have to." The result, we hope, is the best version of a particular recipe, but we realize that only you can be the final judge of our success (or failure). We use the same rigorous approach when we test equipment and taste ingredients.

All of this would not be possible without a belief that good cooking, much like good music, is based on a foundation of objective technique. Some people like spicy foods and others don't, but there is a right way to sauté, there is a best way to cook a pot roast, and there are measurable scientific principles involved in producing perfectly beaten, stable egg whites. Our ultimate goal is to investigate the fundamental principles of cooking to give you the techniques, tools, and ingredients you need to become a better cook. It is as simple as that.

To see what goes on behind the scenes at America's Test Kitchen, check out our social media channels for kitchen snapshots, exclusive content, video tips, and much more. You can watch us work (in our actual test kitchen) by tuning in to *America's Test Kitchen* or *Cook's Country from America's Test Kitchen* on public television or on our websites. Listen in to *America's Test Kitchen Radio* (ATKradio.com) on public radio to hear insights that illuminate the truth about real home cooking. Want to hone your cooking skills or finally learn how to bake—with an America's Test Kitchen test cook? Enroll in one of our online cooking classes. If the big questions about the hows and whys of food science are your passion, join our Cook's Science experts for a deep dive. However you choose to visit us, we welcome you into our kitchen, where you can stand by our side as we test our way to the best recipes in America.

facebook.com/AmericasTestKitchen
twitter.com/TestKitchen
youtube.com/AmericasTestKitchen
instagram.com/TestKitchen
pinterest.com/TestKitchen
google.com/+AmericasTestKitchen

AmericasTestKitchen.com
CooksIllustrated.com
CooksCountry.com
CooksScience.com
OnlineCookingSchool.com

INTRODUCTION

We decided to publish a book on baking with less sugar long before the new dietary guidelines were released by the U.S. Department of Agriculture (USDA) in January 2016. To anyone looking closely, it has been clear for some time that increased sugar consumption is fueling the obesity crisis and other public health issues in this country. In fact, the USDA's new dietary guidelines recommend that most Americans cut their sugar intake by almost half—from an average of about 22 teaspoons a day to a mere 12 teaspoons. With 4 grams of sugar in a teaspoon, that comes to about 48 grams of sugar a day. That may sound like a lot, but the problem goes beyond the sugar we purposely add to homemade baked goods or pour into our morning coffee. There is an incredible amount of hidden sugar in processed foods, from sandwich bread and yogurt to fruit juice and soda. When you consider that your ordinary breakfast muffin may pack around 30 grams of sugar, a glass of orange juice around 20 grams, and a cup of low-fat vanilla yogurt 7 to 10 grams, it's clear that sticking to these guidelines isn't always easy (or obvious); many of us probably surpass the new recommendations before breakfast is even over.

We saw the growing emphasis on reducing sugar consumption as an opportunity to rethink how we prepare our favorite baked goods. Yes, eating fewer baked goods is one way to reduce sugar consumption. But what's a birthday without cake or Thanksgiving without a pie? Moderation is the key to any dietary change and we think the recipes in this book balance great taste (which is, after all, why we eat baked goods) with improved nutrition.

LOW SUGAR MEETS NATURALLY SWEET

Our reader surveys demonstrated that home bakers want to learn how to use less-refined sweeteners like honey, maple syrup, coconut sugar, and Sucanat (an unrefined cane sugar) in their favorite recipes. We take our readers' requests seriously, so we set our sights on developing recipes that not only contain 30 to 50 percent less sugar than their traditional counterparts but also rely on less-processed sweeteners. (Since some bakers might be interested in cutting sweetener usage while sticking with familiar granulated sugar, we also provided information on using white sugar in recipes where this made sense.) While those who have diabetes might appreciate that our recipes contain far less sugar than their traditional counterparts, the sweeteners we are using are not necessarily low on the glycemic index. Rather, the recipes in this book are for an increasingly sugar-wary general public—anyone who is looking to decrease the amount of sugar they're eating without having to give up their favorite baked goods and desserts.

Of course, you can't simply take some of the sugar out of a baking recipe and expect to get decent results (see "The Science of Sugar," page 8). Texture suffers hugely, as does flavor. Add to that the issues inherent in using alternative sweeteners (like different melting points, moisture contents, or absorption capabilities), and we had a sizeable challenge on our hands. But after months of rigorous testing, during which we broke many of the classic rules of baking, we were confident that we had met the challenge head-on: We had created over 100 great-tasting recipes that contained far less sugar than their traditional counterparts and relied on more-flavorful, less-processed sweeteners.

DEFINING NATURAL SWEETENERS

The number of alternative sweeteners available today is staggering—and the landscape just keeps getting more confusing. Sorting through the labeling and the hype helped us refine our goals so we could choose which sweeteners would have a place in our recipes. We sought out sweeteners that were obviously less processed (and, therefore, more natural) than white cane sugar and that would work well in baking; we also wanted to avoid those that were hard to find, manufactured inconsistently across brands, or were nearly as processed as white cane sugar despite marketing claims to the contrary. And we didn't want to go near artificially produced sweeteners like sucralose (Splenda) and aspartame (Equal)—not only are these far from natural, but in all of our past testing, these sweeteners consistently produced baked goods with strange, off-textures and unpleasant flavors. In addition to the granulated and liquid sweeteners we chose, we also wanted to develop recipes using fruit or fruit purees as the main sweetener, with no added sugar of any sort, as well as recipes using chocolate.

While we love the flavor that less processed alternative sweeteners can provide, we knew that some people would simply like to use the granulated sugar they have on hand instead. To that end, we decided to offer regular granulated sugar as a substitution option for the two other dry sugars used in the book: Sucanat and coconut sugar. These three sugars don't behave exactly the same, but they are similar enough to act as effective substitutes for each other. You'll find substitution information as well as notes on flavor and texture differences in the "Sweetener Substitution" boxes, so you can tailor the recipes to your own preferences.

In the pages that follow, you will find highlights of our recipe testing and plentiful information on alternative sweeteners and the best ways to use them. Detailed nutritional information for every recipe is located in the back of the book, and on every recipe page you will see, front and center, the before and after numbers for grams of sugar. The differences are dramatic, but we're confident that even with substantially less sugar, these recipes will more than satisfy your sweet tooth.

HOW SUGAR IS PROCESSED

When choosing which sweeteners to use in this book, we made it our goal to use those that were less processed and more natural than white sugar. But what does that mean exactly? The diagram at right will help you understand how regular white sugar is processed; although it begins as a plant, it requires heavy-duty mechanical and chemical processing. Sweeteners like Sucanat and coconut sugar, on the other hand, require far fewer steps and no chemicals to get from plant to package. The diagrams below illustrate the relatively minimal processing of Sucanat and coconut sugar.

HOW SUCANAT IS MADE

Juice Extraction

Cane Harvested

Straining

Boiling

Paddling

Sucanat

HOW COCONUT SUGAR IS MADE

Flowers Cut

Sap Drained

Filtering

Boiling

Paddling

Coconut Sugar

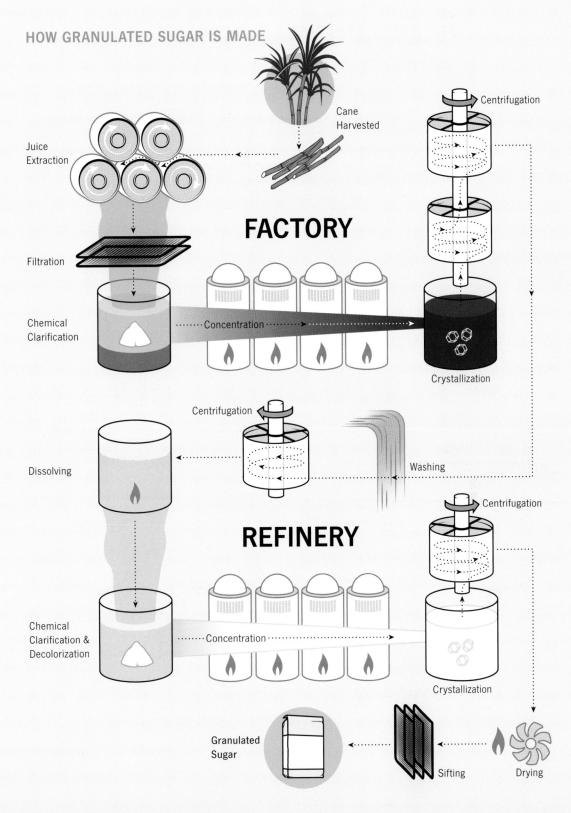

HOW GRANULATED SUGAR IS MADE

Cane Harvested

FACTORY

Juice Extraction

Filtration

Chemical Clarification

Concentration

Crystallization

Centrifugation

REFINERY

Centrifugation

Dissolving

Washing

Chemical Clarification & Decolorization

Concentration

Crystallization

Centrifugation

Granulated Sugar

Sifting

Drying

CHOOSING ALTERNATIVE SWEETENERS

Before we started developing recipes, we headed into the kitchen to test some basic recipes (muffins, cookies, yellow cake) using an array of alternative sweeteners. This helped us learn more about how they worked in baking applications and what their flavors were like. (We ruled out some sweeteners even before this testing because they were clearly artificial or hard to find.) Here is a rundown of the sweeteners we ruled out and the ones we chose to use (and why). For more information about the sweeteners we use in this book, see pages 18–21.

WHAT'S OUT

While this is not an exhaustive list, these are some of the sweeteners that we chose not to use and the reasons why. We did not include obviously artificial sweeteners such as aspartame on this list, since they don't fit the natural profile we were going for.

SWEETENER	WHAT IT IS	WHY WE RULED IT OUT
Turbinado, Demerara, and Muscovado	Historically, these are partially refined cane sugars that still retain some of their natural molasses. Today, they might be partially refined or they may be fully refined sugars with some molasses added back to them.	To create more consistent products, some manufacturers fully refine cane sugar and then add molasses back in, resulting in products that look and taste like traditional versions—but don't meet our standards of being less processed. Because there's no way for consumers to tell the difference, we ruled them out.
Rapadura	Depending on where it's produced and sold, rapadura is also known as panela, piloncillo, papelon, jaggery, gur, evaporated or dehydrated cane juice, whole cane sugar, and other names. It's made by extracting cane juice and drying it in molds, or beating the juice to create a granular sweetener.	With its many names, many forms, and inconsistent flavor profiles, we knew that it would be difficult to develop reliable recipes using this sweetener—and for readers to shop for it. We decided instead to use Sucanat, which is similarly processed and, because it is a brand name, is a more consistent product.
Stevia	This granulated sweetener is made from the stevia plant.	Although it's often touted as "natural," stevia is just as processed as regular sugar. Plus, it's intensely sweet on its own, so it's usually packed with bulking agents (like highly processed erythritol).
Barley Malt	Malted barley is mashed to extract liquid, which is then evaporated into a thick syrup.	We're not fond of the distinct, malty flavor of this sweetener in baked goods.
Brown Rice Syrup	This thick syrup is made by adding enzymes to rice starch and then evaporating the liquid.	The syrup's mild flavor didn't do much for baked goods.
Agave Nectar	Agave nectar is extracted from the heart of the agave plant and then filtered and heated.	Although agave nectar is minimally processed, it is not particularly flavorful—especially when we pitted it against other liquid sweeteners like honey and maple syrup.

WHAT'S IN

After many rounds of testing, we narrowed down our sweetener choices to those listed below, which won tasters over with their standout flavors and versatility. Each one has different advantages, which we took into account when using them in recipes.

SUCANAT

What it is Our go-to sweetener for many of the recipes in this book, Sucanat is an abbreviation for *sucre de canne naturel*, meaning "natural sugar cane." This unrefined cane sugar is made by beating cane juice with paddles to form golden-brown granules. (While regular cane sugar is treated both chemically and mechanically to form regularly shaped and uniform crystals, the minimal processing involved in making Sucanat creates granules, which are irregular in size and shape.)

Why we like it It has a deep molasses flavor, and a small amount goes a long way in developing flavor in recipes.

COCONUT SUGAR

What it is This unrefined, granular (not crystallized) sweetener is made from coconut palm flower sap that is heated and then poured into molds or beaten with paddles to form granules.

Why we like it While its flavor is slightly more neutral than Sucanat's, it still offers a robust and almost nutty flavor to baked goods.

DATE SUGAR

What it is This powder is made by pulverizing dried dates.

Why we like it If you like the flavor of dates, you'll love date sugar. Because it is essentially dried fruit, it retains a lot more nutrients than other sweeteners (relatively speaking). This also means it absorbs a large amount of liquid, and it won't melt or dissolve like other dry sugars. When baking, it is important to take these unique characteristics into account by making adjustments to the recipe, such as adding more liquid.

HONEY

What it is This viscous liquid is made by bees from flower nectar; it is mechanically filtered and strained to remove wax and debris.

Why we like it Honey has an amazing range of flavors that work well in baked goods. It can also be easily incorporated into liquid mixtures where a smooth texture is essential, such as custards or curds.

MAPLE SYRUP

What it is This syrup is made by boiling down sap from maple trees.

Why we like it This versatile liquid sweetener is surprisingly easy to incorporate into a wide range of recipes. It also makes a great stand-in for caramel.

THE SCIENCE OF SUGAR

THE SHAPE OF SUGAR

It's obvious that when you reduce the amount of sugar in a baked good, it will taste less sweet. Yet what most cooks don't realize is that reducing the amount of sugar will also have a huge effect on texture. Before we examine why reducing sugar has such an effect on texture, and how less-processed sugars compare to granulated white sugar, we need to first understand the basic chemical composition of a sweetener.

Sweet-tasting molecules from natural sources (not artificial sweeteners) are composed of hydrogen, oxygen, and carbon. The hydrogen and oxygen atoms link together and then attach to a three-dimensional framework made of carbon. These three-dimensional molecules form specific shapes that bind with the sweet taste receptors in the mouth, which send a "sweet" message to the brain. The three most common sweeteners found in nature are glucose, fructose, and sucrose. Glucose and fructose are simple sugar molecules, called monosaccharides, while sucrose is a larger molecule, called a disaccharide, composed of glucose and fructose bound together. Sucrose is the standard to which all other sweeteners are compared, and granulated white sugar is 99.9 percent sucrose.

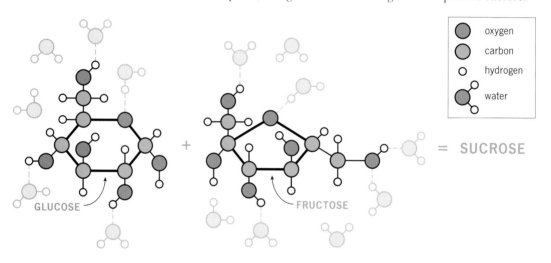

SUGAR MEETS WATER

Glucose, fructose, and sucrose love to be mixed with water. This is because the hydrogen and oxygen atoms found in the water and these sugars are electrostatically attracted to each other; this is known as hygroscopicity. When sugar and water are combined, they quickly form bonds that are very strong. It takes a fair amount of heat energy to break these bonds apart. As a result, the sugar holds on to moisture in baked goods. Because of the tendency for moisture to evaporate in the oven, sugar can make a tremendous difference when it comes to making baked goods that are moist and chewy—rather than dry and crumbly.

The strong sugar-water bond also has an important effect on the flour in a baked good; in particular, it affects the gluten and the starch. Gluten is formed when two proteins in the flour bond together with water to form an elastic network that surrounds the starch granules and pockets of air. When heated, the starch granules absorb water and swell up like little water balloons. This is the basic structure of a baked good; starchy water balloons and pockets of air held in place by an elastic network of gluten. Yet when the gluten and starch are denied water because sugar has been stirred into the mix, this structure becomes weakened. This is why sweet baked goods, such as cakes and cookies, have a more delicate texture and less chew than unsweetened baked goods, such as bread.

COMPARING SWEETENERS

Although the sugar molecules of glucose, fructose, and sucrose all react the same way when combined with water, there are significant differences between them. In terms of being attracted to water (hygroscopicity), fructose is the most hygroscopic, glucose is the least hygroscopic, and sucrose falls somewhere in between. In terms of flavor, fructose is 1.5 times sweeter than sucrose, while glucose is only 75 percent as sweet as sucrose. Also, the length of time that the sweetness is perceived in the mouth is slightly different between these molecules. The flavor of fructose dissipates the most quickly, followed by glucose, while sucrose offers the most sustained sweet flavor.

Below are the five main sweeteners we use throughout the book and their molecular make-up (date sugar is not included here, since it is made from fruit and so has a drastically different molecular structure). These numbers are estimates, and can vary from batch to batch. Given the different molecular designs of these sugars, it is no wonder that they all react a bit differently when added to a recipe.

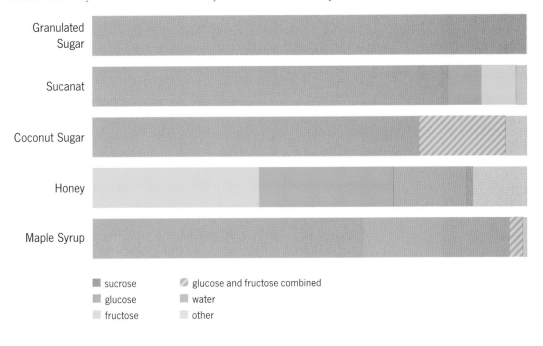

Granulated Sugar

Sucanat

Coconut Sugar

Honey

Maple Syrup

- ▪ sucrose
- ▪ glucose
- ▪ fructose
- ▨ glucose and fructose combined
- ▪ water
- ▪ other

TEST KITCHEN DISCOVERIES

We set the bar pretty high for ourselves with this book. Not only did we want to learn how to bake successfully with less sugar, but we also wanted to learn how to swap granulated white sugar for less-processed sweeteners. Right off the bat, however, we realized that we couldn't tackle both of these issues at the same time in the kitchen because it was too hard to identify which change was causing which result in the finished baked goods. Instead, we found it best to tackle the issue of how to bake with less sugar first. Then, once we had a good low-sugar recipe in hand, we began to experiment with the various white sugar alternatives. Below are some of the discoveries we uncovered as we developed the recipes throughout this book. They fall into two basic categories: baking with less sugar and baking with different sweeteners.

1   NOT EVERY RECIPE WORKS WITH 50 PERCENT LESS SUGAR

For every recipe in this book, we began by reducing the amount of sugar by 50 percent. Some recipes, like muffins, adapted to this alteration very well and required only minor tweaks to fix any resulting flavor or textural issues. Other recipes, however, just couldn't handle such a big change. Cookies, for example, turned irreparably dry and cakey with 50 percent less sugar. We tried many things to restore the texture of these low-sugar cookies, but in the end the only fix was to add a little sugar back into the dough. As a result, the sugar reduction in recipes throughout this book ranges from 30 to 50 percent.

A TRADITIONAL MUFFIN A classic muffin, containing 20 grams of sugar, has a moist, tender crumb.

B SUCCESSFUL MUFFIN WITH 50% LESS SUGAR Reducing the amount of sugar by 50% produced a slightly dry, cakey texture that we could easily fix by swapping cake flour for the all-purpose flour and using melted butter rather than softened butter.

C TRADITIONAL COOKIE This cookie, containing 25 grams sugar, has a moist, chewy texture.

D UNSUCCESSFUL COOKIE WITH 50% LESS SUGAR Reducing the amount of sugar by 50% inhibited spread and produced a dry, cakey texture that was impossible for us to fix without adding back some of the sugar.

2   LESS SUGAR MEANS LESS FLAVOR

We were prepared for all of the recipes in this book to taste less sweet, but we weren't prepared for them to taste dull and bland. Flavors like cinnamon and vanilla seemed to disappear in these less-sweet items. This is because sugar enhances four of our five basic tastes, including sweet, salty, bitter, and umami. There also appears to be a link between sweetness and aroma, which could explain why we perceive some aromas, such as vanilla, as sweet. So, to compensate for the lack of flavor, we often added things like spices, extracts, teas, and citrus zest, as in our recipes for Spiced Shortbread (page 94) and Strawberry-Chamomile Streusel Bars (page 120).

3   LOW SUGAR RECIPES REQUIRE EXTRA LIQUID

When you reduce the amount of sugar in a baking recipe without altering any of the other ingredients, the resulting dough or batter will have too much available moisture. This moisture is then absorbed by the flour. Unlike sugar, which is able to hold on to moisture during baking, the flour isn't able to hold on to the moisture and lets it evaporate in the oven. This is why baked goods made with less sugar often taste dry and crumbly. To combat this, we did a few things to our recipes, such as add extra liquid, increase the number of eggs, and reduce the baking times by a few minutes.

A LOWER-SUGAR SCONE WITH ADDED LIQUID To help keep this 50%-less-sugar scone moist and tender, we replaced the usual ½ cup milk with ¾ cup heavy cream and added a whole egg and a yolk.

B LOWER-SUGAR SCONE WITHOUT ADDED LIQUID If you simply reduce the amount of sugar in a traditional scone recipe by 50%, it will have a very dry, crumbly texture.

4 LESS SUGAR CAN MAKE THINGS GREASY

For some recipes in this book, including many of the cookies, we found that the low-sugar versions were a bit greasier. The reason this happens is that in the absence of sugar, the flour absorbs the excess moisture in the dough and then releases it in the form of steam during baking. Since fat and water repel each other, the steam essentially pushes some of the fat out of the cookies during baking. To curb this effect, we found it helpful to reduce the amount of butter slightly or add a fat that won't melt during baking such as egg yolks.

A LOWER-SUGAR COOKIES WITH LESS BUTTER Although some grease on the sheet is inevitable, reducing the amount of butter to 10 tablespoons minimizes the amount that leaches out during baking.

B LOWER-SUGAR COOKIES WITH TRADITIONAL AMOUNT OF BUTTER With 14 tablespoons of butter, a significant amount leaches out of the cookies.

5 FRUIT IS SUGAR

For many of the fruit-based recipes, like Apple-Pear Pie (page 174), Blueberry Turnovers (page 243), and Raspberry Sorbet (page 274), reducing the sugar was tricky because most of the sugar was coming from the fruit itself. For example, how do you make an apple pie with 50 percent less sugar when the apples represent 56 percent of the sugar in the recipe? You could, of course, skimp on the apples, which would in turn make a smaller pie with smaller portion sizes, but that didn't seem right to us. Instead, we focused on the other sugars in the recipes and reduced them as far as we could.

A TRADITIONAL APPLE PIE This apple pie has 50 grams sugar per portion; 28 grams from fresh fruit and 22 grams from added sugars.

B LOWER-SUGAR APPLE PIE Our reduced-sugar apple pie has 34 grams sugar per portion; 28 grams from fresh fruit and 6 grams from added sugars.

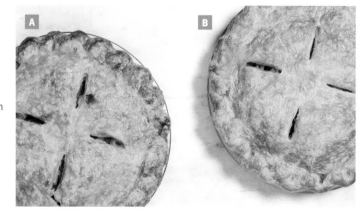

6

YOU MUST USE RIPE BANANAS

Several recipes in the book, including Banana–Trail Mix Muffins (page 40), No-Fuss Banana Ice Cream (page 279), Banana Bread (page 49), Banana Cream Pie (page 191), and Toasted Coconut–Banana Pudding (page 261) rely heavily on bananas for their sweetness. Using underripe bananas in these recipes will make them taste very bland. As bananas ripen, their starch converts to sugar at an exponential rate. In lab tests, we found that heavily speckled bananas had nearly three times the amount of sugar (fructose) of less spotty bananas. (The exact percentage will vary from fruit to fruit.) But the impact of ripeness only goes so far: We found little difference in sweetness between items baked with completely black bananas and those made with heavily speckled ones.

A LIGHTLY SPECKLED A lightly speckled banana contains only a little fructose (about 1.8 percent).

B HEAVILY SPECKLED A heavily speckled banana tastes sweeter because it contains more fructose (about 5.3 percent).

C BLACKENED A blackened banana has the most fructose (about 7.4 percent).

7

EXTRA LEAVENERS HELP MAKE A COOKIE CHEWY

Reducing the amount of sugar in a cookie recipe alters its texture dramatically, turning it from chewy and moist to dry and cakey. An easy way to help these low-sugar cookies achieve a chewier texture is by adding extra leavener, such as baking soda and baking powder, to the dough. This produces excess gas inside the cookies as they bake, but the cookie dough can't hold on to it. As this excess gas escapes during baking and cooling, it causes the cookies to fall flat, which then produces a wonderfully chewy texture.

A LOWER-SUGAR COOKIE WITH TRADITIONAL AMOUNT OF LEAVENER This tall, cakey low-sugar chocolate chip cookie was made with just ¼ teaspoon of baking soda.

B LOWER-SUGAR COOKIE WITH EXTRA LEAVENER This flat, chewy low-sugar chocolate chip cookie was made with 1 teaspoon baking powder and ¾ teaspoon baking soda.

8 ALTERNATIVE SUGARS DON'T WEIGH THE SAME AS WHITE SUGAR

Equal weights of Sucanat, coconut sugar, and granulated sugar do not measure out the same way by volume: Because of its smaller crystal size, a cup of white sugar is heavier than a cup of Sucanat or coconut sugar. We spell out volume substitutions for each sugar in our recipes if you choose not to use a scale. If converting your own recipes from white sugar to alternative sugars, see our chart on page 22.

A GRANULATED WHITE SUGAR
7 ounces = 1 cup
B SUCANAT 7 ounces = 1¼ cups
C COCONUT SUGAR 7 ounces = 1½ cups

9 ALTERNATIVE SUGARS HAVE DRAMATICALLY DIFFERENT FLAVORS, COLORS, AND TEXTURES

At first, it was somewhat surprising how different these sugars looked and tasted in baked goods. White sugar behaved as we expected, but we found its flavor to be milder and less sweet than both Sucanat and coconut sugar. Sucanat has a distinctive earthy molasses flavor, while coconut sugar tastes sweeter with a nutty (and sometimes slightly bitter) aftertaste. Sometimes, we also found that coconut sugar produced a slightly more crumbly texture, especially in low-moisture recipes such as cookies.

A COOKIES MADE WITH GRANULATED SUGAR White sugar has a clean, mild flavor and a very light color.

B COOKIES MADE WITH SUCANAT Sucanat gives the cookies an earthy, molasses flavor and a golden brown color.

C COOKIES MADE WITH COCONUT SUGAR Coconut sugar gives the cookies a nutty, toffee-like flavor and a deep golden brown color.

10 | YOU SHOULD GRIND SUCANAT AND COCONUT SUGAR

Throughout the recipe testing for this book, we noticed that the three different types of dry sugar—Sucanat, coconut sugar, and white granulated sugar—dissolved at different speeds. Granulated white sugar dissolved quickly into various doughs and batters, while Sucanat and coconut sugar took much longer to dissolve, and sometimes never dissolved completely. In some baked goods, such as Blueberry Muffins (page 29), the slow-to-dissolve sugar produced an odd speckled appearance, although the texture of the muffins was relatively unaffected. In other recipes, such as Spiced Shortbread (page 94), the undissolved sugars had a significant effect on the final texture of the cookie. To help the coconut sugar and Sucanat dissolve as easily as granulated sugar, in many recipes we found it necessary to grind these sugars to a fine powder using a spice grinder.

A UNGROUND SUCANAT Sucanat (and coconut sugar) has a tough, granular texture that doesn't always dissolve quickly into batters and doughs.

B MUFFIN MADE WITH UNGROUND SUCANAT This speckled-looking muffin was made with unground Sucanat, which is why it has a speckled appearance.

C COOKIES MADE WITH UNGROUND SUCANAT These shortbread cookies were made with unground Sucanat, which is why they have a coarse, tough, and crumbly texture.

D GROUND SUCANAT After being ground in a spice grinder, the Sucanat has a powdery texture that dissolves more easily into batters and doughs.

E MUFFIN MADE WITH GROUND SUCANAT This evenly colored muffin was made with ground Sucanat.

F COOKIES MADE WITH GROUND SUCANAT These shortbread cookies were made with ground Sucanat and have a fine, tender, and firm texture.

11 HONEY AND MAPLE SYRUP ARE NOT INTERCHANGEABLE

Many cooks think that honey and maple syrup are interchangeable since they are both liquid sugars, but this is simply not true. Honey and maple syrup have very different molecular structures and they react differently in recipes. As shown on page 9, maple syrup is mostly sucrose, and contains about 34 percent water. Honey, on the other hand, is largely composed of glucose and fructose, and contains only about 17 percent water. This is a major factor in why they act differently. For example, fructose browns faster and at lower temperatures than other sugars, so swapping in honey for maple syrup will result in more intense browning, while using maple syrup instead of honey will produce the opposite effect. The other big difference between honey and maple syrup is due to the fact that honey is relatively acidic. When we swapped honey for the maple syrup in our Maple Layer Cake (page 128), we noticed that the cake domed slightly more and its surface was covered with small holes. Our science editor explained that honey's low pH could be to blame: An acidic pH is known to form a more elastic gluten network, so as the cake bakes and the gases in the batter expand, the gluten structure stretches and forms a dome. Eventually, some of the gas breaks through and creates holes.

A CAKE MADE WITH MAPLE SYRUP
Our Maple Layer Cake made with maple syrup has a flat, even top and a lighter color.

B CAKE MADE WITH HONEY When we swap honey for the maple syrup in our Maple Layer Cake recipe, the cake browns significantly more and is speckled with holes.

12

THE TYPE OF HONEY MATTERS

Honey's attributes can range from a mild flavor and golden brown color to a robust flavor and dark brown color, depending on the variety. We tested five varieties of honey—traditional, raw, chestnut, buckwheat, and rosemary—in our recipes and found that their different colors and flavors were noticeable in the final baked goods. We liked all the honey varieties except buckwheat honey: Tasters disliked its distinct, earthy flavor, and it gave baked goods a slightly gummy texture, since it contains a higher ratio of fructose to glucose than other types of honey. This not only causes faster browning but, because fructose holds on to water more effectively than glucose, it also results in a mushy texture. See page 19 for more information on buying honey.

A CAKE MADE WITH BUCKWHEAT HONEY Buckwheat honey gives this cake a strong, earthy flavor and gummy texture.

B CAKE MADE WITH TRADITIONAL HONEY This cake has a mild, sweet flavor and tender texture.

13

YOU CAN STILL MAKE CARAMEL

In recipes such as our Caramel-Nut Tart (page 200) and Maple Flan (page 264) we wanted to achieve the flavor and texture of a traditional caramel without using refined sugar. We found that we could produce a caramel-like texture using Sucanat, coconut sugar, maple syrup, and honey, although the transition to the caramel-like stage happened at much lower temperatures compared to granulated sugar. While tasters weren't fond of the flavor of the honey caramel, the other cooked sugar syrups could be readily substituted in desserts requiring a conventional caramel.

A GRANULATED SUGAR Turns into caramel around 340 degrees. It has a clean, toffee-like flavor.

B SUCANAT Turns caramel-like between 250 and 270 degrees. It has a molasses-y, slightly bitter flavor.

C COCONUT SUGAR Turns caramel-like between 250 and 270 degrees. It is very dark in color, with a nutty, chocolaty flavor.

D MAPLE SYRUP Turns caramel-like between 250 and 270 degrees. It has a rounded, butterscotch flavor.

E HONEY Turns caramel-like between 300 and 320 degrees. It has a bitter, woodsy flavor reminiscent of wet straw.

GETTING TO KNOW NATURAL SWEETENERS

There are many ways to sweeten baked goods without turning to granulated white sugar. Below you'll find more information about the sweeteners we use in this book. Most of these products are available in supermarkets; they are also available online.

SUCANAT

Short for *sucre de canne naturel*, Sucanat is a natural cane sugar that is made by extracting the juice from sugar cane and then beating it with paddles to form granules. Since they retain much of their natural molasses, the granules are a tan-brown color, with a deep, molasses-y flavor that our tasters loved. Sucanat is far more flavorful than regular white sugar, which means that a small amount goes a long way in providing sweetness and flavor to a wide variety of recipes, from Chocolate Chip Cookies (page 76) to Raspberry Sorbet (page 274). In many recipes, we found it necessary to grind Sucanat before using it, which can help ensure that it's well incorporated into doughs or batters and can also eliminate unsightly speckling on finished baked goods (see page 15 for more information on grinding sugars). Because it's a registered trademark, Sucanat is a fairly reliable, consistent product across brands; you can find it in many well-stocked supermarkets or online.

COCONUT SUGAR

Although coconut sugar has just begun making its way onto supermarket shelves, this traditional product has been around for centuries. Sap from the flowers of the coconut palm is collected and then boiled and beaten with paddles to create dark brown granules. We like it because it doesn't really taste like coconut—rather, coconut sugar gives baked goods a deeply rounded, nutty flavor that we like in many applications. Like Sucanat, even a small amount of coconut sugar can provide outsize flavor and sweetness since it is so much more flavorful than regular granulated sugar. We also found it was often necessary to grind coconut sugar before using it to ensure the best flavor, texture, and aesthetic appeal of certain recipes (see page 15 for more information on grinding sugars).

DATE SUGAR

Date sugar isn't really a sugar at all—it's made by grinding dried dates into a powder. This means it's extraordinarily flavorful, but tricky to use—even in the small amounts we needed for our low-sugar recipes. Since the dates are dehydrated, date sugar naturally absorbs a ton of liquid, which can leave baked goods dry and dense if the liquid is not adjusted. And since, chemically speaking, it's a fruit, not a pure sugar, it won't dissolve or melt. We found that date sugar worked well to create date flavor in every bite of our Date-Nut Bread (page 50) and created a perfect, fruit-forward backbone for our

Chocolate Cherry Almond Torte (page 158). We recommend using date sugar only in recipes that are designed to accommodate its distinct qualities. Note that some date sugar contains an extra ingredient to prevent it from clumping. For example, Bob's Red Mill adds oat flour to their date sugar. However, we found that this doesn't affect the way our recipes turn out (and will only minimally affect the sugar content of the recipe).

MAPLE SYRUP

We were amazed at the versatility of maple syrup when developing our low-sugar recipes. From making caramel for flan to sweetening a basic yellow cake to creating a perfectly smooth, gently sweet frozen yogurt, its many uses may surprise you. Although it has a reputation for being expensive, we were happy to find that in tastings of supermarket Grade A Dark Amber syrups, there was almost no discernible difference between products. This is because most syrups on supermarket shelves are blends from a wide range of producers: Since the majority of the world's maple syrup is produced on relatively small-scale farms and it takes 40 gallons of sap to produce just 1 gallon of maple syrup, most producers don't have the resources for national distribution. Small  producers usually sell their syrup to large packagers, which pool hundreds of different products and bottle the blends under a brand name. We recommend choosing the least expensive all-maple product you can find. And don't confuse it with pancake syrup: These highly processed, corn syrup–based products are cloyingly sweet, not at all natural, and we don't like their flavor (in baked goods or otherwise). If you're unsure whether your syrup is pure maple, check the ingredient list: The only ingredient should be maple syrup.

HONEY

Honey's distinct flavor can be a boon in low-sugar recipes, since you only need a small amount to make a big impact. But most traditional baking recipes that call for honey cut it with some granulated sugar, both to balance its strong floral notes and to aid in creating structure. Since we didn't want to rely on white sugar, we found that honey worked best in recipes where its flavor could be the focus, such as Honey Buns (page 66) and Honey-Almond Coffee Cake (page 59), or in recipes where we needed only a small amount, such as our Strawberry Cream Paletas (page 282). It also worked well in applications like lemon curd, since it could incorporate seamlessly into the ultrasmooth custard without disrupting either the color or the texture.

When shopping for honey, there are several important things to know. There are two distinct categories of honey: traditional, which is pressure filtered to remove pollen and create a clear appearance, and raw, which is only lightly filtered and retains much of its pollen. Although both traditional and raw honeys can vary greatly in flavor, we generally prefer raw honey, which is much more nuanced and balanced in flavor than traditional honey. But traditional versus raw is only one piece of the puzzle: The bees' diet also affects the flavor of the honey. While bees who feed mostly on clover will produce a mild-flavored honey, bees with a more varied diet will produce a more complexly flavored honey. Our favorite product, Nature Nate's 100% Pure Raw and Unfiltered Honey, sources its honey from bees that feed on a blend of wildflowers, clover, Chinese tallow, and vetch; it is slightly bitter and floral, with a deep, balanced sweetness.

We also recommend staying away from very strongly flavored honeys, such as buckwheat honey, when baking. The flavor of the honey you use will come through in baked goods and our tasters weren't fond of the distinct, strong flavor of buckwheat, which took away from the other flavors in the recipes (see page 17 for more information on honey types).

DRIED FRUIT

Dried fruit such as cranberries, cherries, raisins, apples, and figs can offer great flavor and sweetness to a wide variety of recipes. The drying process concentrates flavor and sweetness, making them a good choice for several of our low-sugar recipes, whether used for pops of sweetness, as in our Harvest Muffins (page 37), or plumped and pureed for more uniform sweetness and flavor, as in our Apple Cake (page 153). It's important to pay attention to labels when buying dried fruit, as it's often sweetened with sugar. For this book, we use unsweetened dried fruit.

CHOCOLATE

All chocolate begins as cacao beans, which are seeds found in large pods that grow on cacao trees. These beans are fermented, dried, and roasted and then the inner meat (or nib) of the bean is removed from the shell and ground into a paste. This paste is called chocolate liquor (although it contains no alcohol) and consists of cocoa solids and cocoa butter. From there, the chocolate liquor is further processed into the products we're familiar with. The catch: Sweetened chocolate, like semisweet, bittersweet, and milk chocolate, usually does contain white sugar. However, there were certain recipes in this book in which sweetened chocolate was necessary (imagine a chocolate chip cookie with unsweetened chocolate chunks!); in these cases, we used bittersweet when possible (which has the lowest sugar content of all sweetened chocolate) and still reduced the sugar content of the recipe significantly. We supplemented the sweetness where necessary with a natural sweetener like Sucanat. Depending on the brand, cacao percentage, and other factors, sweetened chocolates can contain variable amounts of sugar, so we suggest using our recommended brands for the best results.

White Chocolate: White chocolate is technically not chocolate at all, since it contains no cocoa solids. It does, however, contain quite a bit of sugar: Our favorite brand, Guittard Choc-Au-Lait White Chips, contains 9 grams of sugar per serving. We used white chocolate chips in just one recipe in this book, Honey Blondies (page 111).

Milk Chocolate: Milk chocolate is the sweetest chocolate. Although it must contain at least 10 percent chocolate liquor and 12 percent milk solids, the rest is made up of sweeteners and flavorings (milk chocolate is usually more than 50 percent sugar). Because of this, we used it in only one recipe in this book: Chocolate Pound Cake (page 144), for which a lower-sugar chocolate proved to be simply too bitter. Our favorite brand is Dove Silky Smooth Milk Chocolate.

Dark Chocolate: Encompassing both semisweet and bittersweet chocolates, dark chocolate must contain at least 35 percent chocolate liquor, although most contain more than 55 percent and some go as high as 99 percent. When possible, we use bittersweet chocolate in this book since it generally contains less sugar than semisweet; our favorite brand is Ghirardelli 60% Cacao Bittersweet Chocolate Premium Baking Bar. However, in certain applications, bittersweet chocolate lived up to its name; using it resulted in bitter, unpleasant flavors. In these cases, we used semisweet chocolate. For example, our Chocolate Pudding Cake (page 164) relies only on the chocolate for sweetness—there's no added sweetener at all—so semisweet chocolate was necessary to create big chocolate flavor without any bitterness. We've had good luck with Ghirardelli Semi-Sweet Chocolate Premium Baking Bar.

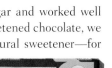

Unsweetened Chocolate: Unsweetened chocolate contains no sugar and worked well when we wanted a bold hit of chocolate flavor. When using unsweetened chocolate, we supplemented it with either sweetened chocolate or another natural sweetener—for example, a small amount of unsweetened chocolate gives the filling for our Dark Chocolate Cream Pie (page 186) a chocolaty boost, while bittersweet chocolate and a very small amount of Sucanat ensure a good level of sweetness. Our favorite brand is Hershey's Unsweetened Baking Bar.

Cocoa Powder: Cocoa powder contains no sugar and is useful in applications like cakes, where a light texture is paramount. Cocoa powder comes in natural and Dutch-processed versions, and we used both in this book. Dutching raises the powder's pH, which neutralizes its acids and astringent notes and rounds out its flavor; it also darkens the color. Our favorite natural cocoa powder is Hershey's Natural Cocoa Unsweetened, and our favorite Dutch-processed cocoa powder is Droste Cocoa.

SUBSTITUTING SWEETENERS

Granulated sugar, Sucanat, and coconut sugar cannot be substituted for one another based on a one-to-one volume measure, so if you choose to use an alternative sugar in place of granulated sugar in your own recipes, you should refer to the chart below for substitution information. Keep in mind that weight is the most accurate way to measure any dry ingredient, so we recommend using a scale when you can. For the recipes in this book that call for Sucanat or coconut sugar, we've provided all the substitution information you'll need, including weight-to-volume conversions and a short description of any differences in texture or flavor should you choose to use one of the alternates.

GRANULATED SUGAR OR BROWN SUGAR	SUCANAT	COCONUT SUGAR	WEIGHT
2 tablespoons	3 tablespoons	3 tablespoons	1 ounce
3 tablespoons	¼ cup	⅓ cup	1½ ounces
¼ cup	⅓ cup	6 tablespoons	1¾ ounces
⅓ cup	6 tablespoons	7 tablespoons	2 ounces
½ cup	½ cup plus 2 tablespoons	¾ cup	3½ ounces
⅔ cup	¾ cup plus 2 tablespoons	1 cup	4⅔ ounces
¾ cup	1 cup	1 cup plus 2 tablespoons	5⅓ ounces
1 cup	1¼ cups	1½ cups	7 ounces
1¼ cups	1⅓ cups plus ¼ cup	1½ cups plus ⅓ cup	8¾ ounces
1⅓ cups	1⅔ cups	1⅔ cups plus ¼ cup	9⅓ cups
1½ cups	1⅔ cups plus ¼ cup	1⅔ cups ½ cup	10½ ounces
1⅔ cups	2 cups plus 2 tablespoons	1¾ cups plus ⅔ cup	11⅔ ounces
1¾ cups	2¼ cups	2⅓ cups plus ¼ cup	12¼ ounces
2 cups	2⅓ cups plus ¼ cup	2⅔ cups plus ¼ cup	14 ounces

WHAT WE ACCOMPLISHED

Before we started this book, we didn't realize just how much sugar was in some of our favorite baked goods—and when we did the calculations, many of the numbers shocked us. We were amazed at the dramatic differences we were able to make for some of these recipes. Below are just a few examples; you'll also find before and after numbers on every recipe page.

RECIPE	SUGAR BEFORE	SUGAR AFTER	PERCENT REDUCTION
Blueberry Muffins	20 g	11 g	45%
Banana Bread	25 g	12 g	52%
Cinnamon Buns	44 g	22 g	50%
Chocolate Chip Cookies	25 g	15 g	40%
Oatmeal Raisin Cookies	23 g	13 g	43%
Honey-Lemon Squares	16 g	9 g	44%
Chocolate Layer Cake	69 g	39 g	43%
Carrot-Honey Layer Cake	49 g	23 g	53%
Blueberry Pie	33 g	13 g	61%
Lemon Cream Pie	64 g	26 g	59%
Strawberry Shortcakes	32 g	22 g	31%
Dark Chocolate Pudding	31 g	20 g	35%
Raspberry Sorbet	26 g	15 g	42%

LIST OF RECIPES BY PRIMARY SWEETENER

When developing recipes, we carefully chose which sweetener to use in each recipe based on our desired flavor and texture. Although many recipes rely on multiple sources of sweetness, like Sucanat and chocolate or honey and fresh fruit, the recipes are listed here by their primary added sweetener—for example, we've listed Apple-Pear Pie under Sucanat, even though the apples and pears also provide sweetness. Where appropriate, some recipes are listed twice, such as Chocolate Cherry Almond Torte, which calls for both date sugar and sweetened chocolate. In the category labeled "No Added Sweetener," you'll find the recipes that rely only on ingredients like fresh or dried fruit for sweetness.

SUCANAT

Blueberry Muffins	(29)
Anise–Poppy Seed Muffins	(30)
Blueberry Scones	(42)
Chai Oat Scones	(46)
Banana Bread	(49)
Pumpkin Bread	(53)
Cardamom-Spiced Zucchini Bread	(55)
Crumb Cake	(56)
Chocolate Chip Cookies	(76)
Oatmeal-Raisin Cookies	(79)
Peanut Butter Cookies	(81)
Fudgy Chocolate Cookies	(83)
Molasses Spice Cookies	(84)
Lemon–Poppy Seed Cookies	(86)
Almond-Cardamom Thins	(91)
Pecan Shortbread Cookies	(93)
Graham Crackers	(101)
Almond Biscotti	(102)
Hazelnut-Orange Biscotti	(103)
Pistachio-Spice Biscotti	(103)
Granola Bars	(106)
Strawberry-Chamomile Streusel Bars	(120)
Chocolate Layer Cake	(124)
Red Velvet Cupcakes	(133)
Strawberry Cupcakes	(134)
Pumpkin Cupcakes	(137)
Easy Vanilla Frosting	(139)
Easy Coffee Frosting	(139)
Easy Almond Frosting	(139)
Easy Coconut Frosting	(139)
Creamy Chocolate Frosting	(140)

Chocolate Pound Cake	(144)
Chai-Spiced Pound Cake	(147)
Summer Peach Cake	(148)
Berry Snack Cake	(151)
Pear Upside-Down Cake	(154)
Spiced-Citrus Bundt Cake	(163)
Blueberry Cheesecake	(170)
Apple-Pear Pie	(174)
Peach Pie	(176)
Summer Berry Pie	(185)
Dark Chocolate Cream Pie	(186)
Banana Cream Pie	(191)
Caramel-Nut Tart	(200)
Peach-Blackberry Free-Form Tart	(208)
Pear-Ginger Free-Form Tart	(212)
Classic Tart Crust	(218)
Apple Crisp	(224)
Cherry-Hazelnut Crisp	(227)
Peach-Raspberry Crumble	(229)
Peach Cobbler	(230)
Strawberry Shortcakes	(233)
Blueberry-Walnut Buckles	(235)
Raspberry-Pistachio Buckles	(235)
Blackberry-Hazelnut Buckles	(235)
Pear Strudel	(236)
Apple Turnovers	(240)
Cherry Clafouti	(244)
Dark Chocolate Pudding	(258)
Strawberry Mousse	(267)
Chocolate-Hazelnut Semifreddo	(269)
Raspberry Sorbet	(274)

SUCANAT (continued)

Raspberry, Ginger, and Mint Sorbet	(275)
Mixed Berry Sorbet	(275)
Pineapple Sorbet	(277)
Piña Colada Sorbet	(277)
Fruit Punch Sorbet	(277)

COCONUT SUGAR

Coconut-Cashew Muffins	(33)
Monkey Bread	(60)
Cinnamon Buns	(64)
Apple-Cinnamon Danish	(70)
Coconut Washboards	(88)
Spiced Shortbread	(94)
Holiday Cookies	(98)
Coconut-Lime Cream Pie	(192)
Toasted Coconut–Banana Pudding	(261)

DATE SUGAR

Date-Nut Bread	(50)
Chocolate Cherry Almond Torte	(158)

HONEY

Honey-Almond Coffee Cake	(59)
Honey Buns	(66)
Honey Blondies	(111)
Honey-Lemon Squares	(116)
Carrot-Honey Layer Cake	(131)
Honey Cream Cheese Frosting	(142)
Honey-Rosemary Polenta Cake with Clementines	(156)
Honey-Oat Bundt Cake	(161)
Roasted Sweet Potato Pie	(183)
Lemon Cream Pie	(189)
Blueberry–Lemon Curd Tart	(194)
Pear and Almond Tart	(198)
Fresh Fruit Tart with Mascarpone and Honey	(203)
Apple, Goat Cheese, and Honey Tart	(204)
Summer Berry Gratin	(246)
Pineapple-Mango Fools	(249)
Strawberry Granita	(280)
Strawberry-Lime Granita	(280)
Strawberry-Basil Granita	(280)
Strawberry Cream Paletas	(282)
Coconut Paletas	(285)
Horchata Paletas	(285)
Coconut, Lime, and Cardamom Paletas	(285)
Striped Fruit Popsicles	(286)

MAPLE SYRUP

Bran Muffins	(34)
Granola with Almonds, Apples, and Cherries	(73)
Granola with Coconut, Blueberries, and Macadamia Nuts	(73)
Maple Pecan Bars	(112)
Maple Layer Cake	(128)
Maple Cream Cheese Frosting	(142)
Maple Whipped Cream	(143)
Mocha-Mascarpone Jelly Roll Cake	(166)
Blueberry Turnovers	(243)
Chilled Maple-Glazed Oranges	(250)
Maple-Caramel Apples with Cinnamon Cream	(253)
Maple Rice Pudding	(263)
Maple Flan	(264)
Vanilla Frozen Yogurt	(270)
Strawberry Frozen Yogurt	(271)
Peach Frozen Yogurt	(271)

CHOCOLATE

Pomegranate and Nut Chocolate Clusters	(108)
Mango and Nut Chocolate Clusters	(108)
Cherry and Nut Chocolate Clusters	(108)
Chocolate Layer Cake	(124)
Creamy Chocolate Frosting	(140)
Chocolate Pound Cake	(144)
Chocolate Cherry Almond Torte	(158)
Chocolate Pudding Cake	(164)
Dark Chocolate Cream Pie	(186)
Dark Chocolate Pudding	(258)
Chocolate-Hazelnut Semifreddo	(269)

NO ADDED SWEETENER

Harvest Muffins	(37)
Cherry-Almond Muffins	(39)
Banana–Trail Mix Muffins	(40)
Fig Bars	(115)
Apple Cake	(153)
Blueberry Pie	(180)
Fig, Cherry, and Walnut Tart*	(207)
Roasted Pears with Cider-Caramel Sauce	(255)
No-Fuss Banana Ice Cream	(279)
No-Fuss Peanut Butter–Banana Ice Cream	(279)
No-Fuss Chocolate-Banana Ice Cream with Walnuts	(279)

*Sucanat in crust

muffins, quick breads, and breakfast treats

Sweetener Substitutions

COCONUT SUGAR	½ cup plus 2 tablespoons (3 ounces) Muffins will taste slightly sweeter; grind sugar as directed in step 1.
GRANULATED SUGAR	7 tablespoons (3 ounces) Muffins will be slightly less sweet and lighter in color; do not grind sugar in step 1.

blueberry muffins

Makes 12 muffins

WHY THIS RECIPE WORKS Blueberry muffins are a classic breakfast staple, but most recipes are loaded with sugar. The first batches we made with a small amount of Sucanat came out of the oven looking a bit speckled, but otherwise beautiful: tall, nicely browned, and studded with juicy berries. After just one bite, however, we knew we had some work to do. They were dense and rubbery and, while the Sucanat lent some rich molasses flavor, the taste fell flat. We focused first on finding a way to re-create the light, tender crumb of the full-sugar muffins. We realized that decreasing the sugar had resulted in too much gluten structure, since sugar usually inhibits some gluten development. We hoped that swapping some of the all-purpose flour for lower-protein cake flour would solve the problem. We tested several flour ratios and found that cake flour alone produced the softest, most appealing texture. To amp up the flavor of the muffins, we browned the butter and added orange zest, cinnamon, and vanilla. Our muffins were almost perfect, but they were still coming out of the oven with speckled tops. Since the Sucanat wasn't completely dissolving in the batter, the granules were leaving marks as they melted in the oven. Pulverizing the Sucanat in a spice grinder easily solved this problem. You can skip grinding the Sucanat in step 1; however, the muffins will have a speckled appearance. Low-fat yogurt can be substituted for the whole-milk yogurt, but the muffins will be slightly drier. Frozen blueberries can be substituted for the fresh blueberries.

⅓ cup plus ¼ cup (3 ounces) Sucanat
8 tablespoons unsalted butter, cut into 8 pieces
1½ cups plain whole-milk yogurt
2 large eggs
1 tablespoon vanilla extract
1 teaspoon grated orange zest
2¾ cups (11 ounces) cake flour
2 teaspoons baking powder
½ teaspoon baking soda
1 teaspoon ground cinnamon
¾ teaspoon salt
¼ teaspoon ground cloves
7½ ounces (1½ cups) blueberries

1. Adjust oven rack to middle position and heat oven to 375 degrees. Grease 12-cup muffin tin. Working in 2 batches, grind Sucanat in spice grinder until fine and powdery, about 1 minute.

2. Melt 6 tablespoons butter in 10-inch skillet over medium-high heat until it begins to turn golden, about 2 minutes. Continue to cook, swirling pan constantly, until butter is dark golden brown and has nutty aroma, 1 to 3 minutes. Transfer browned butter to large bowl and stir in remaining 2 tablespoons butter until melted; let cool slightly.

3. Whisk yogurt, eggs, vanilla, and orange zest into browned butter until smooth. In large bowl, whisk ground Sucanat, flour, baking powder, baking soda, cinnamon, salt, and cloves together until combined. Using rubber spatula, stir in yogurt mixture until combined. Fold in blueberries.

4. Divide batter evenly among prepared muffin cups. Bake until golden brown and toothpick inserted in center of muffin comes out clean, 22 to 27 minutes, rotating muffin tin halfway through baking.

5. Let muffins cool in tin for 20 minutes, then transfer to wire rack and let cool for 10 minutes before serving.

BEFORE 20 grams sugar ⟶ **AFTER** 11 grams sugar

anise–poppy seed muffins

Makes 12 muffins

WHY THIS RECIPE WORKS We wanted to make poppy seed muffins with rich, full flavor; fluffy, tender interiors; and golden crusts. We were amazed to find that our go-to recipe had a whopping 22 grams of sugar per muffin, so we hoped that our new recipe would work with a sugar content of only 11 grams. We turned to Sucanat, which we ground in a spice grinder to ensure that the tops of the finished muffins weren't speckled. Lemon zest seemed like a natural complement to the poppy seeds, but we could only add so much zest before the muffins started to taste soapy, and our muffins were still lacking flavor. To fix this problem and to up the perceived sweetness without adding more sugar, we started by increasing the vanilla. This helped, but tasters still wanted more flavor, so we scoured the pantry for solutions. We found our answer in ground anise seeds, which had a sweet, subtle licorice flavor that rounded out the muffins perfectly. Next, we needed to fix the texture of the muffins; they were a bit dense and tough. To create a finer crumb and a less chewy texture, we switched from all-purpose flour to cake flour. A combination of baking powder and baking soda ensured good rise and good browning, but we also increased the oven temperature and raised the oven rack to help achieve the perfect golden brown crust. You can skip grinding the Sucanat in step 1; however, the muffins will have a speckled appearance. Low-fat yogurt can be substituted for the whole-milk yogurt, but the muffins will be slightly drier.

¾ cup (4 ounces) Sucanat
8 tablespoons unsalted butter, cut into 8 pieces
1½ cups plain whole-milk yogurt
2 large eggs
1 tablespoon vanilla extract
1 tablespoon grated lemon zest
2¾ cups (11 ounces) cake flour
3 tablespoons poppy seeds
2 teaspoons baking powder
¾ teaspoon baking soda
1 teaspoon ground anise seeds
¾ teaspoon salt

1. Adjust oven rack to upper-middle position and heat oven to 425 degrees. Grease 12-cup muffin tin. Working in 3 batches, grind Sucanat in spice grinder until fine and powdery, about 1 minute.

2. Melt 6 tablespoons butter in 10-inch skillet over medium-high heat until it begins to turn golden, about 2 minutes. Continue to cook, swirling pan constantly, until butter is dark golden brown and has nutty aroma, 1 to 3 minutes. Transfer browned butter to large bowl and stir in remaining 2 tablespoons butter until melted; let cool slightly.

3. Whisk yogurt, eggs, vanilla, and lemon zest into browned butter until smooth. In large bowl, whisk ground Sucanat, flour, poppy seeds, baking powder, baking soda, anise, and salt together. Using rubber spatula, stir in yogurt mixture until combined.

4. Divide batter evenly among prepared muffin cups. Bake until golden brown and toothpick inserted in center of muffin comes out clean, 15 to 20 minutes, rotating muffin tin halfway through baking.

5. Let muffins cool in tin for 10 minutes, then transfer to wire rack and let cool for 20 minutes before serving.

BEFORE 22 grams sugar ⟶ **AFTER** 11 grams sugar

Sweetener Substitutions

COCONUT SUGAR ½ cup plus ⅓ cup (4 ounces)
Muffins will taste slightly sweeter and have pronounced anise flavor; grind
sugar as directed in step 1.

GRANULATED SUGAR ⅓ cup plus ¼ cup (4 ounces)
Muffins will be slightly less sweet and lighter in color; do not grind sugar
in step 1.

Sweetener Substitutions

SUCANAT	⅔ cup plus ¼ cup (5¼ ounces) Muffins will have slight molasses flavor.
GRANULATED SUGAR	¾ cup (5¼ ounces) Muffins will be slightly less sweet and lighter in color.

coconut-cashew muffins

Makes 12 muffins

WHY THIS RECIPE WORKS Delicately flavored tropical coconut and buttery, nutty cashews are a perfect pair, but between these sweet add-ins and the even sweeter batter, coconut-cashew muffins can easily begin to veer into dessert territory. To avoid this common pitfall, we started with one of our basic muffin recipes, cut the sugar in half, and used coconut sugar in lieu of granulated. Although the coconut sugar lent subtle coconut flavor to the muffins, it was not nearly enough to satisfy. We wanted to infuse the muffins with big, bold coconut flavor. We found that stirring unsweetened flaked coconut or shredded coconut into the batter produced distractingly chewy bits or unfavorable textures; instead, we opted to pulse the flaked coconut in a food processor to create smaller pieces that distributed evenly throughout the batter. Toasting the coconut brought out its flavor even more. As for the cashews, tossing a full cup of chopped nuts into the batter gave the muffins rich nuttiness and pleasant crunchy contrast. Browned butter, lime zest, and vanilla created a nuanced backbone, and tasters liked a sprinkle of additional coconut and chopped cashews on top. Cake flour in place of all-purpose produced a tender crumb that perfectly showcased the flavors we had developed. Be sure to use unsweetened coconut in this recipe. Low-fat yogurt can be substituted for the whole-milk yogurt, but the muffins will be slightly drier.

1⅔ cups unsweetened flaked coconut

1¼ cups unsalted roasted cashews, chopped

8 tablespoons unsalted butter, cut into 8 pieces

1½ cups plain whole-milk yogurt

2 large eggs

1 tablespoon vanilla extract

1 teaspoon grated lime zest

2¾ cups (11 ounces) cake flour

1 cup plus 2 tablespoons (5¼ ounces) coconut sugar

2 teaspoons baking powder

½ teaspoon baking soda

¾ teaspoon salt

1. Adjust oven rack to middle position and heat oven to 375 degrees. Grease 12-cup muffin tin. Combine ⅓ cup flaked coconut and ¼ cup chopped cashews in bowl; set aside for topping.

2. Spread remaining 1⅓ cups coconut over rimmed baking sheet and bake, stirring often, until lightly golden, about 5 minutes. Let coconut cool for 15 minutes, then pulse in food processor until finely chopped, about 10 pulses; set aside.

3. Melt 6 tablespoons butter in 10-inch skillet over medium-high heat until it begins to turn golden, about 2 minutes. Continue to cook, swirling pan constantly, until butter is dark golden brown and has nutty aroma, 1 to 3 minutes. Transfer browned butter to large bowl and stir in remaining 2 tablespoons butter until melted; let cool slightly.

4. Whisk yogurt, eggs, vanilla, and lime zest into browned butter until smooth. In large bowl, whisk flour, coconut sugar, baking powder, baking soda, and salt together. Using rubber spatula, stir in yogurt mixture until combined. Fold in processed coconut and remaining 1 cup chopped cashews.

5. Divide batter evenly among prepared muffin cups and sprinkle with reserved coconut-cashew mixture. Bake until golden brown and toothpick inserted in center of muffin comes out clean, 20 to 25 minutes, rotating muffin tin halfway through baking.

6. Let muffins cool in tin for 10 minutes, then transfer to wire rack and let cool for 20 minutes before serving.

BEFORE 37 grams sugar ⟶ **AFTER** 16 grams sugar

bran muffins

Makes 12 muffins

WHY THIS RECIPE WORKS Most bran muffins are packed with sugar, but are surprisingly light on their namesake ingredient. We wanted a better bran muffin, with a moist, tender crumb and plenty of deep bran flavor. We found that maple syrup complemented the bran while still allowing its earthy flavor to shine through. Raisins, which provided pops of sweet, fruity flavor throughout, along with plenty of vanilla and warm spices, ensured that tasters didn't miss the sugar (even though we had gone from 27 grams in our classic recipe to only 13 grams). But as we well knew, sugar doesn't just make things taste sweet—reducing the sugar in our muffins also meant reduced moisture. This problem was only compounded by the fact that bran absorbs quite a bit of liquid, making our muffins inedibly dry. Adding a healthy dose of buttermilk helped to alleviate some of the dryness, but the key to the best texture turned out to be in the ratio of bran to flour: Too much bran produced a dry, crumbly muffin; too little and the bran flavor was lost. After testing various proportions, we found that a 1:1 ratio worked best. Finally, for a bit of crunch and an added layer of flavor, we sprinkled the muffins with nutty roasted sunflower seeds.

1½ cups (7½ ounces) all-purpose flour
1½ cups (2½ ounces) wheat bran
1¼ teaspoons baking powder
½ teaspoon baking soda
1 teaspoon ground cinnamon
¾ teaspoon ground allspice
½ teaspoon ground nutmeg
½ teaspoon salt
1¼ cups buttermilk
½ cup maple syrup
6 tablespoons unsalted butter, melted and cooled
2 large eggs
1 tablespoon vanilla extract
½ cup raisins, chopped
2 tablespoons roasted sunflower seeds

1. Adjust oven rack to lower-middle position and heat oven to 375 degrees. Grease 12-cup muffin tin.

2. Whisk flour, wheat bran, baking powder, baking soda, cinnamon, allspice, nutmeg, and salt together in large bowl. In separate bowl, whisk buttermilk, maple syrup, melted butter, eggs, and vanilla together until smooth. Using rubber spatula, stir buttermilk mixture into flour mixture until just combined. Fold in raisins.

3. Divide batter evenly among prepared muffin cups and sprinkle with sunflower seeds. Bake until toothpick inserted in center of muffin comes out with few moist crumbs attached, 16 to 20 minutes, rotating muffin tin halfway through baking.

4. Let muffins cool in tin for 10 minutes, then transfer to wire rack and let cool for 20 minutes before serving.

BEFORE 27 grams sugar ⟶ **AFTER** 13 grams sugar

Portioning Muffin Batter

For neat, evenly sized muffins, portion batter into each cup using measuring cup or ice cream scoop, then circle back and evenly distribute remaining batter with spoon.

harvest muffins

Makes 12 muffins

WHY THIS RECIPE WORKS For this recipe, we set ourselves the lofty goal of making a great muffin without any added sweetener, but this task proved to be even tougher than we anticipated. We hoped that apple cider would provide enough sweetness and depth of flavor to carry the muffins, but quickly realized that this wasn't the case; the first batches, made with apple cider in place of granulated sugar, turned out inedibly bland. To fix this, we added lots of warm, aromatic spices, a full tablespoon of vanilla, and a bit of orange zest, which gave the muffins a flavor profile reminiscent of hot mulled cider. We also found that browning the butter rounded out the muffins' flavor with toasty, nutty notes. But even with the added flavorings, the muffins weren't quite sweet enough. We decided to stir in sweet-tart dried cranberries, which complemented the other flavors in the muffins perfectly and gave us bites of sweet flavor. But it still wasn't enough; tasters wanted more overall sweetness in the muffin batter. We tried pureeing the cranberries and stirring the puree into the batter, but the flavor of the cranberries was lost and we didn't achieve a dramatic increase in sweetness. In search of other sources of sweetness, we came up with an unusual solution: a shredded sweet potato. The potato's natural sugars and subtle, earthy flavor proved to be just what our muffins needed. Simply stirring the raw shreds into the batter dramatically upped the sweetness of the muffins. Be sure to use raw, not cooked, sweet potato in this recipe.

1¼ cups dried cranberries
¾ cup pecans, toasted and chopped fine
6 tablespoons unsalted butter
¾ cup apple cider
⅔ cup buttermilk
2 large eggs
1 tablespoon vanilla extract
¼ teaspoon grated orange zest
2⅓ cups (11⅔ ounces) all-purpose flour
1½ teaspoons baking powder
¾ teaspoon baking soda
1¼ teaspoon ground cinnamon
1 teaspoon ground allspice
½ teaspoon salt
¼ teaspoon ground cloves
1¼ cups peeled and shredded sweet potato (1 small potato)

1. Adjust oven rack to middle position and heat oven to 375 degrees. Grease 12-cup muffin tin. Finely chop ¼ cup cranberries and combine with ¼ cup pecans; set aside for topping.

2. Melt butter in 10-inch skillet over medium-high heat until it begins to turn golden, about 2 minutes. Continue to cook, swirling pan constantly, until butter is dark golden brown and has nutty aroma, 1 to 3 minutes. Transfer browned butter to large bowl; let cool slightly.

3. Whisk apple cider, buttermilk, eggs, vanilla, and orange zest into browned butter until smooth. In large bowl, whisk flour, baking powder, baking soda, cinnamon, allspice, salt, and cloves together. Using rubber spatula, stir in butter mixture until combined. Fold in sweet potato, remaining 1 cup cranberries, and remaining ½ cup pecans.

4. Divide batter evenly among prepared muffin cups and sprinkle with reserved cranberry-pecan mixture. Bake until golden brown and toothpick inserted in center of muffin comes out with few moist crumbs attached, 18 to 20 minutes, rotating muffin tin halfway through baking.

5. Let muffins cool in tin for 10 minutes, then transfer to wire rack and let cool for 20 minutes before serving.

BEFORE 23 grams sugar ⟶ **AFTER** 12 grams sugar

cherry-almond muffins

Makes 12 muffins

WHY THIS RECIPE WORKS Almonds, with their natural sweetness and refined flavor, seemed like a perfect starting point for a no-sugar-added muffin. To ensure that our muffins were chock-full of almond flavor, we started by stirring 1¼ cups of sliced almonds into the batter. Although the almonds added pleasant nuttiness, the lack of sugar meant that the muffins were a little tough and dense. Grinding some of the almonds and whisking them into the flour gave the muffins a more open crumb and a slightly lighter, more tender texture. Even though we didn't want to add sugar, the muffins needed to be sweeter. To avoid muddying the almonds' delicate flavor, we decided to use no-sugar-added white grape juice, which provided sweetness without imparting a distinct flavor of its own. The muffins were improving, but tasters still wanted a bit more sweetness. Dried cherries fit the bill, and chopping them ensured they were evenly distributed, giving us bursts of sweetness in every bite. Finally, we employed a couple of ultraflavorful ingredients that helped to trick the tongue's perception of sweetness: five-spice powder and almond extract. Do not use light white grape juice as it contains an artificial sweetener, called sucralose, that can negatively affect the flavor of the muffins.

1¼ cups sliced almonds, toasted
2⅓ cups (11⅔ ounces) all-purpose flour
1¾ teaspoons baking powder
¾ teaspoon baking soda
1½ teaspoons five-spice powder
¾ teaspoon salt
1½ cups white grape juice
8 tablespoons unsalted butter, melted and cooled
2 large eggs
1 tablespoon vanilla extract
½ teaspoon almond extract
1 cup dried cherries, chopped

1. Adjust oven rack to middle position and heat oven to 375 degrees. Grease 12-cup muffin tin. Pulse ½ cup almonds in food processor until finely ground, about 10 pulses; transfer to large bowl. Whisk in flour, baking powder, baking soda, five-spice powder, and salt.

2. In separate bowl, whisk grape juice, melted butter, eggs, vanilla, and almond extract together. Using rubber spatula, stir grape juice mixture into flour mixture until combined. Fold in ½ cup almonds and dried cherries.

3. Divide batter evenly among prepared muffin cups and sprinkle with remaining ¼ cup almonds. Bake until golden brown and toothpick inserted in center of muffin comes out with few moist crumbs attached, 18 to 20 minutes, rotating muffin tin halfway through baking.

4. Let muffins cool in tin for 10 minutes, then transfer to wire rack and let cool for 20 minutes before serving.

BEFORE 29 grams sugar ⟶ **AFTER** 11 grams sugar

Reheating Pastries

To serve day-old muffins, scones, and coffee cakes, reheat in 300-degree oven for 10 minutes.

banana–trail mix muffins

Makes 12 muffins

WHY THIS RECIPE WORKS Between the granulated sugar and the concentrated sweetness of the dried fruit, traditional banana–trail mix muffins pack a sugary punch. We hoped that the naturally sweet bananas could not only provide flavor, but also eliminate the need for added sugar. To pack in as much banana flavor as we could, we used six very ripe whole bananas. But once mashed, the bananas added too much moisture and made the muffins soggy and mushy. To prevent this, we microwaved the bananas to encourage them to release excess moisture. Rather than toss the liquid (and the flavor) down the drain, we decided to reduce it to concentrate the sweetness and the banana flavor. Our muffins now had deep, bold banana flavor, but without the granulated sugar they turned tough in the oven. To fix this, we switched from all-purpose flour to cake flour. Baking powder and soda provided great rise and helped the muffins turn golden brown. As for the trail mix, we found that the muffins were plenty sweet without the dried fruit. Instead, we added a combination of chopped walnuts, oats, and sunflower seeds to give the muffins depth, pleasant nuttiness, and a warm, toasted flavor without adding any unwanted grams of sugar. Be sure to use very ripe, heavily speckled (or even black) bananas for these muffins. Do not substitute quick oats, instant oats, or steel-cut oats in this recipe.

¾ cup walnuts, chopped

¼ cup (¾ ounces) old-fashioned rolled oats

¼ cup sunflower seeds

6 large very ripe bananas (2¼ pounds), peeled

10 tablespoons unsalted butter, melted and cooled

2 large eggs

2 teaspoons vanilla extract

2 cups (8 ounces) cake flour

2½ teaspoons baking powder

1¼ teaspoons baking soda

½ teaspoon salt

1. Adjust oven rack to upper-middle position and heat oven to 400 degrees. Grease 12-cup muffin tin. Toast walnuts, oats, and sunflower seeds in 12-inch skillet over medium heat until golden and fragrant, 8 to 10 minutes; let cool.

2. Place bananas in bowl, cover, and microwave until bananas are soft and have released liquid, about 5 minutes. Transfer bananas to fine-mesh strainer set over bowl and let drain, stirring occasionally, about 15 minutes; you should have ¾ to 1 cup liquid.

3. Transfer liquid to medium saucepan and transfer bananas to now-empty bowl. Cook banana liquid over medium-high heat until reduced to ⅓ cup, 8 to 10 minutes. Add reduced liquid to bowl with bananas and mash with potato masher until mostly smooth. Whisk in butter, eggs, and vanilla.

4. In large bowl, whisk flour, baking powder, baking soda, and salt together. Using rubber spatula, stir in banana mixture until combined. Fold in walnuts, oats, and sunflower seeds.

5. Divide batter evenly among prepared muffin cups. Bake until toothpick inserted in center of muffins comes out clean, 18 to 22 minutes, rotating muffin tin halfway through baking.

6. Let muffins cool in tin for 10 minutes, then transfer to wire rack and let cool for 20 minutes before serving.

BEFORE 20 grams sugar ⟶ **AFTER** 8 grams sugar

blueberry scones

Makes 8 scones

WHY THIS RECIPE WORKS We wanted our naturally sweetened take on this coffeehouse favorite to be buttery, flaky, and bursting with juicy blueberries. Halving the sugar in a classic recipe and swapping in Sucanat gave the scones a slightly deeper, more rounded flavor. Although tasters were happy with the sweetness level, the reduction in sugar made the scones very dry. The original recipe called for a combination of milk and sour cream, but testing revealed that heavy cream and a bit of extra butter solved the dryness problem without making the scones greasy. For good rise and lightness, we used a generous amount of baking powder and a very hot oven, which encouraged the water in the butter to convert to steam in the scones, fluffing them up nicely. To get the desired flaky layers and to keep the blueberries from turning the scones blue, we rolled out the dough before gently pressing the berries into it. We then rolled the dough like a jelly roll, gently flattened it, and cut out the scones. We reserved some of the cream and egg mixture to brush over the tops of the scones, creating perfect golden-brown exteriors without an extra sprinkling of sugar. Finally, we found it necessary to bake the scones on a double sheet pan to prevent them from overbrowning on the bottom and around the edges as they baked. You can skip grinding the Sucanat in step 1; however, the scones will have a speckled appearance. Frozen blueberries can be substituted for the fresh blueberries.

¾ cup heavy cream

1 large egg plus 1 large yolk

⅓ cup (1¾ ounces) Sucanat

2 cups (10 ounces) all-purpose flour

1 tablespoon baking powder

¾ teaspoon salt

10 tablespoons unsalted butter, cut into ½-inch pieces and chilled

7½ ounces (1½ cups) blueberries

1. Adjust oven rack to middle position and heat oven to 450 degrees. Line rimmed baking sheet with parchment paper and place in second baking sheet. Whisk heavy cream, egg, and yolk together in small bowl. Measure out 1 tablespoon cream mixture and set aside. Grind Sucanat in spice grinder until fine and powdery, about 1 minute.

2. In food processor, pulse ground Sucanat, flour, baking powder, and salt to combine, about 10 pulses. Scatter chilled butter evenly over top and pulse until mixture resembles coarse cornmeal, 12 to 14 pulses. Transfer mixture to large bowl.

3. Fold cream mixture into flour mixture with rubber spatula until just combined. Transfer dough to well-floured counter. Dust dough with flour, and using floured hands, knead dough 2 to 3 times, until it just holds together in ragged ball, adding flour as needed to prevent sticking.

4. Roll dough into rough 12-inch square, sprinkle blueberries over top, and press them lightly into dough. Using bench scraper, loosen dough from counter and roll into tight log. With dough seam side down, gently press into 12 by 4-inch rectangle. Using floured bench scraper or chef's knife, cut dough crosswise into 4 equal rectangles. Cut each rectangle diagonally into 2 triangles.

5. Lay scones on prepared baking sheet, spaced about 2 inches apart, and brush with reserved cream mixture. Bake scones until dark golden brown, 20 to 22 minutes, rotating sheet halfway through baking. Let scones cool on baking sheet for 5 minutes, then transfer to wire rack and let cool for 10 minutes before serving.

BEFORE 18 grams sugar ⟶ **AFTER** 9 grams sugar

Making Blueberry Scones

1 Roll dough into rough 12-inch square on well-floured counter.

2 Sprinkle blueberries over top and press them lightly into dough.

3 Using bench scraper, loosen dough from counter and roll into tight log.

4 With dough seam side down, gently press into 12 by 4-inch rectangle.

5 Using floured bench scraper or chef's knife, cut rectangle crosswise into 4 equal rectangles.

6 Cut each rectangle diagonally to form 2 triangles.

Sweetener Substitutions

COCONUT SUGAR	6 tablespoons (1¾ ounces) Scones will be slightly sweeter and more tender; grind sugar as directed in step 1.
GRANULATED SUGAR	¼ cup (1¾ ounces) Scones will be slightly less sweet and lighter in color; do not grind sugar in step 1.

chai oat scones

Makes 8 scones

WHY THIS RECIPE WORKS To avoid a dry, leaden texture, classic oatmeal scone recipes incorporate copious amounts of sugar. We liked the warm, rounded sweetness of Sucanat and honey, but these scones didn't rise well and were predictably dry and crumbly. Increasing the oven heat was a step in the right direction: The moisture inside the scones quickly converted to steam, which encouraged rise, and the scones baked faster, which meant less time in the oven—and less time to dry out. Although these scones were fluffier, we still wanted them to be moister. Adding cream helped, but we could only add so much before the dough became too difficult to work with. An extra egg yolk solved this problem, contributing richness without added liquid. With the texture issues solved, we turned our attention to the somewhat lackluster flavor. Toasting the oats brought out their natural sweetness and nutty flavor. We then added generous doses of complementary spices like cinnamon, nutmeg, and cloves, but no matter how much we added, tasters complained that their flavors didn't come through. Finally, one taster suggested a surprising solution: chai tea. We were happy to find that briefly steeping two chai tea bags in the cream was a simple way to create complex flavor. You can skip grinding the Sucanat in step 3; however, the scones will have a speckled appearance. Do not substitute quick oats, instant oats, or steel-cut oats in this recipe.

1¼ cups (3¾ ounces) old-fashioned rolled oats
½ cup heavy cream
2 chai tea bags
1 large egg plus 1 large yolk
1 tablespoon vanilla extract
1 tablespoon honey
4 teaspoons Sucanat
1½ cups (7½ ounces) all-purpose flour
1 tablespoon baking powder
¼ teaspoon salt
12 tablespoons unsalted butter, cut into ½-inch pieces and chilled

1. Adjust oven rack to middle position and heat oven to 375 degrees. Spread oats over rimmed baking sheet and bake until fragrant and lightly browned, 8 to 10 minutes; transfer to large bowl and let cool. Increase oven temperature to 450 degrees. Line rimmed baking sheet with parchment paper and place in second baking sheet.

2. Microwave cream and tea bags in covered bowl until hot, about 1 minute; let steep for 5 minutes. Squeeze tea bags to extract as much cream as possible; discard bags. Whisk cream, egg and yolk, vanilla, and honey together in small bowl. Measure out 1 tablespoon cream mixture and set aside.

3. Grind Sucanat in spice grinder until fine and powdery, about 1 minute. In food processor, pulse ground Sucanat, flour, baking powder, and salt until combined, about 10 pulses. Scatter chilled butter evenly over top and pulse until mixture resembles coarse cornmeal, 12 to 14 pulses. Stir mixture into toasted oats. Using rubber spatula, fold in cream mixture until just combined.

4. Transfer dough to well-floured counter. Dust dough with flour and gently pat into 7-inch circle, about 1 inch thick. Using floured bench scraper or chef's knife, cut dough into 8 wedges.

5. Lay scones on prepared baking sheet, spaced about 2 inches apart, and brush with reserved cream mixture. Bake scones until dark golden brown, 12 to 14 minutes, rotating sheet halfway through baking. Let scones cool on baking sheet for 5 minutes, then transfer to wire rack and let cool for 10 minutes before serving.

BEFORE 11 grams sugar ⟶ **AFTER** 5 grams sugar

Making Chai Oat Scones

1 Microwave cream and tea bags until hot. Let steep for 5 minutes; squeeze out tea bags and discard.

2 Whisk cream, egg and yolk, vanilla, and honey together in small bowl. Reserve 1 tablespoon for topping.

3 Pulse ground Sucanat, flour, baking powder, and salt in food processor until combined. Pulse in cold butter until mixture resembles coarse cornmeal.

4 Stir flour-butter mixture into toasted oats. Fold in cream mixture using rubber spatula.

5 Transfer dough to well-floured counter and pat into 7-inch circle. Using floured bench scraper or chef's knife, cut into 8 wedges.

6 Transfer scones to baking sheet, brush with reserved cream mixture, and bake.

Sweetener Substitutions

COCONUT SUGAR	4 teaspoons (do not omit honey) Scones will taste drier and slightly sweeter; grind sugar as directed in step 3.
GRANULATED SUGAR	4 teaspoons (do not omit honey) Scones will be slightly less sweet and lighter in color; do not grind sugar in step 3.

banana bread

Makes 1 loaf; serves 10

WHY THIS RECIPE WORKS We wanted to create a great loaf of banana bread that put the focus squarely on its namesake ingredient. Since we were decreasing the amount of sugar, we wanted to take advantage of the abundance of natural sugars found in overripe bananas to provide sweetness as well as deep banana flavor. To create great flavor without negatively affecting texture, we needed to figure out how many bananas we could include in our recipe. Three turned out to be the magic number; any more and the bread baked up gummy and wet, but with fewer the banana flavor was lost. We replaced the granulated sugar found in many recipes with Sucanat, since its pleasant molasses flavor married well with the other flavors in the bread. A teaspoon of vanilla rounded out the baked bananas' subtle boozy, rum-like flavor. Butter gave our bread a nutty richness while toasted walnuts added a nice textural contrast that tasters liked. Be sure to use very ripe, heavily speckled (or even black) bananas in this recipe. The test kitchen's preferred loaf pan measures 8½ by 4½ inches; if you use a 9 by 5-inch loaf pan, start checking for doneness 5 minutes earlier than advised in the recipe. You can skip grinding the Sucanat in step 1; however, the bread will have a speckled appearance.

7 tablespoons (2½ ounces) Sucanat

2 cups (10 ounces) all-purpose flour

¾ teaspoon baking soda

½ teaspoon salt

3 large very ripe bananas, peeled and mashed

6 tablespoons unsalted butter, melted and cooled

2 large eggs

¼ cup plain whole-milk yogurt

1 teaspoon vanilla extract

½ cup walnuts, toasted and chopped (optional)

1. Adjust oven rack to lower-middle position and heat oven to 350 degrees. Grease 8½ by 4½-inch loaf pan. Working in 2 batches, grind Sucanat in spice grinder until fine and powdery, about 1 minute.

2. Whisk ground Sucanat, flour, baking soda, and salt together in large bowl. In separate bowl, whisk mashed bananas, melted butter, eggs, yogurt, and vanilla until combined. Gently fold banana mixture into flour mixture with rubber spatula until just combined. Fold in walnuts, if using. (Batter will look thick and chunky.)

3. Scrape batter into prepared pan and smooth top. Bake until golden brown and toothpick inserted in center of loaf comes out with few moist crumbs attached, 55 to 65 minutes, rotating pan halfway through baking.

4. Let bread cool in pan for 10 minutes, then transfer to wire rack and let cool for at least 1½ hours before serving.

BEFORE 25 grams sugar ⟶ **AFTER** 12 grams sugar

Sweetener Substitutions

COCONUT SUGAR	½ cup (2½ ounces) Bread will taste similar but will be slightly darker in color; grind sugar as directed in step 1.
LIGHT BROWN SUGAR	6 tablespoons packed (2½ ounces) Bread will be slightly less sweet and lighter in color; do not grind sugar in step 1.

muffins, quick breads, and breakfast treats

date-nut bread

Makes 1 loaf; serves 10

WHY THIS RECIPE WORKS Most date-nut breads suffer from overly dense textures and unmitigated sweetness, so we set out to solve both problems and create a moist, tender loaf studded with soft, sweet dates and crunchy nuts. Our traditional recipe contained 34 grams of sugar in a single serving, so we hoped we could significantly reduce that number. Date sugar, which is made from dried, ground dates, dramatically improved the bread's flavor by ensuring date flavor in every bite. But it had disastrous effects on the bread's texture: Date sugar doesn't melt or dissolve but it does absorb quite a bit of liquid, so our bread turned out terribly dry and dense. Increasing the amount of milk alleviated some of the dryness. To improve the structure of the still-squat loaf, we turned our attention to creating more rise in the batter and developing a more open crumb. We tested different amounts and ratios of baking powder and baking soda, and found that both were necessary to create respectable height and a tender crumb. The texture was improving, but tasters still felt it could be better. Hoping to add structure, we decided to try bread flour in place of the all-purpose flour. This worked perfectly: The bread flour's higher protein content contributed more gluten and helped to create a heartier crumb. With our bread now sturdy enough to support a generous amount of chopped dates and pecans, all we needed was a bit of vanilla extract to round out the flavor. The test kitchen's preferred loaf pan measures 8½ by 4½ inches; if you use a 9 by 5-inch loaf pan, start checking for doneness 5 minutes earlier than advised in the recipe. Watch for pits and stems as you chop the dates.

2 cups (11 ounces) bread flour
1½ teaspoons baking powder
½ teaspoon baking soda
½ teaspoon salt
1 cup whole milk
8 tablespoons unsalted butter, melted and cooled
6 tablespoons (2⅓ ounces) date sugar
2 large eggs
2 teaspoons vanilla extract
6 ounces chopped dates (1 cup)
1 cup pecans or walnuts, toasted and chopped coarse

1. Adjust oven rack to middle position and heat oven to 350 degrees. Grease 8½ by 4½-inch loaf pan.

2. Whisk flour, baking powder, baking soda, and salt together in large bowl. In medium bowl, whisk milk, melted butter, date sugar, eggs, and vanilla until smooth, then stir in chopped dates. Fold milk mixture into flour mixture with rubber spatula until combined. Fold in pecans.

3. Scrape batter into prepared pan and smooth top. Bake until golden brown and toothpick inserted in center of loaf comes out with few moist crumbs attached, 55 minutes to 1 hour, rotating pan halfway through baking.

4. Let bread cool in pan for 10 minutes, then transfer to wire rack and let cool for at least 1½ hours before serving.

BEFORE 34 grams sugar ⟶ **AFTER** 18 grams sugar

Chopping Dates

To make chopping dates and other sticky ingredients easier, spray knife with vegetable oil spray.

pumpkin bread
Makes 1 loaf; serves 10

WHY THIS RECIPE WORKS We set out to develop a naturally sweetened recipe for this autumn favorite with a distinct goal in mind: We wanted rich pumpkin flavor that would be enhanced, not obscured, by sugar. For the sake of simplicity, we wanted to stick with canned pumpkin puree, but knew we would need to boost its flavor and get rid of the raw, metallic taste that can plague canned pumpkin. Cooking down the puree on the stovetop gave it a rich, caramelized flavor and eliminated any off-putting taste. Reducing the puree had another benefit, too: It concentrated the sugars and made the pumpkin taste sweeter, helping to compensate for the reduced amount of sugar. We also stirred ginger, nutmeg, and cloves into the puree as it cooked, which bloomed their flavors. Our bread now had good pumpkin flavor, but was a bit dry; we had driven off a lot of moisture when reducing the puree. Adding buttermilk solved this problem; incorporating cream cheese into the mix underscored the buttermilk's tanginess. To make sure the cream cheese was distributed evenly into the batter, we melted it into the hot puree. Once the puree was cool, we were able to use the pot as the mixing bowl, keeping our recipe streamlined. Be sure to use unsweetened pumpkin puree here, not canned pumpkin pie mix or pie filling, which are sold already spiced and sweetened. The test kitchen's preferred loaf pan measures 8½ by 4½ inches; if you use a 9 by 5-inch loaf pan, start checking for doneness 5 minutes earlier than advised in the recipe.

1¾ cups (8¾ ounces) all-purpose flour

1½ teaspoons baking powder

½ teaspoon baking soda

1 cup canned unsweetened pumpkin puree

1½ teaspoons ground ginger

¾ teaspoon salt

¼ teaspoon ground nutmeg

⅛ teaspoon ground cloves

½ cup plus 2 tablespoons (3½ ounces) Sucanat

6 tablespoons vegetable oil

2½ ounces cream cheese, cut into 8 pieces

2 large eggs

¼ cup buttermilk

½ cup walnuts, toasted and chopped fine

1. Adjust oven rack to middle position and heat oven to 350 degrees. Grease 8½ by 4½-inch loaf pan. Whisk flour, baking powder, and baking soda together in bowl.

2. Combine pumpkin puree, ginger, salt, nutmeg, and cloves in large saucepan. Cook mixture over medium heat, stirring constantly, until reduced to ¾ cup, 6 to 8 minutes. Off heat, stir in Sucanat, oil, and cream cheese. Let mixture stand for 5 minutes, then whisk until smooth and no pieces of cream cheese remain.

3. Whisk eggs and buttermilk together, then whisk into pumpkin mixture. Using rubber spatula, fold in flour mixture until just combined (some small lumps of flour are OK). Fold in walnuts.

4. Scrape batter into prepared pan and smooth top. Bake until toothpick inserted in center of loaf comes out clean, 50 minutes to 1 hour, rotating pan halfway through baking.

5. Let bread cool in pan for 20 minutes, then transfer to wire rack and let cool for at least 1½ hours before serving.

BEFORE 24 grams sugar ⟶ **AFTER** 11 grams sugar

Sweetener Substitutions

COCONUT SUGAR	¾ cup (3½ ounces) Bread will taste similar but will be slightly darker in color.
GRANULATED SUGAR	½ cup (3½ ounces) Bread will taste slightly less sweet and more mild.

Sweetener Substitutions

COCONUT SUGAR	¾ cup (3½ ounces), plus 1 tablespoon for sprinkling Bread will taste similar but will be slightly darker in color.
BROWN SUGAR AND GRANULATED SUGAR	½ cup packed (3½ ounces) brown sugar 1 tablespoon granulated sugar for sprinkling Bread will be slightly less sweet and lighter in color.

cardamom-spiced zucchini bread

Makes 1 loaf; serves 10

WHY THIS RECIPE WORKS Zucchini bread is a great way to use up an overwhelming crop of summer squash, but many recipes use more sugar than zucchini. We found that adding some aromatic, sweet-spicy cardamom complemented the zucchini's flavor without masking it. But this bread was a mushy mess; in typical recipes, the sugar helps to keep the zucchini's abundant moisture in check. Even after we had squeezed a full ⅔ cup of liquid from the grated zucchini and given the bread a long, 75-minute stint in the oven, the bread was inedibly soggy. We couldn't eliminate any more moisture, so instead we added a small amount of whole-wheat flour. The higher-protein flour easily soaked up some of the liquid, giving the bread a much better structure. As an added bonus, the wheat flour contributed a great hearty flavor that perfectly complemented the rustic loaf. Use the large holes of a box grater to shred the zucchini. The test kitchen's preferred loaf pan measures 8½ by 4½ inches; if you use a 9 by 5-inch loaf pan, start checking for doneness 5 minutes earlier than advised in the recipe.

1½ pounds zucchini, shredded

½ cup plus 2 tablespoons (3½ ounces) Sucanat, plus 1 tablespoon for sprinkling

¼ cup vegetable oil

2 large eggs

1 tablespoon vanilla extract

2 cups (10 ounces) all-purpose flour

½ cup (2¾ ounces) whole-wheat flour

2 teaspoons ground cardamom

2 teaspoons baking powder

1 teaspoon baking soda

½ teaspoon salt

¼ teaspoon ground nutmeg

¾ cup walnuts, toasted and chopped

1. Adjust oven rack to middle position and heat oven to 350 degrees. Grease 8½ by 4½-inch loaf pan. Place zucchini in center of dish towel. Gather ends together and twist tightly to drain as much liquid as possible (you should have ½ to ⅔ cup liquid); discard liquid.

2. In medium bowl, whisk ½ cup plus 2 tablespoons Sucanat, oil, eggs, and vanilla together. Stir in zucchini until combined.

3. In large bowl, whisk all-purpose flour, whole-wheat flour, cardamom, baking powder, baking soda, salt, and nutmeg together. Using rubber spatula, stir in zucchini mixture until combined; batter will be thick. Fold in walnuts.

4. Scrape batter into prepared pan, smooth top, and sprinkle with remaining 1 tablespoon Sucanat. Bake until toothpick inserted in center of loaf comes out with few moist crumbs attached, 1 hour 5 minutes to 1¼ hours, rotating pan halfway through baking.

5. Let bread cool in pan for 30 minutes, then transfer to wire rack and let cool for 1½ hours before serving.

BEFORE 27 grams sugar → **AFTER** 13 grams sugar

Removing Moisture From Shredded Zucchini

Place shredded zucchini in center of dish towel, gather ends together, and twist tightly to remove as much liquid as possible.

crumb cake

Serves 9

WHY THIS RECIPE WORKS A perfect New York–style crumb cake consists of only two simple elements: a rich, buttery cake and a lightly spiced crumb topping. But taking out much of the sugar left the topping inedibly sandy. On the plus side, Sucanat gave the crumbs a lovely, balanced butterscotch flavor that tasters liked, so we focused most of our effort on improving the texture. Our original recipe called for cake flour, whose low protein content had ensured that the crumb topping stayed tender by not developing too much gluten structure. But we found that switching back to all-purpose flour provided the extra structure the crumbs needed. With a bit of melted butter, cinnamon, and nutmeg, we had a perfect dough-like crumb that easily broke apart into flavorful, sturdy nuggets. With our topping settled, we turned our attention to the cake itself, which was turning out dense and mushy. We hoped that this would be a simple fix: Since we were already using all-purpose flour in the topping, would all-purpose flour work in the cake too? A bit of testing revealed that the answer was yes. The cake made with all-purpose flour was less dense and was sturdy enough to support the crumb topping. As a final touch, we added cinnamon and nutmeg to the cake to complement the flavors in the topping. Do not skip grinding the Sucanat in steps 1 and 2 or the topping will have a dusty texture and the cake will have a spotty, pockmarked appearance.

topping

- ½ cup (2⅔ ounces) Sucanat
- 8 tablespoons unsalted butter, melted and cooled
- 1 teaspoon ground cinnamon
- ⅛ teaspoon ground nutmeg
- ⅛ teaspoon salt
- 1¼ cups (6¼ ounces) all-purpose flour

cake

- ⅓ cup (1¾ ounces) Sucanat
- 1¼ cups (6¼ ounces) all-purpose flour
- 1 teaspoon baking powder
- ¼ teaspoon baking soda
- ¼ teaspoon ground cinnamon
- ⅛ teaspoon salt
- ⅛ teaspoon ground nutmeg
- 6 tablespoons buttermilk
- 4 tablespoons unsalted butter, melted and cooled
- 1 large egg plus 1 large yolk
- 1 tablespoon vanilla extract

1. FOR THE TOPPING Adjust oven rack to upper-middle position and heat oven to 325 degrees. Working in 2 batches, grind Sucanat in spice grinder until fine and powdery, about 1 minute. Whisk ground Sucanat, melted butter, cinnamon, nutmeg, and salt in medium bowl until smooth. Stir in flour with rubber spatula until mixture resembles thick, cohesive dough; set aside.

2. FOR THE CAKE Grease 8-inch square baking pan and line bottom with parchment paper. Grind Sucanat in spice grinder until fine and powdery, about 1 minute. Whisk ground Sucanat, flour, baking powder, baking soda, cinnamon, salt, and nutmeg together in large bowl. In separate bowl, whisk buttermilk, melted butter, egg and yolk, and vanilla until smooth. Using rubber spatula, stir buttermilk mixture into flour mixture until just combined.

3. Scrape batter into prepared pan and smooth top. Break topping into large pea-size pieces and sprinkle evenly over batter. Bake until crumbs are golden and toothpick inserted in center of cake comes out clean, 25 to 30 minutes, rotating pan halfway through baking.

4. Let cake cool in pan for 30 minutes. Run knife around edge of cake to loosen. Gently flip cake onto large plate, remove parchment, then gently flip again, right side up, onto platter. Serve.

BEFORE 29 grams sugar ⟶ **AFTER** 13 grams sugar

Sweetener Substitutions

COCONUT SUGAR
Topping: ⅓ cup plus ¼ cup (2⅔ ounces)
Cake: 6 tablespoons (1¾ ounces)
Cake will taste slightly sweeter and have mild toffee flavor; grind sugar as directed in steps 1 and 2.

GRANULATED SUGAR
Topping: 6 tablespoons (2⅔ ounces)
Cake: ¼ cup (1¾ ounces)
Cake will be slightly less sweet and lighter in color; do not grind sugar in steps 1 and 2.

honey-almond coffee cake

Serves 6

WHY THIS RECIPE WORKS Coffee cakes can come in many shapes, sizes, and flavors, from towering Bundt-style cakes to yeasted Danish rings to simpler, cinnamon-laced butter cakes. For our version, we had our minds set on creating a golden honey-sweetened cake with a flavorful, unique topping. We were happy to find that a relatively small amount of honey gave the cake plenty of rounded, floral, earthy sweetness while also keeping the cake moist. We decided to go with a simple topping that would provide big flavor, lots of textural contrast, and enough visual interest to make the cake worthy of company. Sliced almonds worked like a charm; we combined the nuts with some melted butter and additional honey and spread the mixture over the cake batter. Since we were using only a small amount of honey for both the cake and the topping, it was important that we made the most of it. A few tests revealed that tasters preferred equal amounts of honey in the topping and in the cake, finding its flavor and sweetness to be most pronounced that way. All-purpose flour, baking powder, and a little baking soda gave the cake enough structure to easily support the almond topping and ensured that the cake baked up with an even-textured crumb. Melted butter, eggs, and sour cream provided much-needed richness, and the sour cream had the added benefit of providing just enough tang to balance the sweetness. Finally, 2 teaspoons of cinnamon along with a dash of vanilla and almond extracts boosted the flavor of the cake and complemented the almond topping perfectly.

1½ cups (7½ ounces) all-purpose flour

2 teaspoons ground cinnamon

1½ teaspoons baking powder

½ teaspoon baking soda

½ teaspoon salt

¾ cup sour cream

½ cup honey

2 large eggs

7 tablespoons unsalted butter, melted and cooled

2 teaspoons vanilla extract

½ teaspoon almond extract

½ teaspoon grated lemon zest

⅔ cup sliced almonds

1. Adjust oven rack to middle position and heat oven to 350 degrees. Grease 9-inch round cake pan.

2. Whisk flour, cinnamon, baking powder, baking soda, and ¼ teaspoon salt together in large bowl. In separate bowl, whisk sour cream, ¼ cup honey, eggs, 3 tablespoons melted butter, vanilla, almond extract, and lemon zest until smooth. Using rubber spatula, stir sour cream mixture into flour mixture until just combined. Scrape batter into prepared pan and smooth top (batter will be quite thick); set aside.

3. Bring remaining ¼ teaspoon salt, remaining ¼ cup honey, and remaining 4 tablespoons melted butter to simmer in small saucepan over medium heat and whisk to combine. Once simmering, stir in almonds to coat. Spread almond mixture evenly over top of batter.

4. Bake until top is golden brown and toothpick inserted in center comes out with few moist crumbs attached, 22 to 27 minutes, rotating pan halfway through baking.

5. Let cake cool in pan for 30 minutes. Run knife around edge of cake to loosen. Gently flip cake onto large plate, then gently flip again, right side up, onto platter. Serve.

BEFORE 45 grams sugar ⟶ **AFTER** 23 grams sugar

monkey bread

Serves 8

WHY THIS RECIPE WORKS Monkey bread is a knotty-looking loaf made by stacking buttery, sugar-coated balls of yeasted dough into a Bundt pan. It's traditionally served warm so that the sweet, gooey pieces can be easily pulled apart with your hands. Our ambitious goal was to cut down on the hefty 49 grams of sugar in our traditional recipe and use only natural sweeteners—without losing any of that hallmark sticky-sweet appeal. We tested both Sucanat and coconut sugar in place of the traditional brown sugar; tasters found Sucanat's strong molasses flavor to be out of place and preferred the more neutral flavor of the coconut sugar. Even with the relatively small amount, tasters didn't miss any sweetness; just a light coating of coconut sugar gave the balls of dough great caramel flavor. Though the glaze is usually made with 1 whole cup of confectioners' sugar, we found that a mere 3 tablespoons of coconut sugar, along with some vanilla extract, made for a nicely balanced, flavorful glaze that imparted a sweet finish to the bread. The dough should be sticky, but if you find it's too wet and not coming together in the mixer, add 2 tablespoons more flour and mix until the dough forms a cohesive mass. After baking, don't let the bread cool in the pan for more than 5 minutes or it will stick to the pan and come out in pieces. Do not skip grinding the coconut sugar in step 7, or the glaze will have a grainy texture. You can thin the glaze with an extra teaspoon of milk if necessary. The monkey bread is best served warm.

dough

- 1 cup warm whole milk (110 degrees)
- ⅓ cup warm water (110 degrees)
- 2 tablespoons unsalted butter, melted and cooled
- 2¼ teaspoons instant or rapid-rise yeast
- 2 teaspoons coconut sugar
- 3¼ cups (16¼ ounces) all-purpose flour
- 1 teaspoon salt

sugar coating

- 1 cup (4⅔ ounces) coconut sugar
- 1 tablespoon ground cinnamon
- ¼ teaspoon ground nutmeg
- 5 tablespoons unsalted butter, melted and cooled

glaze

- 3 tablespoons coconut sugar
- 2 teaspoons milk
- ½ teaspoon vanilla extract

1. FOR THE DOUGH Adjust oven rack to lower-middle position and heat oven to 200 degrees. As soon as oven reaches 200 degrees, turn it off. (This will be warm proofing box for dough. Do not begin step 2 until oven has been turned off.) Thoroughly grease 12-cup nonstick Bundt pan.

2. Whisk warm milk, warm water, melted butter, yeast, and coconut sugar together in 2-cup liquid measuring cup until yeast dissolves. In bowl of stand mixer, whisk flour and salt together. Using dough hook on low speed, slowly add milk mixture and mix until dough comes together, about 3 minutes. Increase speed to medium and knead until dough is shiny and smooth, about 6 minutes.

3. Transfer dough to lightly floured counter and knead by hand to form smooth, round ball, about 1 minute. Place dough in large, lightly greased bowl, cover tightly with greased plastic wrap, and let rise in warmed oven until doubled in size, about 1 hour.

4. FOR THE SUGAR COATING While dough is rising, combine coconut sugar, cinnamon, and nutmeg in small bowl. Place melted butter in separate small bowl.

5. Transfer dough to lightly floured counter and pat into 8-inch square. Using bench scraper or chef's knife, cut dough into 64 even pieces (½ ounce each). Working with 1 piece of dough at a time, roll into tight ball, dip in butter to coat, roll in sugar mixture, then place in prepared Bundt pan. Stagger dough balls so that seams do not line up. Cover Bundt pan tightly with plastic and place in warmed oven until dough balls are puffy and have risen 1 to 2 inches from top of pan, about 1 hour.

6. Remove pan from oven and heat oven to 350 degrees. Discard plastic and bake until top is light golden brown, 25 to 30 minutes, rotating pan halfway through baking. Let monkey bread cool in pan for 5 minutes, then turn out on large platter and let cool for 10 minutes before glazing.

7. FOR THE GLAZE While bread cools, grind coconut sugar in spice grinder until fine and powdery, about 1 minute. Whisk ground sugar, milk, and vanilla together in bowl until smooth. Drizzle glaze over monkey bread and serve warm.

BEFORE 49 grams sugar $\longrightarrow$ **AFTER** 25 grams sugar

Making Monkey Bread

1 Using bench scraper or chef's knife, cut dough into 64 even pieces (½ ounce each) on lightly floured counter.
2 Roll 1 piece of dough into tight ball.
3 Dip ball of dough in butter to coat, then roll in sugar mixture.
4 Place dough balls in prepared Bundt pan, staggering them so that seams do not line up.

Sweetener Substitutions

SUCANAT	Dough: 2 teaspoons Sugar Coating: ¾ cup plus 2 tablespoons (4⅔ ounces) Glaze: 3 tablespoons Monkey bread will have strong molasses flavor and glaze will be slightly grainy; grind Sucanat as directed in step 7.
LIGHT BROWN SUGAR AND CONFECTIONERS' SUGAR	Dough: 2 teaspoons packed brown sugar Sugar Coating: ⅔ cup packed (4⅔ ounces) brown sugar Glaze: ¼ cup (1 ounce) confectioners' sugar Monkey bread will be slightly less sweet and lighter in color. Do not grind confectioners' sugar in step 7.

cinnamon buns

Makes 8 buns

WHY THIS RECIPE WORKS There's nothing like a warm, decadent, homemade cinnamon bun, but we were shocked when we realized that our favorite recipe contained a whopping 44 grams of sugar. Could we cut that number down while still maintaining the integrity of these treats? First, we swapped in coconut sugar, since its neutral sweetness was a better fit for this recipe than bold, molasses-y Sucanat. We were happy to find that the dough tasted plenty sweet with just a tablespoon of coconut sugar, allowing us to use more in the filling and glaze. We also found that a refined drizzle of vanilla-spiked cream cheese glaze gave the buns plenty of gooey appeal. For the filling, we used a hefty amount of cinnamon and ¾ cup of coconut sugar to ensure plenty of flavor and sweetness. As an added bonus, we sped up the normally lengthy prep time by using both yeast and baking powder in the dough, so we needed only a single 30-minute rise time before our buns could be baked. Do not skip grinding the coconut sugar in step 7, or the glaze will have a grainy texture.

filling

- ¾ cup (3½ ounces) coconut sugar
- 1 tablespoon ground cinnamon
- ⅛ teaspoon salt
- 2 tablespoons unsalted butter, melted and cooled
- 1 teaspoon vanilla extract

dough

- 1¼ cups warm whole milk (110 degrees)
- 4 teaspoons instant or rapid-rise yeast
- 1 tablespoon coconut sugar
- 2¾ cups (13¾ ounces) all-purpose flour
- 2½ teaspoons baking powder
- ¾ teaspoon salt
- 5 tablespoons unsalted butter, melted and cooled

glaze

- 3 tablespoons coconut sugar
- 1½ ounces cream cheese, softened
- 2 tablespoons whole milk, plus extra as needed
- 1 tablespoon unsalted butter, melted and cooled
- ¼ teaspoon vanilla extract
- ⅛ teaspoon salt

1. FOR THE FILLING Combine coconut sugar, cinnamon, and salt in bowl. Stir in melted butter and vanilla until mixture resembles wet sand; set aside.

2. FOR THE DOUGH Grease 9-inch round cake pan, line with parchment paper, and grease parchment. Whisk warm milk, yeast, and coconut sugar in bowl and let sit until bubbly, about 5 minutes.

3. Whisk flour, baking powder, and salt together in large bowl. Stir in yeast mixture and 2 tablespoons melted butter until dough forms (dough will be sticky). Transfer dough to well-floured counter and knead until smooth ball forms, about 2 minutes.

4. Roll dough into 12 by 9-inch rectangle, with long side parallel to counter edge. Brush dough completely with 1 tablespoon melted butter, leaving ½-inch border on far edge. Sprinkle filling over butter and press filling firmly into dough. Using bench scraper, loosen dough from counter and roll away from you into tight log, then pinch seam to seal.

5. Roll log seam side down and cut into 8 equal pieces using serrated knife. Turn buns cut-side up and reshape gently as needed. Place 1 bun in center of prepared pan and others around perimeter, seam sides facing in. Brush tops with remaining 2 tablespoons melted butter, cover loosely with plastic wrap, and let rise for 30 minutes, until dough springs back when gently pressed. Adjust oven rack to middle position and heat oven to 350 degrees.

6. Discard plastic and bake buns until edges are well browned, 23 to 25 minutes, rotating pan halfway through baking. Loosen buns from sides of pan with paring knife and let cool for 5 minutes. Flip buns out of pan, then flip again, right side up, onto platter. Let cool for 5 minutes.

7. FOR THE GLAZE While buns cool, grind coconut sugar in spice grinder until fine and powdery, about 1 minute. In bowl, whisk cream cheese, milk, melted butter, vanilla, and salt until smooth. Whisk in ground sugar until smooth. Add additional milk as needed to adjust consistency. Drizzle glaze evenly over buns and serve.

BEFORE 44 grams sugar ⟶ **AFTER** 22 grams sugar

Making Cinnamon Buns

1 Roll dough into 12 by 9-inch rectangle, with long side parallel to counter edge.

2 Brush dough completely with 1 tablespoon melted butter, leaving ½-inch border on far edge, then cover with filling; press on filling firmly to adhere to dough.

3 Using bench scraper, loosen dough from counter and roll away from you into tight log, then pinch seam to seal.

4 Roll log seam side down and cut into 8 equal pieces using serrated knife.

5 Place 1 bun in center of prepared pan and others around perimeter, seam sides facing in.

6 Brush buns with 2 tablespoons melted butter. Cover with plastic wrap and let rise for 30 minutes before baking.

Sweetener Substitutions

SUCANAT	Filling: ½ cup plus 2 tablespoons (3½ ounces) Dough: 1 tablespoon Glaze: 3 tablespoons Cinnamon buns will have strong molasses flavor; grind Sucanat as directed in step 7.
LIGHT BROWN SUGAR AND CONFECTIONERS' SUGAR	Filling: ½ cup packed (3½ ounces) brown sugar Dough: 1 tablespoon packed brown sugar Glaze: ¼ cup (1 ounce) confectioners' sugar Cinnamon buns will be slightly less sweet and lighter in color. Do not grind confectioners' sugar in step 7.

honey buns

Makes 9 buns

WHY THIS RECIPE WORKS Honey buns, with their nostalgic charm and luscious, sticky appeal, seemed like a perfect candidate for a unique, naturally sweet alternative to warm-spiced cinnamon buns. However, most honey bun recipes call for hefty amounts of corn syrup and granulated sugar along with the honey, obscuring the honey's flavor almost completely. We wanted to build a better honey bun by decreasing the amount of sweetener, eliminating the extraneous corn syrup and granulated sugar, and letting the flavor of the honey shine through. We started with a rich, buttery yeasted dough, which required only a small amount of honey to activate the yeast and give the dough a subtle sweetness. Tasters liked a dough made with buttermilk over one with regular milk, since the slight tang complemented the honey's rich flavor. We thought the filling and glaze would be easy—we simply combined honey, butter, and vanilla. But tasters found the flavor of the honey mixture to be a bit flat. Not wanting to overshadow the honey, we turned to orange blossom water, which added a subtle, floral backbone and gave our honey buns a distinctly "grown-up" flavor profile. A sprinkling of pecans over the filling and in the baking pan gave the buns pleasant crunch and nuttiness. If you don't have orange blossom water, you can substitute ½ teaspoon orange zest.

dough

- 6 tablespoons unsalted butter, melted and cooled
- ⅓ cup buttermilk
- 2 large eggs
- 1½ teaspoons honey
- 1⅛ teaspoons instant or rapid-rise yeast
- 2 cups (10 ounces) all-purpose flour, plus extra as needed
- ½ teaspoon salt

filling and glaze

- ⅔ cup honey
- 4 tablespoons unsalted butter
- 1 teaspoon vanilla
- 1 teaspoon orange blossom water
- 1 cup pecans, chopped coarse

1. FOR THE DOUGH Whisk melted butter, buttermilk, eggs, honey, and yeast in medium bowl until combined. In bowl of stand mixer, whisk flour and salt together. Fit stand mixer with dough hook and slowly add buttermilk mixture on low speed; mix until dough comes together, about 2 minutes. Increase speed to medium and knead until dough is smooth and elastic, about 10 minutes. (If, after 5 minutes, dough is still very sticky, add 1 to 2 tablespoons extra flour; dough should clear sides of bowl but stick to bottom.)

2. Transfer dough to lightly floured counter and knead by hand to form smooth, round ball, about 1 minute. Place dough in large, lightly greased bowl, cover tightly with greased plastic wrap, and let rise until doubled in size, about 1 hour.

3. FOR THE FILLING AND GLAZE Cook honey, butter, vanilla, and orange blossom water together in small saucepan over medium heat until butter is melted, then whisk to combine. Measure out ¼ cup mixture and set aside for filling. Pour remaining mixture over bottom of 8-inch square baking pan, then sprinkle with ½ cup pecans.

4. Transfer dough to lightly floured counter and roll into 12 by 9-inch rectangle, with long side parallel to counter edge. Brush dough completely with reserved ¼ cup honey mixture, leaving ½-inch border on far edge. Sprinkle remaining ½ cup pecans over top and press filling firmly into dough. Using bench scraper, loosen dough from counter and roll away from you into tight log, then pinch seam to seal.

5. Roll log seam side down and cut into 9 equal pieces using serrated knife. Turn buns cut side up and reshape gently as needed. Arrange buns in pan, cover with plastic, and let rise until doubled in size, about 1 hour. Adjust oven rack to middle position and heat oven to 350 degrees.

6. Bake buns until golden brown, 20 to 25 minutes, rotating pan halfway through baking. Loosen buns from sides of pan with paring knife and let cool for 5 minutes. Flip buns out of pan onto platter. Drizzle with glaze left in pan and let cool for 15 to 20 minutes before serving.

BEFORE 39 grams sugar $\longrightarrow$ **AFTER** 21 grams sugar

Making Honey Buns

1 After reserving ¼ cup of glaze for filling, pour remaining glaze into 8-inch square baking pan.

2 Sprinkle ½ cup chopped pecans into pan.

3 After assembling and cutting buns, place them on top of glaze and nuts in baking pan.

4 When buns are finished baking, loosen buns from sides of pan with paring knife; let cool for 5 minutes. Flip buns out of pan onto platter.

apple-cinnamon danish

Makes 6 Danish

WHY THIS RECIPE WORKS Apple Danish are often no-holds-barred confections, with sticky-sweet fillings that barely resemble fruit. They're also a production to make; the flaky dough alone can take hours, not to mention the time required to make the filling. Luckily, store-bought puff pastry proved to be a perfect base for our Danish: It's easy to work with, takes no time to prep, and contains very little sugar. But that was only half the battle. We also wanted a simple, fruit-forward filling that wasn't laden with sugar but still tasted pleasantly sweet. We decided to brush a small amount of apricot jelly onto the puff pastry to give the Danish a sweet-tart base. A sprinkle of cinnamon sugar gave us the sweetness we craved without going overboard; tasters preferred coconut sugar over Sucanat, since its neutral sweetness allowed the fruit flavor to shine through. Sliced apples, tossed with ginger, lemon juice, and a bit more cinnamon, made a perfect filling. Rolling the puff pastry around the apple slices created rose-like Danishes that were as pretty as they were delicious. Parbaking the apple slices ensured that they were pliable enough to roll without breaking. To thaw frozen puff pastry, let it sit either in the refrigerator for 24 hours or on the counter for 30 minutes to 1 hour. For an especially pretty presentation, sprinkle with confectioners' sugar before serving.

2 apples (6 ounces each), cored, halved, and sliced thin

1 tablespoon unsalted butter, melted and cooled

2 teaspoons lemon juice

1 teaspoon ground cinnamon

½ teaspoon ground ginger

¼ teaspoon salt

2 tablespoons coconut sugar

1 (9½ by 9-inch) sheet puff pastry, thawed

2 tablespoons apricot preserves

1. Adjust oven rack to middle position and heat oven to 375 degrees. Toss apples with melted butter, lemon juice, ½ teaspoon cinnamon, ginger, and salt in bowl. Spread apples in single layer on parchment paper–lined baking sheet and bake until softened, about 10 minutes. Set aside until cool enough to handle, about 10 minutes.

2. Line clean baking sheet with parchment and spray with vegetable oil spray. Combine coconut sugar with remaining ½ teaspoon cinnamon in bowl.

3. On floured counter, roll pastry into 12 by 10-inch rectangle, with long side parallel to counter edge. Brush preserves evenly over top and sprinkle with cinnamon sugar. Using sharp knife or pizza wheel, cut pastry lengthwise into six 10 by 2-inch strips.

4. Working with 1 strip of dough at a time, shingle 12 apple slices, peel side out, down length of dough, leaving 1-inch border of dough along bottom. Fold bottom inch of dough over bottom of apple slices, leaving top of apple slices exposed. Roll up dough and apples into tight pinwheel and place, apple side up, on prepared sheet.

5. Bake until golden brown and crisp, 22 to 26 minutes, rotating sheet halfway through baking. Let Danish cool on sheet for 15 minutes before serving.

BEFORE 21 grams sugar → **AFTER** 14 grams sugar

Making Apple-Cinnamon Danish

1 On floured counter, roll pastry into 12 by 10-inch rectangle, with long side parallel to counter edge.

2 Brush preserves evenly over top and sprinkle with cinnamon sugar.

3 Using sharp knife or pizza wheel, cut pastry lengthwise into six 10 by 2-inch strips.

4 Working with 1 strip of dough at a time, shingle 12 apple slices down length of dough, leaving 1-inch border of dough along bottom.

5 Fold bottom inch of dough over bottom of apple slices, leaving top of apple slices exposed.

6 Roll up dough and apples into tight pinwheel and place, apple side up, on prepared sheet.

Sweetener Substitutions

SUCANAT	**2 tablespoons** Danish will taste similar.
GRANULATED SUGAR	**2 tablespoons** Danish will taste similar.

granola with almonds, apples, and cherries

Makes 9 cups

WHY THIS RECIPE WORKS Granola may seem like a healthy breakfast alternative to sugary-sweet cereals, but most granolas contain a ton of sugar, too (even our homemade recipe had 22 grams per serving). We sought to remedy this by using only a small amount of a natural sweetener while still creating a lightly sweet glaze for the oats and nuts. We found that a mere ½ cup of pure maple syrup for 5 cups of oats provided plenty of flavor and sweetness. Although many granola recipes call for granulated sugar as well as maple syrup, we found it unnecessary, especially after adding a generous 4 teaspoons of vanilla. Pressing the granola mixture down into the sheet pan and baking it at a relatively low oven temperature helped keep the granola fuss-free: We didn't need to mix or stir during baking, and we didn't have to worry about it burning. Once we let the mixture cool, we tossed it with dried fruit to give it extra sweetness. Dried apples and cherries, although pleasantly sweet, are surprisingly low in sugar, and their flavors worked perfectly with the subtleness of the maple and vanilla. Do not substitute quick oats, instant oats, or steel-cut oats in this recipe.

½ cup vegetable oil
½ cup maple syrup
4 teaspoons vanilla extract
½ teaspoon salt
5 cups (15 ounces) old-fashioned
   rolled oats
2 cups whole almonds, chopped coarse
1 cup dried apples, chopped
½ cup dried cherries, chopped

1. Adjust oven rack to upper-middle position and heat oven to 325 degrees. Line rimmed baking sheet with parchment paper. Whisk oil, maple syrup, vanilla, and salt together in large bowl. Fold in oats and almonds until thoroughly coated.

2. Transfer mixture to prepared baking sheet and spread evenly into thin layer. Using stiff metal spatula, compress mixture until very compact. Bake until lightly browned, 40 to 45 minutes, rotating pan halfway through baking.

3. Let granola cool in pan, about 1 hour, then break into pieces of desired size. Stir in dried apples and dried cherries and serve.

BEFORE 22 grams sugar ⟶ **AFTER** 11 grams sugar (per ½ cup)

granola with coconut, blueberries, and macadamia nuts
Substitute coconut flakes for cherries, dried blueberries for dried apples, and macadamia nuts for almonds.
BEFORE 22 grams sugar ⟶ **AFTER** 10 grams sugar (per ½ cup)

cookies and bars

chocolate chip cookies

Makes 16 cookies

WHY THIS RECIPE WORKS A great chocolate chip cookie should have crisp edges, a chewy center, complex toffee flavor, and chocolate in every bite. To make our low-sugar version, we decided to use Sucanat, since its molasses flavor fit the cookie's profile nicely. Swapping the typical semisweet chocolate chips for bittersweet helped to further reduce sugar content, but tasters found that the flavor of the chips was a bit muted; chopped bar chocolate had much better chocolate flavor. Even with the reduced sugar, these cookies had great flavor—but their texture was disappointing. They didn't spread enough during baking and they were dry, crumbly, and stale tasting. To encourage spread, we tried adding milk and tweaking the number of eggs; these cookies spread well but they were too tender and cakey. We backtracked and decided to take a closer look at how we were treating the liquid—specifically the butter—already present in our recipe. Our traditional recipe called for melted butter, but in a side-by-side test of melted butter versus softened butter, it was clear that softened butter was the way to go—the cookies spread beautifully. However, they were still a bit cakey. Our solution was twofold: First, we found that size made a big difference. Smaller cookies were more uniform in texture, while larger cookies tended to have softer centers and crisper edges. Second, we adjusted the leaveners: In our traditional recipe, we used only ½ teaspoon of baking soda to give the cookies a small amount of lift. But a few tests revealed that increasing the amount of baking soda and adding a teaspoon of baking powder caused the cookies to "overleaven," so the cookies rose high in the oven and then fell. This encouraged the pleasantly dense, chewy centers we were after. Our cookies were almost perfect, but a 30-minute rest pushed them over the top; it hydrated the Sucanat and ensured the best texture and fullest flavor. Our favorite brand of bittersweet chocolate is Ghirardelli 60% Cacao Bittersweet Chocolate Premium Baking Bar (see page 21 for more information); other brands may contain different amounts of sugar. Do not shortchange the dough's 30-minute resting time in step 2 or the cookies will be drier and slightly bland.

1¾ cups (8¾ ounces) all-purpose flour
1 teaspoon baking powder
¾ teaspoon baking soda
½ teaspoon salt
10 tablespoons unsalted butter, softened
⅔ cup plus ½ cup (6⅔ ounces) Sucanat
1 large egg plus 1 large yolk
1 tablespoon vanilla extract
5 ounces bittersweet chocolate, chopped

1. Combine flour, baking powder, baking soda, and salt in medium bowl. Using stand mixer fitted with paddle, beat butter and Sucanat together on medium-high speed until pale and fluffy, about 3 minutes. Add egg and yolk and vanilla and mix until combined, about 1 minute. Reduce speed to low, add flour mixture, and mix until combined, about 1 minute, scraping down bowl as needed. Add chocolate and mix until combined, about 30 seconds. Give dough final stir by hand.

2. Cover bowl with plastic wrap and let rest at room temperature for 30 minutes. Adjust oven rack to middle position and heat oven to 350 degrees. Line 2 baking sheets with parchment paper.

3. Working with scant 3 tablespoons of dough at a time, roll into balls and space 2 inches apart on prepared sheets.

4. Bake cookies, 1 sheet at a time, until light golden brown and edges have begun to set but centers are still soft, 12 to 15 minutes, rotating sheet halfway through baking. Let cookies cool completely on sheet. Serve.

BEFORE 25 grams sugar $\longrightarrow$ **AFTER** 15 grams sugar

Sweetener Substitutions

COCONUT SUGAR	1¼ cups plus 2 tablespoons (6⅔ ounces) Cookies will spread more, have crisper edges, and be darker in color.
DARK BROWN SUGAR	⅔ cup packed plus ¼ cup packed (6⅔ ounces) Cookies will have milder flavor and spread more.

Sweetener Substitutions

COCONUT SUGAR	**1½ cups (7 ounces)** Cookies will be darker in color and have slightly deeper flavor; grind sugar as directed in step 1.
LIGHT BROWN SUGAR	**1 cup packed (7 ounces)** Cookies will be lighter in color and have crisper texture; do not grind sugar in step 1.

oatmeal-raisin cookies

Makes 24 cookies

WHY THIS RECIPE WORKS When we set out to develop a low-sugar, naturally sweetened recipe for oatmeal-raisin cookies, we realized that their hallmark crisp edges and chewy centers are usually made possible by a generous amount of sugar. Our first attempts turned out dry, unappealing cookies with disappointing oat flavor and an overwhelming spice profile. To boost the oat flavor, we tested various flour-to-oat ratios; 1½ cups of flour for 3 cups of old-fashioned rolled oats provided the best flavor without making the cookies tough. Although traditional, cinnamon had an overpowering flavor; we preferred the cleaner, subtler flavor of nutmeg. Making big cookies encouraged the edges to crisp while the centers stayed soft. To ensure good spread, we pressed the dough balls to a ½-inch thickness before baking them. Do not substitute quick oats, instant oats, or steel-cut oats in this recipe. You can skip grinding the Sucanat in step 1; however, the cookies will have a speckled appearance. Do not shortchange the dough's 30-minute resting time in step 3 or the cookies will be drier and slightly bland.

1½ cups (7½ ounces) all-purpose flour
½ teaspoon salt
½ teaspoon baking powder
¼ teaspoon ground nutmeg
1¼ cups (7 ounces) Sucanat
16 tablespoons unsalted butter, softened
2 large eggs
3 cups (9 ounces) old-fashioned rolled oats
1 cup raisins

1. Combine flour, salt, baking powder, and nutmeg in bowl. Working in 4 batches, grind Sucanat in spice grinder until fine and powdery, about 1 minute.

2. Using stand mixer fitted with paddle, beat butter and ground Sucanat together on medium-high speed until light and fluffy, about 3 minutes. Add eggs, one at a time, and mix until combined, about 30 seconds. Reduce speed to low, add flour mixture, and mix until combined, about 1 minute, scraping down bowl as needed. Add oats and raisins and mix until combined, about 30 seconds. Give dough final stir by hand.

3. Cover bowl with plastic wrap and let rest at room temperature for 30 minutes. Adjust oven rack to middle position and heat oven to 350 degrees. Line 2 baking sheets with parchment paper.

4. Working with 2 heaping tablespoons of dough at a time, roll into balls and space 2 inches apart on prepared sheets. Press dough to ½-inch thickness using bottom of greased drinking glass.

5. Bake cookies, 1 sheet at a time, until edges begin to turn golden and firm, 12 to 15 minutes, rotating sheet halfway through baking. Let cookies cool completely on sheet. Serve.

BEFORE 23 grams sugar ⟶ **AFTER** 13 grams sugar

Pressing Cookies Flat

1 Roll 2 heaping tablespoons of dough into balls and space 2 inches apart on prepared sheets.
2 Press dough balls to ½-inch thickness using bottom of greased drinking glass to ensure dough doesn't stick to cup.

Sweetener Substitutions

COCONUT SUGAR
1¼ cups plus 2 tablespoons (6⅔ ounces)
Cookies will be darker in color and taste less rich; grind sugar as directed in step 1.

LIGHT BROWN SUGAR
⅔ cup packed plus ¼ cup packed (6⅔ ounces)
Cookies will have drier texture and have milder flavor; do not grind sugar in step 1.

peanut butter cookies

Makes 24 cookies

WHY THIS RECIPE WORKS We wanted a naturally sweetened peanut butter cookie that would be bursting at the seams with peanut flavor and have an appealingly chewy texture. We started by using honey as our sweetener; tasters loved the flavor of honey with the peanut butter, but we found it gave the cookies a tough, cakey texture that we couldn't overcome. Switching to Sucanat was the best solution: Because a granulated sweetener like Sucanat is more hygroscopic (water-retaining) than honey, it holds in more moisture from the dough throughout baking, resulting in a chewier cookie overall. Additionally, the Sucanat's deep flavor gave the peanut butter a nice backbone; resting the dough before baking produced the deepest, roundest flavor since the Sucanat had time to dissolve and distribute. But our work was far from done. The traditional creaming method yielded pale, dry cookies; a one-bowl mixing method using melted butter contributed a better density and texture, and cutting down on the amount of butter ensured the cookies weren't greasy. Further hydrating the dough with an additional ¼ cup of milk encouraged spread. A splash of vanilla rounded out the cookies' flavor, and a sprinkle of ground peanuts on top added a subtle crunch to our perfect low-sugar peanut butter cookies. The type of peanut butter you use here makes a difference; our recommended brand of crunchy peanut butter is Jif Natural Crunchy Peanut Butter Spread. Other brands may contain different amounts of sugar. You can skip grinding the Sucanat in step 1; however, the cookies will have a speckled appearance. Do not shortchange the dough's 30-minute resting time in step 3 or the cookies will taste slightly bland.

½ cup unsalted dry-roasted peanuts

⅔ cup plus ½ cup (6⅔ ounces) Sucanat

1 cup (5 ounces) all-purpose flour

1 teaspoon baking powder

¾ teaspoon baking soda

½ teaspoon salt

⅔ cup extra-crunchy peanut butter

¼ cup milk

1 large egg plus 1 large yolk

3 tablespoons unsalted butter, melted and cooled

2 teaspoons vanilla extract

1. Pulse peanuts in food processor until finely ground, about 14 pulses; measure out and reserve 2 tablespoons ground peanuts for topping. Working in 4 batches, grind Sucanat in spice grinder until fine and powdery, about 1 minute.

2. Combine flour, baking powder, baking soda, and salt in bowl. In large bowl, whisk ground Sucanat, peanut butter, milk, egg and yolk, melted butter, and vanilla together until combined. Using rubber spatula, stir in flour mixture until combined. Fold in ground peanuts.

3. Cover bowl with plastic wrap and let rest at room temperature for 30 minutes. Adjust oven racks to upper-middle and lower-middle positions and heat oven to 350 degrees. Line 2 baking sheets with parchment paper.

4. Working with heaping tablespoon dough at a time, use your wet hands to roll into balls and space 2 inches apart on prepared sheets (dough will be sticky). Sprinkle reserved ground peanuts over tops of cookies. Press dough to ½-inch thickness using bottom of greased drinking glass.

5. Bake cookies until just beginning to brown and firm, about 12 minutes, switching and rotating sheets halfway through baking. Let cookies cool completely on sheets. Serve.

BEFORE 12 grams sugar ⟶ **AFTER** 8 grams sugar

cookies and bars

fudgy chocolate cookies

Makes 24 cookies

WHY THIS RECIPE WORKS Fudgy chocolate cookies often pack in the sugar to get the perfect chew; we set out to use less sugar but still achieve the same big chocolate flavor and chewy texture. Since the traditional recipe called for both brown sugar and sweetened chocolate, we had to change the type of sugar as well as the type of chocolate to sweeten these cookies naturally. Unsurprisingly, our first attempts using Sucanat and unsweetened chocolate were unacceptable: They lacked good chocolate flavor and had a pronounced bitter taste; plus, they were overly tender and cakey. The key to perfectly balanced chocolate flavor turned out to be doubling up on chocolate: Cocoa powder gave the cookies a bold hit of chocolate flavor, while the unsweetened chocolate, which contains cocoa butter, prevented the cookies from drying out. Next, we set our sights on improving the structure. Switching from all-purpose flour to higher-protein bread flour gave the cookies better chew, but didn't solve all our issues. The fat in the butter was making the cookies crumbly, but decreasing the butter resulted in cookies that lacked richness. In the end, adding a small amount of heavy cream provided moisture and richness without the high fat content of butter. Do not skip grinding the Sucanat in step 1, or the cookies will be overly delicate. Do not substitute natural cocoa or the cookies will be dry and spread less. Our favorite Dutch-processed cocoa powder is Droste Cocoa and our favorite unsweetened chocolate is Hershey's Unsweetened Baking Bar (see page 21 for more information). Do not shortchange the dough's 30-minute resting time in step 3 or the cookies will be drier and slightly bland.

2 ounces unsweetened chocolate, chopped

½ cup (1½ ounces) Dutch-processed cocoa powder

4 tablespoons unsalted butter, cut into 4 pieces

¾ cup plus ⅔ cup (7¾ ounces) Sucanat

1¼ cups (6¾ ounces) bread flour

1 teaspoon baking powder

¾ teaspoon baking soda

½ teaspoon salt

⅓ cup heavy cream

1 large egg plus 1 large yolk

2 teaspoons vanilla extract

1. Microwave chocolate, cocoa, and butter in bowl at 50 percent power, stirring often, until melted and smooth, 2 to 4 minutes; let cool slightly. Working in 4 batches, grind Sucanat in spice grinder until fine and powdery, about 1 minute.

2. Combine ground Sucanat, flour, baking powder, baking soda, and salt in bowl. In large bowl, whisk cream, egg and yolk, and vanilla together. Whisk in cooled chocolate mixture. Stir in flour mixture using rubber spatula until combined; dough will be stiff and dry.

3. Cover bowl with plastic wrap and let rest at room temperature for 30 minutes. Adjust oven racks to upper-middle and lower-middle positions and heat oven to 350 degrees. Line 2 baking sheets with parchment paper.

4. Working with scant 2 tablespoons dough at a time, roll into balls and space 2 inches apart on prepared sheets.

5. Bake cookies until edges have just begun to set but centers are still very soft, about 10 minutes, switching and rotating sheets halfway through baking. Let cookies cool completely on sheets. Serve.

BEFORE 15 grams sugar ⟶ **AFTER** 9 grams sugar

Sweetener Substitutions

COCONUT SUGAR	1½ cups plus 2 tablespoons (7¾ ounces) Cookies will be slightly drier; grind sugar as directed in step 1.
LIGHT BROWN SUGAR	1 cup packed plus 2 tablespoons packed (7¾ ounces) Cookies will have milder flavor; do not grind sugar in step 1.

cookies and bars

molasses spice cookies

Makes 16 cookies

WHY THIS RECIPE WORKS Molasses spice cookies should be ultramoist, soft yet chewy, with a warm, tingling spiciness and the dark bittersweet flavor of molasses. But the granulated sugar, dark brown sugar, and generous amount of mild molasses meant that our traditional recipe was loaded with sugar. Our first move was to switch out the usual combination of white and brown sugars for Sucanat and omit the molasses altogether, hoping that the natural molasses present in the Sucanat would be enough to flavor our cookies. While tasters were fairly happy with the flavor of the cookies, taking out the molasses had also eliminated a lot of moisture, so the cookies were very dry. To fix this, we added in some milk, and found that a mere ¼ cup was enough to create a moist, chewy cookie. But the milk also had an unexpected consequence: The dairy had muted the bold, bittersweet flavor that is the hallmark of a great molasses cookie. No matter what spices we added, we could not re-create the robust molasses flavor we were after. In the end, the solution was to add just a small amount of molasses back to our cookies. To get the most impact while keeping the amount as small as possible, we used blackstrap molasses, which has much bolder flavor and contains less sugar than mild or medium molasses. Do not shortchange the dough's 30-minute resting time in step 3 or the cookies will taste slightly bland. You can substitute mild or medium molasses for the blackstrap molasses, but the sugar content of the cookies will be different.

2¼ cups (11¼ ounces) all-purpose flour
1½ teaspoons ground cinnamon
1½ teaspoons ground ginger
 1 teaspoon baking soda
½ teaspoon ground cloves
¼ teaspoon ground allspice
¼ teaspoon pepper
¼ teaspoon salt
12 tablespoons unsalted butter, softened
¾ cup plus ⅔ cup (7¾ ounces) Sucanat
¼ cup whole milk
 1 large egg yolk
 1 tablespoon blackstrap molasses
 1 teaspoon vanilla extract

1. Combine flour, cinnamon, ginger, baking soda, cloves, allspice, pepper, and salt in bowl.

2. Using stand mixer fitted with paddle, beat butter and Sucanat on medium-high speed until pale and fluffy, about 3 minutes. Add milk, egg yolk, molasses, and vanilla and mix until combined, about 1 minute. Reduce speed to low, add flour mixture, and mix until combined, about 1 minute, scraping down bowl as needed. Give dough final stir by hand.

3. Cover bowl with plastic wrap and let rest at room temperature for 30 minutes. Adjust oven rack to middle position and heat oven to 350 degrees. Line 2 baking sheets with parchment paper.

4. Working with scant 3 tablespoons dough at a time, roll into balls and space 2 inches apart on prepared sheets.

5. Bake cookies, 1 sheet at a time, until browned and edges have begun to set but centers are still soft and puffy, 10 to 12 minutes, rotating sheet halfway through baking. Let cookies cool completely on sheet. Serve.

BEFORE 20 grams sugar ⟶ **AFTER** 14 grams sugar

Sweetener Substitutions

COCONUT SUGAR	1½ cups plus 2 tablespoons (7¾ ounces) Cookies will be darker in color and have drier texture.
GRANULATED SUGAR AND BROWN SUGAR	½ cup plus 2 tablespoons (4⅓ ounces) granulated sugar and ½ cup packed (3½ ounces) brown sugar Cookies will be lighter in color and have milder flavor.

lemon–poppy seed cookies

Makes 36 cookies

WHY THIS RECIPE WORKS Lemon and poppy seeds are a classic combination in the baker's repertoire. We wanted to incorporate these two ingredients into a small, slightly chewy cookie perfect for afternoon tea or snacking. We started by adapting our traditional lemon sugar cookie recipe, but as we well knew, simply reducing the sugar wouldn't cut it. Moreover, the Sucanat's molasses undertone overpowered the relatively mild lemon flavor. We tried boosting the lemon flavor with lemon zest, juice, and extract, but tasters found that the lemon extract tasted artificial. We ditched it and used as much lemon juice as we could afford—just enough before the cookies began to spread too much—and rested the dough before baking to ensure that it wasn't too sticky to work with. To combat the dry, cakey quality of the cookies, we tried decreasing the baking powder—thus far the only leavening agent in the recipe. The resulting cookies were flatter and chewier with crisp edges, but the bottoms were still comparatively soft and cakey. To impart more crispness to the bottoms and to get a bit more spread, we introduced baking soda. These cookies were the best yet: pleasantly zesty, nicely sized, and slightly sophisticated. You can skip grinding the Sucanat in step 1; however, the cookies will be speckled in appearance. Do not shortchange the dough's 30-minute resting time in step 3 or the dough will be difficult to work with and the cookies will spread unevenly and taste slightly bland.

1⅓ cups (6⅔ ounces) all-purpose flour
4 teaspoons poppy seeds
½ teaspoon salt
½ teaspoon baking soda
¼ teaspoon baking powder
¾ cup plus ⅓ cup (6 ounces) Sucanat
10 tablespoons unsalted butter, softened
1 large egg plus 1 large yolk
4 teaspoons grated lemon zest plus 2 tablespoons juice (2 lemons)

1. Combine flour, 1 tablespoon poppy seeds, salt, baking soda, and baking powder in bowl. Working in 4 batches, grind Sucanat in spice grinder until fine and powdery, about 1 minute.

2. Using stand mixer fitted with paddle, beat butter and ground Sucanat together on medium-high speed until pale and fluffy, about 3 minutes. Add egg and yolk and lemon zest and juice and mix until thoroughly combined and emulsified, about 2 minutes. Reduce speed to low, add flour mixture, and mix until combined, about 1 minute, scraping down bowl as needed. Give dough final stir by hand. (Dough will be very sticky.)

3. Cover bowl with plastic wrap and let rest at room temperature for 30 minutes. Adjust oven rack to middle position and heat oven to 350 degrees. Line baking sheet with parchment paper.

4. Using 2 spoons, drop dough 1 scant tablespoon at a time onto prepared sheet, spaced 2 inches apart (you should have 12 cookies on sheet). Sprinkle ⅓ of remaining poppy seeds over tops of cookies.

5. Bake cookies, 1 sheet at a time, until light golden brown and edges have begun to set but centers are still soft, 8 to 10 minutes, rotating sheet halfway through baking. Let cookies cool completely on sheet. Repeat with remaining dough and poppy seeds. Serve.

BEFORE 8 grams sugar ⟶ **AFTER** 5 grams sugar

Sweetener Substitutions

COCONUT SUGAR	1¼ cups (6 ounces) Cookies will be darker in color and have slight caramel flavor; grind sugar as directed in step 1.
GRANULATED SUGAR	¾ cup plus 2 tablespoons (6 ounces) Cookies will be paler and have milder flavor; do not grind sugar in step 1.

coconut washboards

Makes 36 cookies

WHY THIS RECIPE WORKS Crisp and crunchy washboard cookies, named for their resemblance in shape and line design to old-fashioned washboards, make an ideal accompaniment to coffee or tea. We wanted our version of this classic to rely on a mere 3 grams of sugar. Our first move was to replace the sweetened shredded coconut, which contains a whopping 40 grams of sugar per cup, with unsweetened, which contains only 5 grams per cup. Coconut sugar lent a rich, toasted flavor, and tasters found that the reduced sweetness level allowed the flavor of coconut to come through unhindered. To create the "washboard" ridges that stripe the top of each cookie, we used a fork with moistened tines to easily imprint the pattern on the dough. You can skip grinding the coconut sugar in step 1; however, the cookies will have a speckled appearance.

2 cups (10 ounces) all-purpose flour
½ teaspoon baking powder
¼ teaspoon baking soda
¼ teaspoon salt
¼ teaspoon ground nutmeg
¾ cup (3½ ounces) coconut sugar
8 tablespoons unsalted butter, softened
1 large egg
2 tablespoons milk
1 cup (3 ounces) unsweetened shredded coconut

1. Combine flour, baking powder, baking soda, salt, and nutmeg in bowl. Working in 3 batches, grind coconut sugar in spice grinder until fine and powdery, about 1 minute.

2. Using stand mixer fitted with paddle, beat butter and ground sugar on medium-high speed until pale and fluffy, about 3 minutes. Add egg and milk and mix until combined, about 1 minute. Reduce speed to low, add flour mixture, and mix until combined, scraping down bowl as needed, about 1 minute. Add shredded coconut and mix until combined, about 1 minute. Give dough final stir by hand.

3. Transfer dough to lightly floured counter. Using your floured hands and bench scraper, shape dough into 9 by 3-inch rectangle (about 1 inch tall). Wrap dough tightly with plastic wrap and refrigerate until firm, at least 45 minutes or up to 24 hours.

4. Adjust oven rack to middle position and heat oven to 350 degrees. Line 2 rimmed baking sheets with parchment paper. Cut dough into ¼-inch-thick cookies and space 1 inch apart on prepared sheets. Using dinner fork dipped in water, press fork across center of each cookie to make ridged washboard-style design.

5. Bake cookies, 1 sheet at a time, until firm, 13 to 15 minutes, rotating sheet halfway through baking. Let cookies cool on sheet for 5 minutes, then transfer to wire rack and let cool completely. Serve.

BEFORE 7 grams sugar ⟶ **AFTER** 3 grams sugar

Making Coconut Washboards

1 Cut chilled dough into ¼-inch-thick cookies using chef's knife.
2 Using dinner fork dipped in water, press fork across center of each cookie to make ridged washboard-style design.

Sweetener Substitutions

SUCANAT	½ cup plus 2 tablespoons (3½ ounces) Cookies will have slightly deeper flavor and will spread slightly; grind sugar as directed in step 1.
LIGHT BROWN SUGAR	½ cup packed (3½ ounces) Cookies will have milder flavor; do not grind sugar in step 1.

Sweetener Substitutions

COCONUT SUGAR	¾ cup (3½ ounces) Cookies will be darker in color and have nuttier flavor; grind sugar as directed in step 2.
GRANULATED SUGAR	½ cup (3½ ounces) Cookies will be lighter in color and have slightly crumbly texture; do not grind sugar in step 2.

almond-cardamom thins

Makes 36 cookies

WHY THIS RECIPE WORKS For a refined take on a classic slice-and-bake cookie, we wanted a buttery, robustly flavored treat. We swapped the granulated sugar for Sucanat and, to give greater complexity to the cookie, we introduced citrusy cardamom and toasted almonds. We also browned the butter to contribute deeper flavor. This step required switching from the traditional creaming method to a bowl method, but the cookies turned out exceptionally nutty and aromatic. Still, we found these cookies much shorter and far less sturdy than the original version. We needed moisture to hydrate the flour, develop gluten, and give structure to the cookies. Luckily, simply adding water did the trick: The resulting thins were perfectly crisp. You can skip grinding the Sucanat in step 2; however, the cookies will have a speckled appearance.

14 tablespoons unsalted butter, cut into 14 pieces

1½ teaspoons ground cardamom

½ cup plus 2 tablespoons (3½ ounces) Sucanat

3 tablespoons water

2 large egg yolks

2 teaspoons vanilla extract

½ teaspoon salt

2¼ cups (11¼ ounces) all-purpose flour

⅔ cup sliced almonds, toasted

1. Heat 10 tablespoons butter in 10-inch skillet over medium-high heat until it begins to turn golden, about 2 minutes. Continue to cook, swirling pan constantly, until butter is dark golden brown and has nutty aroma, 1 to 3 minutes; transfer to large bowl. Stir in remaining 4 tablespoons butter and cardamom until butter is completely melted; let cool for 15 minutes.

2. Working in 2 batches, grind Sucanat in spice grinder until fine and powdery, about 1 minute. Whisk ground Sucanat, water, egg yolks, vanilla, and salt into melted butter until smooth. Using rubber spatula, stir in flour until combined. Fold in almonds.

3. Transfer dough to clean counter and knead until it forms cohesive mass, about 1 minute. Divide dough into 2 equal pieces and roll each into 6-inch log, about 2 inches thick. Wrap each log tightly in plastic wrap, twisting ends to help compact log, and place upright in tall drinking glass. Refrigerate until firm, at least 2 hours or up to 2 days.

4. Adjust oven racks to upper-middle and lower-middle positions and heat oven to 350 degrees. Line 2 baking sheets with parchment paper. Working with 1 log of dough at a time, slice into ¼-inch-thick cookies, turning log every few slices to prevent sides from flattening, and space ¾ inch apart on prepared sheets.

5. Bake cookies until edges just begin to brown, 12 to 15 minutes, switching and rotating sheets halfway through baking. Let cookies cool completely on sheets. Serve.

BEFORE 4 grams sugar → **AFTER** 2 grams sugar

Making Almond-Cardamom Thins

1 Roll each piece of dough into 6-inch log, about 2 inches thick.
2 Place wrapped dough upright in tall drinking glass and refrigerate for at least 2 hours; glass helps to protect dough's round shape as it chills.

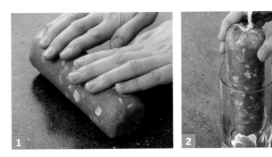

Sweetener Substitutions

COCONUT SUGAR   ½ cup plus ⅓ cup (4 ounces)
Cookies will be darker in color and lightly speckled; grind sugar as directed
in step 1.

LIGHT BROWN SUGAR   ⅓ cup packed plus ¼ cup packed (4 ounces)
Cookies will look pale, taste dry, and be slightly crumbly when slicing; do not
grind sugar in step 1.

pecan shortbread cookies

Makes 40 cookies

WHY THIS RECIPE WORKS Whimsical and festive, these pecan-laden icebox cookies are perfect for any occasion, especially because they're simple to make and can be prepared in advance. We cut the sugar from 6 grams to just 3 and replaced the typical brown sugar with Sucanat to give the cookies a gentle molasses flavor. To boost flavor further, we added cinnamon for its bold, warm presence along with a little nutmeg for depth. The addition of vanilla helped to round out the flavors. Tasters liked the nutty flavor of browned butter, but it negatively affected the texture of the cookies—with so little liquid already in the recipe, we couldn't afford to cook the water out of the butter. Instead, we decided to process some of the pecans in a food processor and incorporate them into the dough to provide some of the nuttiness we would have gotten from browned butter. To streamline the recipe, we processed the rest of the dry ingredients in the food processor, followed by the wet. Chilling the dough logs for at least 2 hours ensured that the dough could be sliced and baked into cookies with clean, crisp edges. A pretty pecan half placed on top of each cookie made them look worthy of company (and a quick egg wash ensured they stayed firmly on the cookies). Do not skip grinding the Sucanat in step 1 or the cookies will have a dense, hard texture.

¾ cup (4 ounces) Sucanat
1 cup pecans
8 tablespoons unsalted butter, melted and cooled
2 large egg yolks
2 tablespoons water
2 teaspoons vanilla extract
2¼ cups (11¼ ounces) all-purpose flour
1 teaspoon ground cinnamon
½ teaspoon salt
⅛ teaspoon ground nutmeg
1 large egg white mixed with 2 tablespoons water

1. Working in 3 batches, grind Sucanat in spice grinder until fine and powdery, about 1 minute. Reserve 40 prettiest pecan halves for garnishing. Whisk melted butter, egg yolks, water, and vanilla in bowl until combined.

2. Process remaining pecans in food processor until nuts are coarsely ground, about 20 seconds. Add ground Sucanat, flour, cinnamon, salt, and nutmeg and process until combined, about 10 seconds. With processor running, add butter mixture and process until dough comes together, about 25 seconds.

3. Transfer dough to clean counter, knead until smooth and cohesive, and divide into 2 equal pieces. Roll each piece of dough into 6-inch log, about 2 inches thick. Wrap each log tightly in plastic wrap and place upright in tall drinking glass. Refrigerate until firm, at least 2 hours or up to 2 days.

4. Adjust oven rack to middle position and heat oven to 325 degrees. Line 2 baking sheets with parchment paper. Working with 1 log of dough at a time, slice into ¼-inch-thick cookies, turning log every few slices to prevent sides from flattening, and space ¾ inch apart on prepared sheets. Brush cookies with egg white mixture, then gently press reserved pecan halves into center of each cookie.

5. Bake, 1 sheet at a time, until edges of cookies are beginning to brown and set, 16 to 19 minutes, rotating sheet halfway through baking. Let cookies cool completely on sheet. Serve.

BEFORE 5 grams sugar ⟶ **AFTER** 3 grams sugar

spiced shortbread

Makes 16 cookies

WHY THIS RECIPE WORKS The basics of making shortbread haven't changed much over the past five centuries: Combine flour, sugar, butter, and salt; pat the dough into a round; and bake. With so few ingredients, each one has a big impact, so taking out half the sugar meant we had to abandon this time-honored formula. However, we still wanted all the best elements of classic shortbread: a pleasantly crumbly texture and plenty of buttery richness offset by subtle sweetness. Reverse creaming (combining the flour and sugar before adding the butter) created less aeration and produced a more substantial shortbread. To solve the persistent problem of blandness, we added a hefty dose of cinnamon and vanilla along with some nutmeg and cloves. The spices gave the shortbread an identity and complemented the buttery flavor. Although tasters liked the flavor of Sucanat, the texture of the shortbread made with coconut sugar was more on par with their expectations. To bake the shortbread, we started the oven at a hot 425 degrees, which helped set the crust, and then lowered the temperature to 300 degrees to allow the shortbread to gently bake through. To form the shortbread into a neat round, we used a springform pan collar as a mold. We started with the collar in the closed position to help shape the raw dough and then opened the collar before baking to allow the shortbread to expand slightly. Do not skip grinding the coconut sugar in step 1 or the shortbread will have a very dense, dry texture.

6 tablespoons (1¾ ounces) coconut sugar

2 cups (10 ounces) all-purpose flour

2½ teaspoons ground cinnamon

¼ teaspoon ground nutmeg

¼ teaspoon ground cloves

½ teaspoon salt

14 tablespoons unsalted butter, sliced ⅛ inch thick and chilled

2 tablespoons vanilla extract

1. Adjust oven rack to middle position and heat oven to 425 degrees. Place collar of 9- or 9½-inch springform pan on parchment paper–lined rimmed baking sheet (do not use springform pan bottom). Grind coconut sugar in spice grinder until fine and powdery, about 1 minute.

2. Using stand mixer fitted with paddle attachment, mix ground sugar, flour, cinnamon, nutmeg, cloves, and salt on low speed until combined, about 1 minute. Add chilled butter, 1 piece at a time, and mix until only pea-size pieces remain, about 1 minute. Add vanilla and mix until dough comes together, about 5 minutes. Give dough final stir by hand.

3. Press dough evenly into springform collar and smooth top of dough with back of spoon. Using 2-inch biscuit cutter, cut out dough in center; place extracted dough on baking sheet and replace cutter in center of dough. Open springform collar, but leave it in place.

4. Place shortbread in oven and immediately reduce oven temperature to 300 degrees. Bake shortbread until edges are deep golden brown, about 20 minutes.

5. Remove baking sheet from oven and remove springform pan collar and biscuit cutter. Using chef's knife, score surface of shortbread into 16 even wedges, cutting halfway through shortbread. Using blunt end of wooden skewer, poke 8 to 10 holes in each wedge. Return shortbread to oven and continue to bake until golden brown, about 40 minutes.

6. Let shortbread cool completely on sheet, about 2 hours. Cut shortbread along scored lines and serve.

BEFORE 5 grams sugar ⟶ **AFTER** 3 grams sugar

Making Shortbread

1 After pressing dough into springform collar, smooth top of dough with back of spoon.

2 Using 2-inch biscuit cutter, cut out dough in center; place extracted dough on rimmed baking sheet and replace cutter in center of dough.

3 Open springform collar, but leave it in place.

4 After baking shortbread for 20 minutes, remove springform collar and biscuit cutter and score shortbread into 16 even wedges, cutting halfway through shortbread.

5 Using blunt end of wooden skewer, poke 8 to 10 holes in each wedge, then continue to bake shortbread for 40 minutes longer.

6 Once cooled, cut shortbread into individual cookies along scored lines.

Sweetener Substitutions

SUCANAT	⅓ cup (1¾ ounces) Shortbread will be lighter in color; grind sugar as directed in step 1.
CONFECTIONERS' SUGAR	7 tablespoons (1¾ ounces) Shortbread will taste slightly pasty, less sweet, and have milder flavor; do not grind sugar in step 1.

holiday cookies
Makes forty 2½-inch cookies

WHY THIS RECIPE WORKS For us, it's hard to imagine the holidays without a batch of festively decorated cookies. We were pleasantly surprised that halving the sugar of our traditional recipe yielded buttery, toothsome cookies with a pleasant, mild sweetness. But without the added sugar, the cookies domed considerably during baking, producing an unsightly (and undecoratable) hump on each cookie. Without the tenderizing power of the extra sugar, the cookies were developing too much gluten structure, and the initial burst of heat in the oven was causing water in the dough to quickly turn to steam, an effect called "oven spring." We tried lowering the oven temperature to diminish the oven spring, but the cookies still had noticeable—if slightly smaller—domes. Next, we tried weakening the gluten structure by switching to lower protein cake flour. This seemed to do the trick: The cookies were beautifully flat and uniform. Unfortunately, they were also pasty and far too delicate to decorate. We switched back to all-purpose flour and turned our attention to fat instead. Our traditional recipe contained both butter and cream cheese; the cream cheese was intended to give the cookies richness without making them greasy, but we wondered if it was contributing to our textural issues. But manipulating ratios of butter and cream cheese made no difference. In the end, we arrived at a solution through a happy accident: Halfway through baking, if we jostled the baking sheet, some of the cookies would deflate and bake up perfectly flat. By striking the pan against a surface partway through baking, we could create flat, uniform shapes every time. Using this simple but unconventional method, we were able to cut the sugar in half without sacrificing texture or aesthetics. A tangy cream cheese frosting rounded out our versatile, delicious holiday cookies. Note that glaze made with coconut sugar will be dark brown in color and require 6 hours to set. For a bright white glaze that is easier to tint with food coloring and requires only 30 minutes to dry, omit the cornstarch and substitute ¾ cup (3 ounces) confectioners' sugar for the ground coconut sugar in the glaze. Do not skip grinding the coconut sugar in step 1 or step 6 or the cookies will have a crumbly texture and the glaze will be grainy.

cookies

- ⅓ cup plus ¼ cup (2⅔ ounces) coconut sugar
- 2½ cups (12½ ounces) all-purpose flour
- ⅛ teaspoon salt
- 16 tablespoons unsalted butter, cut into 16 pieces and softened
- 2 tablespoons cream cheese, softened
- 2 teaspoons vanilla extract

glaze

- ½ cup plus 2 tablespoons (3 ounces) coconut sugar
- 4 teaspoons cornstarch
- 2 tablespoons cream cheese, softened
- 1–2 tablespoons milk
- ⅛ teaspoon salt

1. FOR THE COOKIES Working in 2 batches, grind coconut sugar in spice grinder until fine and powdery, about 1 minute. Using stand mixer fitted with paddle, mix ground sugar, flour, and salt together on low speed until combined, about 1 minute. Add butter, 1 piece at a time, and mix until only pea-size pieces remain, about 1 minute. Add cream cheese and vanilla and mix until dough just begins to form large clumps, about 30 seconds.

2. Transfer dough to clean counter, knead until dough forms cohesive mass, then divide into 2 equal pieces. Shape each piece into 4-inch disk, then wrap in plastic wrap and refrigerate until firm, at least 30 minutes or up to 3 days.

3. Adjust oven rack to middle position and heat oven to 375 degrees. Working with 1 piece of dough at a time, roll ⅛ inch thick between 2 sheets of parchment paper. Slide dough, still between parchment, onto baking sheet and refrigerate until firm, about 20 minutes.

4. Line 2 baking sheets with parchment. Working with 1 sheet of dough at a time, remove top sheet of parchment and cut dough as desired using cookie cutters; space ¾ inch apart on prepared sheets. (Dough scraps can be patted together, chilled, and rerolled once.)

5. Bake cookies, 1 sheet at a time, until lightly puffed but still underdone, about 5 minutes. Remove partially baked cookies from oven and, holding sheet firmly with both hands, rap pan flat against open oven door 3 to 5 times until puffed cookies flatten. Rotate pan, return cookies to oven, and continue to bake until light golden brown around edges, 4 to 6 minutes longer. Let cookies cool completely on sheet.

6. FOR THE GLAZE Working in 2 batches, grind coconut sugar in spice grinder until fine and powdery, about 1 minute. Whisk ground sugar and cornstarch together in small bowl. In separate bowl, whisk cream cheese, 1 tablespoon milk, and salt together until smooth. Whisk in coconut sugar mixture until smooth, adding remaining 1 tablespoon milk as needed until glaze is thin enough to drizzle. Drizzle or decorate each cookie with glaze as desired. Let glaze set for at least 6 hours before serving.

BEFORE 10 grams sugar $\longrightarrow$ **AFTER** 5 grams sugar

Making Holiday Cookies

1 Working with 1 piece of dough at a time, roll ⅛ inch thick between 2 sheets of parchment paper.

2 Slide dough, still between parchment, onto baking sheet and refrigerate until firm, about 20 minutes.

3 Working with 1 sheet of dough at a time, remove top sheet of parchment and cut dough as desired using cookie cutters; space ¾ inch apart on prepared sheets.

4 Halfway through baking, remove cookies from oven and, holding sheet firmly with both hands, rap pan flat against oven door 3 to 5 times until puffed cookies flatten.

Sweetener Substitutions

SUCANAT	Cookies: ½ cup (2⅔ ounces) Glaze: ⅓ cup plus ¼ cup (3 ounces) Cookies and glaze will be light brown in color and have earthy, molasses aftertaste; grind sugar as directed in steps 1 and 6.
GRANULATED SUGAR AND CONFECTIONERS' SUGAR	Cookies: 6 tablespoons (2⅔ ounces) granulated sugar Glaze: ¾ cup (3 ounces) confectioners' sugar Cookies will be lighter in color and glaze will be bright white in color; omit cornstarch and do not grind sugar in steps 1 and 6.

cookies and bars

Sweetener Substitutions

COCONUT SUGAR
½ cup plus 2 tablespoons (3 ounces)
Crackers will be darker in color and taste drier; grind sugar as directed in step 1.

GRANULATED SUGAR
7 tablespoons (3 ounces)
Crackers will have milder flavor and be slightly crumbly; do not grind sugar in step 1.

graham crackers

Makes 36 crackers

WHY THIS RECIPE WORKS Despite their name, graham crackers are a decidedly sweet treat. Making graham crackers is surprisingly easy and we loved the idea of being able to control how much and what type of sugar went into them. Although the flavor of honey was nice, we found the added moisture made the dough too soft to work with; Sucanat tasted great and ensured that our dough was easy to roll. Rolling the dough between sheets of parchment made it easy to transfer from the counter to the baking sheet. To achieve a short, flaky texture, we cut chilled butter into the dough using a food processor. Cinnamon and vanilla rounded out the flavor of our crackers. You can skip grinding the Sucanat in step 1; however, the crackers will have a speckled appearance. Do not shortchange the dough's 30-minute resting time in step 2 or the dough will be difficult to handle.

⅓ cup plus ¼ cup (3 ounces) Sucanat
¼ cup water
1 tablespoon vanilla extract
1¾ cups (9⅔ ounces) graham flour
½ cup (2½ ounces) all-purpose flour
1 teaspoon ground cinnamon
1 teaspoon baking powder
½ teaspoon baking soda
½ teaspoon salt
8 tablespoons unsalted butter, cut into ½-inch pieces and chilled

1. Working in 2 batches, grind Sucanat in spice grinder until fine and powdery, about 1 minute. Combine water and vanilla in bowl.

2. Process ground Sucanat, graham flour, all-purpose flour, cinnamon, baking powder, baking soda, and salt in food processor until combined, about 3 seconds. Add chilled butter and process until mixture resembles coarse cornmeal, about 15 seconds. Add vanilla mixture and process until dough comes together, about 20 seconds. Transfer to bowl, cover with plastic wrap, and let dough rest at room temperature for 30 minutes.

3. Adjust oven racks to upper-middle and lower-middle positions and heat oven to 300 degrees. Divide dough into 2 equal pieces, shape each piece into 4-inch square, and cover with plastic wrap.

4. Working with 1 piece of dough at a time, roll between 2 large sheets of parchment paper into 16 by 8-inch rectangle (⅛ inch thick); loosen pieces of parchment from dough occasionally when rolling out. Remove top sheet parchment. Using sharp knife, score dough into eighteen 2⅔-inch squares, then prick each square several times with fork. Slide each parchment with dough onto rimmed baking sheet.

5. Bake crackers until firm to touch and just beginning to brown around edges, 30 to 35 minutes, switching and rotating sheets halfway through baking. Let crackers cool completely on sheets, then break apart along scored lines. Serve.

BEFORE 4 grams sugar → **AFTER** 2 grams sugar

Making Graham Crackers

1 Roll dough into 16 by 8-inch rectangle (⅛ inch thick) between 2 large sheets of parchment paper, then remove top sheet of parchment.

2 Using sharp knife, score dough into eighteen 2⅔-inch squares, then prick each square several times with fork.

almond biscotti

Makes 30 cookies

WHY THIS RECIPE WORKS Our ideal low-sugar biscotti had to meet the perfect afternoon coffee requirements: bold, nutty flavor; satisfying (but not tooth-breaking) crunch; good for dipping but equally delicious on its own. We found that cutting the sugar of our traditional recipe from 7 grams to just 3 produced a satisfactory flavor, and we did not miss the extra sweetness. We chose Sucanat to sweeten our biscotti because of its slight molasses undertone that paired well with a bold almond taste. But while the cookies were certainly flavorful, they were drier and a bit harder than we wanted. With less sugar, the dough was unable to hold on to as much moisture. The typical two-step baking process—once to set the log, and a second time to toast the slices—only exacerbated the problem. To account for the loss in moisture, we reduced the baking time in both stages. The resulting biscotti were less dry and sandy, but they were still a bit hard to bite. Whipping the eggs helped alleviate this problem by imparting lift and aeration to the cookies. But too much gluten was still developing in the dough; in order to temper the gluten development and contribute a slight crumbliness, we cut the flour with ground toasted almonds—with the added benefit of extra nutty flavor. Be sure to toast the nuts lightly before making the dough, as they will continue to toast as the biscotti bake.

1¼ cups whole almonds, lightly toasted

1¾ cups (8¾ ounces) all-purpose flour

2 teaspoons baking powder

¼ teaspoon salt

2 large eggs, plus 1 large white lightly beaten

½ cup plus 2 tablespoons (3½ ounces) Sucanat

4 tablespoons unsalted butter, melted and cooled

1½ teaspoons almond extract

½ teaspoon vanilla extract

1. Adjust oven rack to middle position and heat oven to 325 degrees. Line rimmed baking sheet with parchment paper and spray with vegetable oil spray. Pulse 1 cup almonds in food processor until coarsely chopped, 8 to 10 pulses; transfer to bowl.

2. Process remaining ¼ cup almonds in now-empty food processor until finely ground, about 45 seconds. Add flour, baking powder, and salt and process to combine, about 15 seconds; transfer to separate bowl.

3. Process 2 eggs in now-empty food processor until lightened in color and almost doubled in volume, about 3 minutes. With processor running, slowly add Sucanat until thoroughly combined, about 15 seconds. Add melted butter, almond extract, and vanilla and process until combined, about 10 seconds; transfer to large bowl.

4. Sprinkle half of flour mixture over egg mixture and, using rubber spatula, fold until just combined. Add remaining flour mixture and chopped almonds and fold until just combined.

5. Divide batter in half. Using your floured hands, press dough into two 8 by 3-inch loaves on prepared baking sheet, spaced about 4 inches apart. Brush loaves with beaten egg white. Bake loaves until golden and just beginning to crack on top, 20 to 25 minutes, rotating sheet halfway through baking.

6. Let loaves cool on sheet for 30 minutes, then transfer loaves to cutting board. Using serrated knife, slice each loaf on slight bias into ½-inch-thick slices. Lay slices, cut side down, about ¼ inch apart on wire rack set in rimmed baking sheet. Bake cookies until crisp and light golden brown on both sides, 25 to 30 minutes, flipping slices and rotating sheet halfway through baking. Let biscotti cool completely on rack before serving.

BEFORE 7 grams sugar ⟶ **AFTER** 3 grams sugar

hazelnut-orange biscotti

Substitute lightly toasted and skinned hazelnuts for almonds. Add 2 tablespoons minced fresh rosemary to food processor with flour. Substitute orange-flavored liqueur for almond extract and add 1 tablespoon grated orange zest to egg mixture.

BEFORE 7 grams sugar $\longrightarrow$ **AFTER** 3 grams sugar

pistachio-spice biscotti

Substitute shelled pistachios for almonds. Add 1 teaspoon ground cardamom, ½ teaspoon ground cloves, ½ teaspoon pepper, ¼ teaspoon ground cinnamon, and ¼ teaspoon ground ginger to food processor with flour. Substitute 1 teaspoon water for almond extract and increase vanilla extract to 1 teaspoon.

BEFORE 7 grams sugar $\longrightarrow$ **AFTER** 4 grams sugar

Making Biscotti

1 Using your floured hands, press dough into two 8 by 3-inch loaves on prepared baking sheet, spaced about 4 inches apart.
2 Bake loaves until golden and just beginning to crack on top, 20 to 25 minutes.
3 Let loaves cool for 30 minutes, then slice each loaf on slight bias into ½-inch-thick slices using serrated knife.
4 Lay slices, cut side down, about ¼ inch apart on wire rack set in rimmed baking sheet and bake until crisp and light golden brown on both sides, 25 to 30 minutes.

Sweetener Substitutions

COCONUT SUGAR	¾ cup (3½ ounces) Biscotti will taste slightly less sweet and be darker in color.
GRANULATED SUGAR	½ cup (3½ ounces) Biscotti will be slightly less sweet and have stronger almond flavor.

granola bars

Makes 16 bars

WHY THIS RECIPE WORKS It can be hard to find store-bought granola bars that aren't packed with refined sugars, and even homemade, naturally sweetened versions tend to be overzealous with ingredients like honey and dried fruit. We wanted a low-sugar version of this on-the-go snack. Honey seemed like a perfect option, but its relatively high sugar content meant we couldn't use nearly enough to hold the bars together. Sucanat was a better option: During baking, the Sucanat melted, glazing the oats, seeds, and nuts and helping to bind everything together. But the holding power of the Sucanat wasn't enough on its own, and the bars were still far too delicate, breaking apart in tasters' hands. To supplement, we turned to egg whites, which contain both water and protein. The egg whites were able to fully coat the nuts and seeds, and when the water baked off, the protein that was left formed a crisp binding layer. To keep our bars from drying out too much, we decided to grind some of the oats into an oat flour, which helped hold on to some of the moisture. For our nuts and seeds, we chose a flavorful combination of pecans, pepitas, sunflower seeds, and unsweetened flaked coconut. To pump up the flavor even more, we added vanilla, a little cinnamon, and a pinch of nutmeg. Our bars were now so flavorful that tasters didn't miss the dried fruit, so we opted to leave it out entirely. You can substitute extra-virgin olive oil or melted coconut oil for the vegetable oil. Do not substitute quick oats, instant oats, or steel-cut oats in this recipe.

2 cups (6 ounces) old-fashioned rolled oats

7 tablespoons (2¼ ounces) Sucanat

3 large egg whites

⅓ cup vegetable oil

1 tablespoon vanilla extract

¼ teaspoon salt

¼ teaspoon ground cinnamon
Pinch ground nutmeg

½ cup pecans, chopped fine

½ cup raw pepitas

½ cup raw sunflower seeds

½ cup (1 ounce) unsweetened flaked coconut

1. Adjust oven rack to middle position and heat oven to 300 degrees. Make foil sling for 13 by 9-inch baking pan by folding 2 long sheets of aluminum foil; first sheet should be 13 inches wide and second sheet should be 9 inches wide. Lay sheets of foil in pan perpendicular to each other, with extra foil hanging over edges of pan. Push foil into corners and up sides of pan, smoothing foil flush to pan. Grease foil.

2. Process ½ cup oats in food processor until finely ground, about 30 seconds. Whisk Sucanat, egg whites, oil, vanilla, salt, cinnamon, and nutmeg together in large bowl. Stir in processed oats, remaining 1½ cups oats, pecans, pepitas, sunflower seeds, and coconut until thoroughly coated.

3. Transfer mixture to prepared pan and spread into even layer. Using greased metal spatula, press firmly on mixture until very compact. Bake granola bars until light golden brown and fragrant, about 40 minutes, rotating pan halfway through baking.

4. Remove bars from oven and let cool in pan for 15 minutes; do not turn oven off. Using foil overhang, lift bars from pan and transfer to cutting board. Cut into 16 bars. Space bars evenly on parchment paper–lined baking sheet and continue to bake until deep golden brown, 15 to 20 minutes, rotating sheet halfway through baking.

5. Transfer bars to wire rack and let cool completely, about 1 hour. Serve.

BEFORE 8 grams sugar ⟶ **AFTER** 5 grams sugar

Making Granola Bars

1 Make aluminum foil sling for 13 by 9-inch baking pan using 2 sheets foil, pushing foil into corners and up sides of pan, and grease foil.

2 Process ½ cup oats in food processor until finely ground, about 30 seconds; this helps keep bars from drying out.

3 Whisk Sucanat, egg whites, oil, vanilla, salt, cinnamon, and nutmeg together in large bowl. Stir in processed oats, remaining 1½ cups oats, pecans, pepitas, sunflower seeds, and coconut until thoroughly coated.

4 Transfer mixture to prepared pan and spread into even layer. Using greased metal spatula, press firmly on mixture until very compact.

5 After baking bars for 40 minutes, remove from oven and let cool slightly. Transfer granola bars to cutting board using foil sling and cut into 16 bars.

6 Space parbaked bars evenly on parchment-lined baking sheet and continue to bake until deep golden brown, 15 to 20 minutes.

Sweetener Substitutions

COCONUT SUGAR	½ cup (2¼ ounces) Granola bars will be darker in color and have delicate texture.
BROWN SUGAR	⅓ cup packed (2¼ ounces) Granola bars will have milder flavor and be less sweet.

pomegranate and nut chocolate clusters

Makes 12 clusters

WHY THIS RECIPE WORKS More candy than cookie, chocolate-enrobed clusters of nuts, seeds, and fruit are a gift-worthy holiday confection. But their small size belies their high sugar content. For our low-sugar version, we set out to create beautiful, elegant, and tasty treats that could adorn any holiday platter. We knew we couldn't use enough chocolate to create fully enrobed clusters, so we opted instead to simply top dollops of melted chocolate with a variety of nuts, seeds, and fruit. We found that semisweet chocolate had the best balance of deep, rich chocolate flavor without any bitterness. We tried quickly melting all of the chocolate in the microwave, but this resulted in melty, gooey chocolate that never fully hardened. To ensure that the chocolate resolidified, we needed to melt it slowly and gently. To do this, we microwaved most of the chocolate at 50 percent power until it was partially melted and then stirred in the remaining chocolate, relying on additional short bursts in the microwave to melt all of the chocolate. Finally, we came up with several colorful combinations of nuts, seeds, and fruit to give our clusters both dimension and textural contrast. We've had good luck using Ghirardelli Semi-Sweet Chocolate Premium Baking Bar in this recipe (see page 21 for more information); other brands may contain different amounts of sugar.

⅓ cup pecans, toasted and chopped

¼ cup shelled pistachios, toasted and chopped

2 tablespoons unsweetened flaked coconut, toasted

2 tablespoons pomegranate seeds

3 ounces semisweet chocolate, chopped fine

1. Line rimmed baking sheet with parchment paper. Combine pecans, pistachios, coconut, and pomegranate seeds in bowl.

2. Microwave 2 ounces chocolate in bowl at 50 percent power, stirring often, until about two-thirds melted, 45 to 60 seconds. Remove bowl from microwave; stir in remaining 1 ounce chocolate until melted. If necessary, microwave chocolate at 50 percent power for 5 seconds at a time until melted.

3. Working quickly, measure 1 teaspoon melted chocolate onto prepared sheet and spread into 2½-inch wide circle using back of spoon. Repeat with remaining chocolate, spacing circles 1½ inches apart.

4. Sprinkle pecan mixture evenly over chocolate and press gently to adhere. Refrigerate until chocolate is firm, about 30 minutes. Serve.

BEFORE 7 grams sugar ⟶ **AFTER** 4 grams sugar

mango and nut chocolate clusters
Substitute cashews for pecans, pepitas for pistachios, and 4 teaspoons chopped unsweetened dried mango for pomegranate seeds.
BEFORE 7 grams sugar ⟶ **AFTER** 4 grams sugar

cherry and nut chocolate clusters
Substitute almonds for pecans, walnuts for pistachios, and 4 teaspoons chopped dried cherries for pomegranate seeds.
BEFORE 7 grams sugar ⟶ **AFTER** 4 grams sugar

honey blondies

Makes 16 blondies

WHY THIS RECIPE WORKS Surprised to learn that our traditional blondie recipe had 25 grams of sugar per square, we set out to create a lower-sugar version. Honey lent itself perfectly to a classic blondie flavor profile. The texture, however, was a different story: We had lost the hearty crumb and chewy, brownie-like texture of a classic blondie. Because of the honey's moisture content, we were getting a much fluffier, cake-like crumb. And textural issues aside, tasters also noticed that the bars were overly greasy. Since the greasiness seemed like a simpler problem to fix, we turned our attention there first. We tried cutting back on butter but found these blondies were lacking richness. Since reducing the overall amount of fat was clearly not the solution, we needed to find a different source of fat. We found our answer in egg yolks, which better emulsified the batter and didn't leach fat when baked. We were also happy to find that the extra egg yolks greatly improved the texture of the blondies by giving the bars better structure and therefore better chew. Although tasters were happy with the sweetness, we wanted to further amp up the flavor of the blondies. To this end, we added several teaspoons of vanilla, toasted the nuts, and used a mixture of white chocolate and semisweet chocolate chips. All told, each bar contained only 13 grams of sugar. Be very careful not to overbake the blondies; they dry out easily and will turn hard. Start checking for doneness a couple minutes early.

1¼ cups (6¼ ounces) all-purpose flour

½ teaspoon salt

¼ teaspoon baking powder

8 tablespoons unsalted butter, melted and cooled

6 tablespoons honey

1 large egg plus 2 large yolks

4 teaspoons vanilla extract

½ cup pecans, toasted and chopped coarse

½ cup (3 ounces) semisweet chocolate chips

½ cup (3 ounces) white chocolate chips

1. Adjust oven rack to middle position and heat oven to 350 degrees. Make foil sling for 8-inch square baking pan by folding 2 long sheets of aluminum foil so each is 8 inches wide. Lay sheets of foil in pan perpendicular to each other, with extra foil hanging over edges of pan. Push foil into corners and up sides of pan, smoothing foil flush to pan. Grease foil.

2. Combine flour, salt, and baking powder in bowl. In large bowl, whisk melted butter, honey, egg and yolks, and vanilla together. Whisk in flour mixture until combined. Fold in pecans, chocolate chips, and white chocolate chips. Scrape batter into prepared pan and smooth top.

3. Bake blondies until toothpick inserted in center comes out with few moist crumbs attached, 22 to 25 minutes, rotating pan halfway through baking. Let blondies cool in pan for 20 minutes. Using foil overhang, lift blondies from pan and transfer to cutting board. Cut into squares and serve.

BEFORE 25 grams sugar ⟶ **AFTER** 13 grams sugar

Working with a Foil Sling

1 Lay 2 sheets foil into pan, perpendicular to one another, and let extra hang over edges of pan. Push foil flat into corners and up sides of pan and grease foil.

2 After bars have baked and cooled, use foil sling to transfer them to cutting board.

maple pecan bars

Makes 16 bars

WHY THIS RECIPE WORKS A perfect pecan bar should balance sweet, gooey caramel, crunchy, nutty pecans, and a sturdy yet flaky shortbread crust. But most versions of this classic confection are brimming with refined sugar and corn syrup. We wanted to keep all the classic elements of pecan bars intact, but decrease the overall sugar and use only maple syrup, since its warm flavor was a natural fit for the buttery nuts. We started with the shortbread crust. Replacing the sugar with maple syrup resulted in a crumbly crust that simply couldn't support the hefty topping. Adding water helped to create a better crumb by hydrating the dough, and parbaking the crust before adding the topping was essential to ensuring that it stayed crisp. As for the topping, we found that we could use a mere ⅓ cup of maple syrup (cutting the overall sugar content by more than half). We bolstered the syrup's flavor with vanilla extract and a shot of bourbon. Although traditional recipes call for sprinkling the pecans over the caramel, we found that the nuts didn't stay on the finished bars. Mixing the pecans into the caramel before pouring it over the crust ensured that our bars were cohesive.

crust

- 1 cup (5 ounces) all-purpose flour
- ½ teaspoon salt
- ¼ teaspoon baking powder
- 8 tablespoons unsalted butter, cut into ½-inch pieces and chilled
- 2 tablespoons maple syrup
- 1 tablespoon water

pecan filling

- ⅓ cup maple syrup
- 4 tablespoons unsalted butter, melted and cooled
- 1 large egg
- 1 tablespoon bourbon or dark rum (optional)
- 2 teaspoons vanilla extract
- ¼ teaspoon salt
- 1¾ cups pecans, toasted and chopped coarse

1. FOR THE CRUST Adjust oven rack to middle position and heat oven to 350 degrees. Make foil sling for 8-inch square baking pan by folding 2 long sheets of aluminum foil so each is 8 inches wide. Lay sheets of foil in pan perpendicular to each other, with extra foil hanging over edges of pan. Push foil into corners and up sides of pan, smoothing foil flush to pan. Grease foil.

2. Pulse flour, salt, and baking powder in food processor until combined, about 5 pulses. Add chilled butter, maple syrup, and water and pulse until mixture forms small balls of dough, 10 to 12 pulses. Transfer mixture to prepared pan and press into even layer with bottom of dry measuring cup. Bake until crust is light golden brown, 20 to 24 minutes, rotating pan halfway through baking.

3. FOR THE PECAN FILLING Whisk maple syrup; melted butter; egg; bourbon, if using; vanilla; and salt together in medium bowl until combined. Stir in pecans. Pour filling over top of hot crust and spread to coat evenly. Bake until top is bubbling, 22 to 25 minutes, rotating pan halfway through baking.

4. Let bars cool completely in pan, about 1 hour. Using foil overhang, lift bars from pan and transfer to cutting board. Cut into bars and serve.

BEFORE 13 grams sugar ⟶ **AFTER** 6 grams sugar

fig bars

Makes 16 bars

WHY THIS RECIPE WORKS Dried figs make a great bar cookie filling: They're naturally supersweet and have great depth of flavor; plus, they're available year-round. Because dried figs are relatively low in sugar compared to other dried fruits, we were amazed to find that traditional recipes had as much as 20 grams of sugar in every bar. We wanted to take advantage of figs' inherent sweetness to create a bar with no added sugar. The filling was simple: We hydrated the figs (soft, sweet Turkish or Calimyrna figs worked best) with a little no-sugar-added apple juice and then pureed the mixture to create a jammy, ultraflavorful fig filling. But we ran into problems with the crust. We wanted a shortbread-like crust and topping that would provide balanced, buttery flavor and nice textural contrast. But with no sugar at all, the crust tasted floury and flat and the texture was far too soft. We first tried incorporating some of the pureed fig mixture into the crust for sweetness, but found it only made the base mushy. The simplest solution turned out to be the best one: We used a bit of the no-sugar-added apple juice to impart a slight sweetness and give us the shortbread texture we were after. Baking the crust on its own ensured a flaky texture; once it cooled, all we had to do was spread the fig filling over the crust. A simple sprinkling of toasted nuts on top gave us the extra crunch we craved, for a bar that now had only 6 grams of sugar. Do not use dried Black Mission figs in this recipe.

1 cup (5 ounces) all-purpose flour

2 teaspoons ground allspice

½ teaspoon salt

¼ teaspoon baking powder

8 tablespoons unsalted butter, cut into ½-inch pieces and chilled

½ cup plus 3 tablespoons no-sugar-added apple juice

1 cup dried Turkish or Calimyrna figs, stemmed and quartered

¼ cup sliced almonds, toasted

¼ cup shelled pistachios, toasted and chopped

1. Adjust oven rack to middle position and heat oven to 375 degrees. Make foil sling for 8-inch square baking pan by folding 2 long sheets of aluminum foil so each is 8 inches wide. Lay sheets of foil in pan perpendicular to each other, with extra foil hanging over edges of pan. Push foil into corners and up sides of pan, smoothing foil flush to pan. Grease foil.

2. Pulse flour, allspice, salt, and baking powder in food processor until combined, about 3 pulses. Scatter chilled butter over top and pulse until mixture resembles wet sand, about 10 pulses. Add 3 tablespoons apple juice and pulse until dough comes together, about 8 pulses.

3. Transfer mixture to prepared pan and press into even layer with bottom of dry measuring cup. Bake crust until golden brown, 35 to 40 minutes, rotating pan halfway through baking. Let crust cool completely in pan, about 45 minutes.

4. Microwave figs and remaining ½ cup apple juice in covered bowl until slightly softened, about 2 minutes. Puree fig mixture in now-empty food processor until smooth, about 15 seconds. Spread fig mixture evenly over cooled crust, then sprinkle with almonds and pistachios, pressing to adhere. Using foil overhang, lift bars from pan and transfer to cutting board. Cut into squares and serve.

BEFORE 20 grams sugar ⟶ **AFTER** 6 grams sugar

honey-lemon squares

Makes 16 bars

WHY THIS RECIPE WORKS Lemon squares are a favorite in the American household, but they are so often ruined by soggy crusts and grainy, muddled curds. We wanted a lemon square with a mouthwateringly tart, lusciously smooth curd coupled with a sturdy, buttery crust. We chose honey to sweeten both components, both for its subtle flavor and its smooth texture that makes it perfect for liquid mixtures. For the crust, we chose a simple press-in crust. By mixing softened butter and flour to a sandy texture, we produced a crust with a texture between short and flaky. A small amount of honey provided sweetness, while a bit of water hydrated the dough just enough to make it workable. For the curd, we started with traditional flour-thickened mixtures that were cooked in the oven. But these versions were consistently grainy, pale, and muted in lemon flavor. Without the aid of granulated sugar to disperse the flour in the mixture, clumps formed in the curd. Moreover, the curd's appearance was unreasonably sensitive to minute variations in baking time and temperature: If the curd was cooked 1 minute too long or the oven was running a bit too hot, the result was an unsightly cracked surface. We opted instead for the more foolproof method of starting the curd on the stovetop and then finishing it in the oven. Rather than rely on flour for thickening power, this method took advantage of the honey's viscosity to produce a smooth, velvety curd. A generous number of egg yolks produced a vibrant yellow color and rich flavor, and also provided great emulsifying power. To boost the lemon flavor, we introduced a hefty amount of lemon zest. Finishing the curd with a small amount of butter and cream gave the curd a silky consistency and good dimension. Finally, straining the curd ensured an irresistibly smooth texture. When eaten together with the buttery crust, our lemon squares had a welcome textural contrast and enticing pucker perfect for lemon lovers. To avoid air bubbles in the curd, stir in the cream with a spatula.

crust

- 1 cup (5 ounces) all-purpose flour
- ¼ teaspoon salt
- 6 tablespoons unsalted butter, cut into 6 pieces and softened
- 2 teaspoons water
- 1 teaspoon honey

lemon curd

- 2 large eggs plus 7 large yolks
- ½ cup honey
- ¼ cup grated lemon zest plus ⅔ cup juice (4 lemons)
- ⅛ teaspoon salt
- 4 tablespoons unsalted butter, cut into 4 pieces
- 3 tablespoons heavy cream

1. FOR THE CRUST Adjust oven rack to middle position and heat oven to 350 degrees. Make foil sling for 8-inch square baking pan by folding 2 long sheets of aluminum foil so each is 8 inches wide. Lay sheets of foil in pan perpendicular to each other, with extra foil hanging over edges of pan. Push foil into corners and up sides of pan, smoothing foil flush to pan. Grease foil.

2. Using stand mixer fitted with paddle, mix flour and salt on low speed until combined, about 30 seconds. Add butter, 1 piece at a time, and mix until only pea-size pieces remain, about 1 minute. Add water and honey and continue to mix until mixture begins to clump and resembles wet sand, about 30 seconds.

3. Transfer mixture to prepared pan and press into even layer with bottom of dry measuring cup. Bake crust until golden brown, 20 to 25 minutes, rotating pan halfway through baking.

4. FOR THE LEMON CURD Meanwhile, whisk eggs and yolks, honey, lemon zest and juice, and salt together in medium saucepan until smooth. Cook over medium-low heat, stirring constantly with rubber spatula, until mixture thickens slightly and registers 165 degrees, about 5 to 7 minutes. Off heat, whisk in butter until melted. Strain lemon curd through fine-mesh strainer into bowl, then gently stir in cream with rubber spatula.

5. Pour warm lemon curd over hot crust. Bake until filling is shiny and opaque and center jiggles slightly when shaken, 10 to 12 minutes, rotating pan halfway through baking. Let bars cool completely in pan, about 2 hours. Using foil overhang, lift bars from pan and transfer to cutting board. Cut into squares and serve.

BEFORE 16 grams sugar ⟶ **AFTER** 9 grams sugar

Making Honey-Lemon Squares

1 Whisk eggs and yolks, honey, lemon zest and juice, and salt together in medium saucepan. Cook, stirring constantly with rubber spatula, until mixture thickens and registers 165 degrees.

2 Whisk in butter until melted. Strain curd through fine-mesh strainer, then gently stir in cream with spatula to avoid incorporating air bubbles.

3 Pour warm curd over hot crust.

4 Bake until filling is shiny and opaque and jiggles slightly when shaken.

strawberry-chamomile streusel bars

Makes 24 bars

WHY THIS RECIPE WORKS We wanted a perfect balance of bright, tangy fruit filling and rich, buttery shortbread crust for these bars, and we wanted to sweeten them naturally using much less sugar than in traditional recipes. For a fresh-tasting filling, we ditched the sugar-packed store-bought jams and made our own quick jam using frozen strawberries, which were of reliable quality and sweetness year-round. We added a dash of lemon juice and a bit of Sucanat to round out the filling, but tasters wanted deeper flavor. We tried reducing the mixture further to concentrate the flavor, but this made the filling overly thick and leathery. Instead, we set out to find an additional component that would complement the berry notes. We tested herbs, citrus, rose water, and even black pepper; in the end, we found an unconventional solution in chamomile teabags. While the chamomile didn't impart a pronounced flavor, it nicely underscored the berry flavor. We then made a butter-rich shortbread dough, which we hoped would pull double duty as the bottom crust and the foundation for our streusel topping. After pressing part of the mixture into the pan, we added more Sucanat along with oats, nuts, and a little extra butter to the remaining dough, which we pinched into clumps to create a chunky streusel. Do not substitute quick oats, instant oats, or steel-cut oats in this recipe. Do not skip grinding the Sucanat in steps 4 and 6 or the crust will have a speckled appearance and the topping will be dense and dry.

filling

- 1 pound frozen strawberries
- 2 teaspoons Sucanat
- 1 teaspoon lemon juice
- 2 chamomile tea bags, strings and tags removed
- 2 teaspoons cornstarch
- 1 tablespoon water

crust

- ½ cup plus 2 tablespoons (3½ ounces) Sucanat
- 2½ cups (12½ ounces) all-purpose flour
- ¾ teaspoon salt
- 16 tablespoons unsalted butter, cut into 16 pieces and softened

topping

- ⅓ cup (1¾ ounces) Sucanat
- ½ cup (1½ ounces) old-fashioned rolled oats
- ½ cup pecans, chopped fine
- 2 tablespoons unsalted butter, cut into 2 pieces and softened

1. FOR THE FILLING Microwave frozen strawberries in covered bowl at 50 percent power, stirring occasionally, until completely thawed, about 6 minutes. Combine thawed strawberry mixture, Sucanat, lemon juice, and tea bags in medium saucepan. Whisk cornstarch into water to dissolve, then stir into pot.

2. Bring mixture to simmer over medium heat, whisking often and being careful not to break tea bags. Cook, mashing berries with potato masher, until mixture is mostly smooth, thickened, and measures 2 cups, about 5 minutes. Off heat, squeeze teabags to extract as much liquid as possible and discard. Cover pot and set aside until needed.

3. FOR THE CRUST Meanwhile, adjust oven rack to middle position and heat oven to 375 degrees. Make foil sling for 13 by 9-inch baking pan by folding 2 long sheets of aluminum foil; first sheet should be 13 inches wide and second sheet should be 9 inches wide. Lay sheets of foil in pan perpendicular to each other, with extra foil hanging over edges of pan. Push foil into corners and up sides of pan, smoothing foil flush to pan. Grease foil.

4. Working in 2 batches, grind Sucanat in spice grinder until fine and powdery, about 1 minute. Using stand mixer fitted with paddle, mix ground Sucanat, flour, and salt on low speed until combined, about 1 minute. Add butter, 1 piece at a time, and mix until mixture resembles damp sand, about 2 minutes. Measure out and reserve 1¼ cups of mixture separately in medium bowl for topping.

5. Transfer remaining mixture to prepared pan and press into even layer with bottom of dry measuring cup. Bake crust until just beginning to brown, 14 to 18 minutes, rotating pan halfway through baking.

6. FOR THE TOPPING Grind Sucanat in spice grinder until fine and powdery, about 1 minute. Add ground Sucanat, oats, and pecans to reserved topping mixture and toss to combine. Using your fingers, rub softened butter into mixture until incorporated, then pinch mixture into hazelnut-size clumps of streusel.

7. Spread strawberry filling evenly over hot crust, then sprinkle with streusel. Bake bars until topping is deep golden brown, 22 to 25 minutes, rotating pan halfway through baking. Let bars cool completely in pan, about 2 hours. Using foil overhang, lift bars from pan and transfer to cutting board. Cut into squares and serve.

BEFORE 14 grams sugar ⟶ **AFTER** 7 grams sugar

Making Strawberry-Chamomile Streusel Bars

1 Simmer strawberry filling, mashing berries with potato masher until mixture is mostly smooth, thickened, and measures 2 cups, about 5 minutes.

2 Remove teabags from filling and squeeze between tongs to extract as much liquid as possible; discard tea bags.

3 Firmly press crust into pan using bottom of measuring cup, then bake until crust is just beginning to brown, 14 to 18 minutes.

4 Spread cooked strawberry filling evenly over hot crust using rubber spatula, then sprinkle evenly with streusel. Bake bars until topping is deep golden brown, 22 to 25 minutes.

Sweetener Substitutions

COCONUT SUGAR	Filling: 2 teaspoons Crust: ¾ cup (3½ ounces) Topping: 6 tablespoons (1¾ ounces) Bars will be darker in color; grind sugar as directed in steps 4 and 6.
GRANULATED SUGAR AND BROWN SUGAR	Filling: 2 teaspoons granulated sugar Crust: ½ cup (3½ ounces) granulated sugar Topping: ¼ cup packed (1¾ ounces) brown sugar Bars will be lighter in color and have slightly milder flavor; do not grind sugar in steps 4 and 6.

cakes

chocolate layer cake

Serves 12

WHY THIS RECIPE WORKS A good chocolate cake should be rich and ultrachocolaty; it also must have a moist and tender yet sturdy crumb. Swapping Sucanat for the sugar in our traditional recipe produced a decent cake with abundant chocolate flavor. However, this cake was a bit dense: The original recipe called for bread flour to give the cake better structure, but without the tenderizing power of the sugar, the crumb was too heavy. We tested all-purpose and cake flours, but tasters missed the more substantial texture of the cake made with bread flour. Instead, we increased the amount of baking powder to open up the crumb. This cake was lighter, but it was also drier and had muted chocolate flavor. We made cakes using butter and oil and found that oil produced a moister cake than butter. We couldn't add more chocolate without sacrificing texture, so we turned to coffee since its robust flavor enhances chocolate flavor. A few teaspoons of vinegar helped to activate the leavening power of the baking soda, ensuring a perfect texture. If you use natural cocoa powder for this recipe, the cake will be lighter in appearance and have a milder chocolate flavor. Our favorite brand of bittersweet chocolate is Ghirardelli 60% Cacao Bittersweet Chocolate Premium Baking Bar (see page 21 for more information); other brands may contain different amounts of sugar. Do not skip grinding the Sucanat in step 1 or large air pockets will appear inside the cake and on the surface of the cake. If using dark colored cake pans, start checking the cakes for doneness 5 to 10 minutes earlier. We prefer the flavor of Creamy Chocolate Frosting on this cake; however, Easy Vanilla Frosting (page 139) will also work well.

¾ cup plus ⅓ cup (6 ounces) Sucanat

6 ounces bittersweet chocolate, chopped

⅔ cup (2 ounces) Dutch-processed cocoa powder

1½ cups hot brewed coffee

1½ cups (8¼ ounces) bread flour

1 teaspoon salt

1 teaspoon baking soda

1 teaspoon baking powder

¾ cup vegetable oil

4 large eggs

4 teaspoons distilled white vinegar

2 teaspoons vanilla extract

1 recipe Creamy Chocolate Frosting (page 140)

1. Adjust oven rack to middle position and heat oven to 350 degrees. Grease two 9-inch round cake pans, line with parchment paper, grease parchment, and flour pans. Working in 4 batches, grind Sucanat in spice grinder until fine and powdery, about 1 minute.

2. Place chocolate and cocoa in medium bowl, add hot coffee, and whisk until melted and smooth. Refrigerate mixture until completely cool, about 20 minutes. In separate bowl, whisk ground Sucanat, flour, salt, baking soda, and baking powder together.

3. Whisk oil, eggs, vinegar, and vanilla into cooled chocolate mixture until smooth. Add flour mixture and whisk until smooth.

4. Divide batter evenly among prepared cake pans. Bake until cakes are set and center is just firm to touch, 20 to 22 minutes, rotating pans halfway through baking. Let cakes cool in pans for 10 minutes. Remove cakes from pans, discard parchment, and let cool completely on wire rack, about 1 hour. (Cake layers can be wrapped in plastic wrap and stored at room temperature for up to 3 days.)

5. Line edges of cake platter with 4 strips of parchment to keep platter clean and place dab of frosting in center to anchor cake. Place 1 cake layer on platter and spread 1 cup frosting evenly over top. Top with second cake layer, press lightly to adhere, then spread 1 cup frosting evenly over top. Spread remaining frosting evenly over sides of cake. To smooth frosting, run edge of offset spatula around cake sides and over top. Carefully remove parchment strips and serve.

BEFORE 69 grams sugar ⟶ **AFTER** 39 grams sugar

chocolate sheet cake

Substitute 13 by 9-inch baking pan for 9-inch cake pans; prepare pan as directed. Scrape all of batter into pan and increase baking time to 22 to 25 minutes. Let cake cool completely in pan, about 2 hours. Remove cake from pan, spread frosting evenly over top and sides, and serve. Serves 16.

BEFORE 52 grams sugar ⟶ **AFTER** 29 grams sugar

chocolate cupcakes

Substitute two 12-cup muffin tins for 9-inch cake pans; line tins with paper or foil liners. Portion batter evenly into prepared muffin tins and reduce baking time to 17 to 19 minutes. Let cupcakes cool in tin for 10 minutes, then transfer to wire rack and let cool completely, about 1 hour. Spread frosting evenly over cupcakes and serve. Makes 24 cupcakes.

BEFORE 34 grams sugar ⟶ **AFTER** 19 grams sugar

Frosting Layer Cake

1 Place cake layer on platter and spread 1 cup frosting evenly over top.
2 Place second cake layer on top and press lightly to adhere.
3 Spread 1 cup frosting evenly over top of cake.
4 Spread remaining frosting evenly over sides of cake. To smooth frosting, run edge of offset spatula around cake sides and over top.

Sweetener Substitutions

COCONUT SUGAR	1¼ cups (6 ounces) Cake will taste slightly sweeter with caramel notes; grind sugar as directed in step 1.
GRANULATED SUGAR	¾ cup plus 2 tablespoons (6 ounces) Cake will taste less sweet and have slightly milder flavor; do not grind sugar in step 1.

maple layer cake

Serves 12

WHY THIS RECIPE WORKS Moist, tender yellow layer cake is a classic, timeless treat. But unlike decadent chocolate cakes or flavorful, spice-laden carrot cakes, the flavor of yellow cake has nothing to hide behind—so we knew that making a low-sugar version that still tasted great would be quite a challenge. We hoped that using an ultraflavorful natural sweetener like Sucanat, honey, or maple syrup would counteract the fact that we were using less sugar overall. Since the cake has such a basic ingredient list, the sweetener would have a big impact on flavor, so it had to be just right. Although the cake made with Sucanat tasted good, it turned out dry, sandy, and riddled with holes—problems we couldn't fix no matter what we tried. Honey's flavor was overpowering in this simple context. But maple syrup proved to be a hit with tasters: It gave the cake a pleasant yet subtle maple flavor and aroma. Plus, the liquid sweetener helped to ensure that the cake wasn't too dry. Although many yellow cakes rely on butter as the fat, a simple test revealed that oil worked much better; it produced a cake that was not only tender and rich but also sturdy enough to support the frosting. As an added bonus, using oil meant that we didn't have to get out the stand mixer and could simply stir everything together by hand. A maple-kissed cream cheese frosting made for a perfect finishing touch on our flavorful maple cake. If using dark colored cake pans, start checking the cakes for doneness 5 to 10 minutes earlier. We prefer the flavor of Maple Cream Cheese Frosting on this cake; however, Easy Vanilla Frosting (page 139) or Creamy Chocolate Frosting (page 140) will also work well.

2½ cups (10 ounces) cake flour

2 teaspoons baking powder

½ teaspoon salt

¾ cup plus 2 tablespoons vegetable oil

1¼ cups maple syrup

3 large eggs

4 teaspoons vanilla extract

1 recipe Maple Cream Cheese Frosting (page 142)

1. Adjust oven rack to middle position and heat oven to 325 degrees. Grease two 9-inch round cake pans, line with parchment paper, grease parchment, and flour pans.

2. Whisk flour, baking powder, and salt together in bowl. In large bowl, whisk oil, maple syrup, eggs, and vanilla together until smooth. Whisk in flour mixture until smooth. Divide batter evenly among prepared cake pans. Bake until cakes are set and center is just firm to touch, 22 to 25 minutes, rotating pans halfway through baking.

3. Let cakes cool in pans for 10 minutes. Remove cakes from pans, discard parchment, and let cool completely on rack, about 1 hour. (Cake layers can be wrapped in plastic wrap and stored at room temperature for up to 3 days.)

4. Line edges of cake platter with 4 strips of parchment to keep platter clean and place dab of frosting in center to anchor cake. Place 1 cake layer on platter and spread 1 cup frosting evenly over top. Top with second cake layer, press lightly to adhere, then spread 1 cup frosting evenly over top. Spread remaining frosting evenly over sides of cake. To smooth frosting, run edge of offset spatula around cake sides and over top. Carefully remove parchment strips and serve.

BEFORE 52 grams sugar ⟶ **AFTER** 28 grams sugar

maple sheet cake

Substitute 13 by 9-inch baking pan for 9-inch cake pans; prepare pan as directed. Scrape all of batter into pan and increase baking time to about 30 minutes. Let cake cool completely in pan, about 2 hours. Remove cake from pan, spread frosting evenly over top and sides, and serve. Serves 16.

BEFORE 35 grams sugar ⟶ **AFTER** 21 grams sugar

Making Layer Cake

1 Using softened butter or shortening (or baking spray with flour), grease inside of cake pan thoroughly.

2 Line bottom of cake pan with piece of parchment that has been cut to fit, then grease parchment.

3 Sprinkle flour inside pan and shake pan to coat it evenly with flour. Knock any excess flour out of pan. (You can skip this step if using baking spray with flour.)

4 After removing baked cakes from oven, let them cool in cake pans for 10 minutes.

5 To remove cakes from cake pans, place plate over top of each pan and, holding it firmly in place, flip cake over.

6 After removing cake pan and parchment, transfer to wire rack and let cool completely before frosting.

carrot-honey layer cake

Serves 12

WHY THIS RECIPE WORKS For a naturally sweetened version of our traditional carrot cake, our goal was twofold: to keep the recipe as simple as possible, and to sweeten the cake only with honey, since its floral nuances seemed like a natural pair with the sweet carrots and warm spices. To keep the recipe streamlined, we wanted to avoid getting out the electric mixer and instead rely on an easy bowl method. Tasters preferred cakes made with neutral-flavored oil over those made with melted butter, since the oil didn't detract from the other flavors in the cake. Our traditional recipe called for four whole carrots and we found that this amount worked perfectly to contribute both flavor and sweetness to the cake without impacting the texture. Finally, we bolstered the cake's flavor by increasing the amounts of cinnamon, nutmeg, and cloves. Shred the carrots on the large holes of a box grater or in a food processor fitted with the shredding disk. If using dark colored cake pans, start checking the cakes for doneness 5 to 10 minutes earlier. We prefer the flavor of Honey Cream Cheese Frosting on this cake; however, Easy Vanilla Frosting (page 139) will also work well.

1¾ cups (8¾ ounces) all-purpose flour
2 teaspoons baking powder
1 teaspoon baking soda
2 teaspoons ground cinnamon
1 teaspoon ground nutmeg
½ teaspoon ground cloves
½ teaspoon salt
⅓ cup plus ¼ cup honey
¾ cup vegetable oil
3 large eggs
1 tablespoon vanilla extract
2⅔ cups shredded carrots (4 carrots)
1 recipe Honey Cream Cheese Frosting (page 142)

1. Adjust oven rack to middle position and heat oven to 350 degrees. Grease two 9-inch round cake pans, line with parchment paper, grease parchment, and flour pans.

2. Whisk flour, baking powder, baking soda, cinnamon, nutmeg, cloves, and salt together in bowl. In large bowl, whisk honey, oil, eggs, and vanilla together until smooth. Stir in carrots. Add flour mixture and fold with rubber spatula until mixture is just combined.

3. Divide batter evenly among prepared cake pans and smooth tops. Bake until cakes are set and center is just firm to touch, 16 to 20 minutes, rotating pans halfway through baking.

4. Let cakes cool in pans for 10 minutes. Remove cakes from pans, discard parchment, and let cool completely on wire rack, about 1 hour. (Cake layers can be wrapped in plastic wrap and stored at room temperature for up to 3 days.)

5. Line edges of cake platter with 4 strips of parchment to keep platter clean and place dab of frosting in center to anchor cake. Place 1 cake layer on platter and spread 1 cup frosting evenly over top. Top with second cake layer, press lightly to adhere, then spread 1 cup frosting evenly over top. Spread remaining frosting evenly over sides of cake. To smooth frosting, run edge of offset spatula around cake sides and over top. Carefully remove parchment strips and serve.

BEFORE 49 grams sugar ⟶ **AFTER** 23 grams sugar

carrot-honey sheet cake

Substitute 13 by 9-inch baking pan for 9-inch cake pans; prepare pan as directed. Scrape all of batter into pan and increase baking time to 20 to 22 minutes. Let cake cool completely in pan, about 2 hours. Remove cake from pan, spread frosting evenly over top and sides, and serve. Serves 16.

BEFORE 31 grams sugar ⟶ **AFTER** 17 grams sugar

red velvet cupcakes

Makes 12 cupcakes

WHY THIS RECIPE WORKS Although their vibrant color seems to get most of the attention, red velvet cupcakes are more than just a novelty. The cupcakes themselves are extra tender, light, and moist, which is typically achieved through the use of vinegar, baking soda, and natural cocoa powder. The acidity of the cocoa powder and vinegar reacts with the baking soda to create a fine and tender crumb; this reaction also contributes to the red color. Unfortunately, cutting out half of the sugar left our cupcakes bland. To remedy this, we upped the amount of cocoa powder for some extra chocolate kick, and used Sucanat for its deep flavor. Increasing the amount of vanilla extract gave our cupcakes more backbone. To add some extra richness to our cupcakes, we replaced the classic buttermilk (which is low in fat) with regular whole milk; happily, our cupcakes still got just enough tang from the vinegar. Our favorite natural cocoa powder is Hershey's Natural Cocoa Unsweetened; do not use Dutch-processed cocoa powder in this recipe. We prefer the flavor of Honey Cream Cheese Frosting on these cupcakes; however, Easy Vanilla Frosting (page 139) will also work well. You can skip grinding the Sucanat in step 1; however, the cupcakes will have a speckled appearance.

1 cup plus 2 tablespoons (5⅔ ounces) all-purpose flour

2 tablespoons natural unsweetened cocoa powder

¾ teaspoons baking soda

⅛ teaspoon salt

½ cup whole milk

1 large egg

1 tablespoon vanilla extract

1 tablespoon red food coloring

1½ teaspoons distilled white vinegar

7 tablespoons (2½ ounces) Sucanat

6 tablespoons unsalted butter, softened

1 recipe Half-Batch Honey Cream Cheese Frosting (page 142)

1. Adjust oven rack to middle position and heat oven to 350 degrees. Line 12-cup muffin tin with paper or foil liners. Whisk flour, cocoa, baking soda, and salt together in bowl. In separate bowl, whisk milk, egg, vanilla, food coloring, and vinegar together. Working in 2 batches, grind Sucanat in spice grinder until fine and powdery, about 1 minute.

2. Using stand mixer fitted with paddle, beat ground Sucanat and butter together on medium-high speed until fluffy, about 2 minutes, scraping down bowl as needed. Reduce speed to low and add flour mixture in 3 additions, alternating with milk in 2 additions, scraping down bowl as needed. Using rubber spatula, give batter final stir.

3. Portion batter evenly into prepared muffin tin. Bake cupcakes until toothpick inserted in center comes out with few crumbs attached, 14 to 18 minutes, rotating muffin tin halfway through baking.

4. Let cupcakes cool in tin for 10 minutes, then transfer to wire rack and let cool completely, about 1 hour. (Unfrosted cupcakes can be stored at room temperature for up to 3 days.) Spread frosting evenly over cupcakes and serve.

BEFORE 20 grams sugar ⟶ **AFTER** 11 grams sugar

Sweetener Substitutions	
COCONUT SUGAR	½ cup (2½ ounces) Cupcakes will be slightly sweeter; grind sugar as directed in step 1.
GRANULATED SUGAR	6 tablespoons (2½ ounces) Cupcakes will be lighter in color and taste slightly less sweet; do not grind sugar in step 1.

strawberry cupcakes

Makes 12 cupcakes

WHY THIS RECIPE WORKS We were shocked to find that many recipes for strawberry cupcakes rely on a packet of strawberry-flavored Jell-O. For our low-sugar, naturally sweetened version, we resolved to pack in the berry flavor using real strawberries. We put together a quick cake base by creaming butter with ground Sucanat, adding a couple eggs, and stirring in cake flour (which we knew would give our cupcakes the tenderness we were after). We started by stirring chopped frozen strawberries (which were of reliable quality year-round) into the cake batter, but were unsurprised when the chunks disrupted the fine crumb of the cake and left behind mushy pockets. For our next round of testing, we pressed the liquid out of the strawberries and added the juice to the batter. This time our cake had good flavor but was mushy. To rid the batter of excess moisture without compromising on flavor, we reduced the liquid on the stovetop to a mere ¼ cup, which concentrated the strawberry flavor beautifully. A couple teaspoons of baking powder ensured that the concentrated liquid wouldn't weigh down our cakes. Instead of discarding the strawberry solids left behind from straining the berries, we added them to our cream cheese frosting, giving our cupcakes even more strawberry flavor. We prefer the flavor of Honey Cream Cheese Frosting for this recipe; however, Easy Vanilla Frosting (page 139) will also work well. You can skip grinding the Sucanat in step 1; however, the cupcakes will have a speckled appearance.

⅓ cup plus ¼ cup (3 ounces) Sucanat

1 cup plus 2 tablespoons (4½ ounces) cake flour

2 teaspoons baking powder

½ teaspoon salt

10 ounces (2 cups) frozen whole strawberries

6 tablespoons whole milk

2 large eggs

2 teaspoons vanilla extract

6 tablespoons unsalted butter, softened

1 recipe Half-Batch Honey Cream Cheese Frosting (page 142)

1. Adjust oven rack to middle position and heat oven to 350 degrees. Line 12-cup muffin tin with paper or foil liners. Working in 2 batches, grind Sucanat in spice grinder until fine and powdery, about 1 minute. Whisk flour, baking powder, and salt together in bowl. Microwave strawberries in covered bowl until softened and very juicy, about 4 minutes.

2. Transfer strawberries to fine-mesh strainer set over small saucepan and press firmly with rubber spatula to extract as much liquid as possible; set solids aside for frosting. Boil strained strawberry juice over medium-high heat, stirring occasionally, until syrupy and measures ¼ cup, about 8 minutes. Transfer juice to medium bowl and let cool for 5 minutes. Whisk in milk until combined, followed by eggs and vanilla.

3. Using stand mixer fitted with paddle, beat ground Sucanat and butter on medium-high speed until pale and fluffy, about 3 minutes. Slowly add juice mixture and beat until well combined, about 1 minute, scraping down bowl as needed (mixture will look soupy). Reduce speed to low, add flour mixture, and mix until combined, about 1 minute. Give batter final stir by hand.

4. Portion batter evenly into prepared muffin tin. Bake cupcakes until toothpick inserted in center comes out with few crumbs attached, 15 to 20 minutes, rotating muffin tin halfway through baking.

5. Let cupcakes cool in tin for 10 minutes, then transfer to wire rack and let cool completely, about 1 hour. (Unfrosted cupcakes can be stored at room temperature for up to 3 days.) Stir reserved strawberry solids into frosting until combined. Spread frosting evenly over cupcakes and serve.

BEFORE 27 grams sugar ⟶ **AFTER** 13 grams sugar

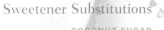

Sweetener Substitutions

COCONUT SUGAR	½ cup plus 2 tablespoons (3 ounces) Cupcakes will be brown in color and have nutty flavor; grind sugar as directed in step 1.
GRANULATED SUGAR	7 tablespoons (3 ounces) Cupcakes will be slightly paler and have slightly milder flavor; do not grind sugar in step 1.

pumpkin cupcakes

Makes 12 cupcakes

WHY THIS RECIPE WORKS Many pumpkin-flavored desserts fall into the same traps: They're overly sweet and so heavily seasoned with pumpkin pie spice that the pumpkin flavor is completely hidden. To avoid the same mistakes, we started with unsweetened pumpkin puree, avoiding cans of overly sweet preseasoned pumpkin pie filling. This allowed us to completely control the sweetness level and the spices that went into our cake. Cinnamon, allspice, nutmeg, cloves, and ginger are the go-to seasonings for anything pumpkin-flavored, but we wanted to keep the profile more simple and streamlined. We found that 1 teaspoon of cinnamon was plenty, while small amounts of allspice and ginger added the right background flavor. With the pumpkin and spice flavorings nailed down, we turned our attention to the texture of our cupcakes. Perfect pumpkin cupcakes should be moist and velvety, but our cakes were ending up damp and leaden. To help open the crumb and make the cake more tender, we used 1 teaspoon of baking powder and ½ teaspoon of baking soda. Achieving the right moisture level was a matter of finding the right combination of oil and eggs. Too much of either (or both) would weigh the cupcakes down further, but with too little the cakes would be dry and overly crumbly. We finally settled on a combination of two eggs and ½ cup of vegetable oil for cupcakes that were tender, fine-crumbed, and perfectly moist. We prefer the flavor of Honey Cream Cheese Frosting on these cupcakes; however, Easy Vanilla Frosting (page 139) will also work well. You can skip grinding the Sucanat in step 1; however, the cupcakes will have a speckled appearance.

⅓ cup plus ¼ cup (3 ounces) Sucanat

1 cup (5 ounces) all-purpose flour

1 teaspoon ground cinnamon

1 teaspoon baking powder

½ teaspoon baking soda

½ teaspoon salt

⅛ teaspoon ground allspice

⅛ teaspoon ground ginger

¾ cup canned unsweetened pumpkin puree

½ cup vegetable oil

2 large eggs

1 recipe Half-Batch Honey Cream Cheese Frosting (page 142)

1. Adjust oven rack to middle position and heat oven to 350 degrees. Line 12-cup muffin tin with paper or foil liners. Working in 2 batches, grind Sucanat in spice grinder until fine and powdery, about 1 minute.

2. Whisk flour, cinnamon, baking powder, baking soda, salt, allspice, and ginger together in large bowl. In separate bowl, whisk Sucanat, pumpkin puree, oil, and eggs until smooth. Using rubber spatula, stir Sucanat mixture into flour mixture until combined.

3. Portion batter evenly into prepared muffin tin. Bake cupcakes until toothpick inserted in center comes out with few crumbs attached, 15 to 20 minutes, rotating muffin tin halfway through baking.

4. Let cupcakes cool in tin for 10 minutes, then transfer to wire rack and let cool completely, about 1 hour. (Unfrosted cupcakes can be stored at room temperature for up to 3 days.) Spread frosting evenly over cupcakes and serve.

BEFORE 22 grams sugar ⟶ **AFTER** 12 grams sugar

Sweetener Substitutions

COCONUT SUGAR	½ cup plus 2 tablespoons (3 ounces) Cupcakes will taste slightly less sweet; grind sugar as directed in step 1.
GRANULATED SUGAR	7 tablespoons (3 ounces) Cupcakes will be paler and have slightly milder flavor; do not grind sugar in step 1.

cakes

Sweetener Substitutions

COCONUT SUGAR   **1¼ cups (6 ounces)**
Frosting will have golden brown color and strong caramel flavor; grind sugar as directed in step 1.

CONFECTIONERS' SUGAR   **1½ cups (6 ounces)**
Frosting will have bright, white color and milder flavor.

easy vanilla frosting

Makes 3 cups

WHY THIS RECIPE WORKS A cake or cupcake is only really complete once it's been topped with a fluffy, rich frosting. While sophisticated flavors certainly have their place, a great vanilla frosting is sure to please every palate and pair with any cake. For this simplest of toppings, we decided to keep the method simple to match. Since we were only using a few ingredients, the flavor of the sugar could really shine through, an added bonus when using highly flavorful sugars like Sucanat and coconut sugar. Many frosting recipes call for milk, but we found that heavy cream gave us the silkiest texture. Usually, making frosting is as easy as whipping everything together until it's light and fluffy, but the key to the smoothest texture lay in an added step: grinding the Sucanat in small batches for a full minute. Since vanilla works well as a base for other flavors, we decided to create a few flavor variations to make our simple frosting even more versatile. While we love the hearty molasses flavor that Sucanat adds to this frosting, it produces a light brown–colored frosting. For a more mild flavor and traditional, white-colored frosting, use confectioners' sugar in place of Sucanat. Do not use salted butter or omit the heavy cream or you will ruin the frosting. Do not skip grinding the Sucanat in step 1 or the frosting will be gritty.

¾ cup plus ⅓ cup (6 ounces) Sucanat
24 tablespoons (3 sticks) unsalted butter, softened
3 tablespoons heavy cream
1 tablespoon vanilla extract
¼ teaspoon salt

1. Working in 4 batches, grind Sucanat in spice grinder until fine and powdery, about 1 minute. Using stand mixer fitted with whisk attachment, whip butter, cream, vanilla, and salt together on medium-high speed until smooth, 1 to 2 minutes.

2. Reduce mixer speed to low, slowly add ground Sucanat, and whip until incorporated and smooth, 1 to 2 minutes. Increase speed to medium-high and whip frosting until light and fluffy, 3 to 5 minutes.

BEFORE 21 grams sugar ⟶ **AFTER** 14 grams sugar (per ¼ cup)

half-batch easy vanilla frosting
This recipe will make 1½ cups frosting; enough for 12 cupcakes. Halve all ingredients; mixing times will not change.

easy coffee frosting
Add 1½ tablespoons instant espresso or instant coffee to butter mixture before whipping. (For half-batch variation, add 2 teaspoons instant espresso or instant coffee.)

easy almond frosting
Add 1 teaspoon almond extract to butter mixture before whipping. (For half-batch variation, add ½ teaspoon almond extract.)

easy coconut frosting
Add 2 teaspoons coconut extract to butter mixture before whipping. (For half-batch variation, add 1 teaspoon coconut extract.)

creamy chocolate frosting

Makes 4 cups

WHY THIS RECIPE WORKS To create a silky smooth, decadent chocolate frosting, we looked to Swiss meringue buttercream. This style of frosting achieves its ethereal texture by cooking egg whites with sugar before whipping in knobs of softened butter. We swapped Sucanat for the granulated sugar, and were happy to find that cooking the Sucanat with the egg whites eliminated the need to grind the Sucanat. Melted bittersweet chocolate provided perfect chocolate flavor. The melted chocolate should be cooled to between 85 and 100 degrees before being added to the frosting. If the frosting seems too soft after adding the chocolate, chill it briefly in the refrigerator and then rewhip it until creamy. Our favorite brand of bittersweet chocolate is Ghirardelli 60% Cacao Bittersweet Chocolate Premium Baking Bar (see page 21 for more information); other brands may contain different amounts of sugar.

8 ounces bittersweet chocolate, chopped

1 teaspoon vanilla extract

¾ cup plus 2 tablespoons (4⅔ ounces) Sucanat

4 large egg whites

⅛ teaspoon salt

24 tablespoons (3 sticks) unsalted butter, cut into 24 pieces and softened

1. Microwave chocolate in bowl at 50 percent power, stirring occasionally, until melted, about 4 minutes. Stir in vanilla and let cool, about 10 minutes.

2. Combine Sucanat, egg whites, and salt in bowl of stand mixer and set over saucepan filled with 1 inch of barely simmering water. Whisking gently but constantly, heat mixture until slightly thickened, foamy, and registers 150 degrees, about 8 minutes.

3. Fit stand mixer with whisk attachment and whip warmed Sucanat mixture on medium speed until slightly cooled and has consistency of shaving cream, about 2 minutes. Add butter, 1 piece at a time, until smooth and creamy. (Frosting may look curdled after half of butter has been added; it will smooth with additional butter.)

4. Once all butter is added, add cooled melted chocolate mixture and mix until combined. Increase speed to medium-high and whip until light, fluffy, and well combined, about 2 minutes, scraping down whisk and bowl as needed. (Frosting can be refrigerated for up to 24 hours. To refresh, microwave until just slightly softened, about 15 seconds, then whip on medium-high speed in stand mixer until light and creamy, about 2 minutes.)

BEFORE 29 grams sugar ⟶ **AFTER** 14 grams sugar (per ¼ cup)

half-batch creamy chocolate frosting

This recipe will make 2 cups frosting; enough for 12 cupcakes. Halve all ingredients; mixing times will not change.

Sweetener Substitutions	
COCONUT SUGAR	1 cup (4⅔ ounces) Frosting will have nutty, slightly bitter flavor.
GRANULATED SUGAR	⅔ cup (4⅔ ounces) Frosting have will have milder flavor.

honey cream cheese frosting

Makes 3 cups

WHY THIS RECIPE WORKS We set our sights on developing a perfectly balanced cream cheese frosting that would pair well with our carrot cake, red velvet cupcakes, pumpkin cupcakes, and more. But cream cheese frostings very often veer into sugar bomb territory, so overly sweet and cloying that the cream cheese tang is lost. We took it down a notch by not only using less sugar than usual, but also replacing the sugar with honey. Honey paired nicely with the tang of the cream cheese, giving this frosting a more distinct, nuanced, and well-rounded flavor profile. Do not substitute low-fat cream cheese here or the frosting will have a soupy consistency. If the frosting becomes too soft to work with, refrigerate it until firm.

12 ounces cream cheese, softened
8 tablespoons unsalted butter, cut into 8 pieces and softened
2 teaspoons vanilla extract
⅛ teaspoon salt
6 tablespoons honey

1. Using stand mixer fitted with whisk attachment, whip cream cheese, butter, vanilla, and salt on medium-high speed until smooth, 1 to 2 minutes.

2. Reduce mixer speed to medium-low, add honey, and whip until smooth, 1 to 2 minutes. Increase speed to medium-high and whip frosting until light and fluffy, 3 to 5 minutes.

BEFORE 15 grams sugar ⟶ **AFTER** 9 grams sugar (per ¼ cup)

half-batch honey cream cheese frosting
This recipe will make 1½ cups frosting; enough for 12 cupcakes.
Halve all ingredients; mixing times will not change.

maple cream cheese frosting
Substitute maple syrup for honey.
BEFORE 15 grams sugar ⟶ **AFTER** 7 grams sugar (per ¼ cup)

maple whipped cream

Makes 2 cups

WHY THIS RECIPE WORKS Fluffy, decadent whipped cream is a great way to dress up any unfrosted cake, so we set out to create a luscious, naturally sweetened version with a clean, creamy flavor. We tried variations flavored with Sucanat, coconut sugar, honey, and maple syrup. Sucanat and coconut sugar gave the whipped cream a slightly darker appearance, as well as a mildly nutty flavor that we found distracting. Honey's overt floral notes detracted from the overall fresh cream flavor. The whipped cream sweetened with maple syrup won our tasters over with its straightforward flavor, smooth texture, and clean appearance. To ensure that the cream whipped to a smooth, light, and stable consistency, we whipped it on high speed until we achieved soft peaks. A splash of vanilla and a pinch of salt added just a bit of depth to this satisfying take on the classic dessert accompaniment.

1 cup heavy cream
2 tablespoons maple syrup
½ teaspoon vanilla
Pinch salt

Using stand mixer fitted with whisk attachment, whip cream, maple syrup, vanilla, and salt on medium-low speed until foamy, about 1 minute. Increase speed to high and whip until soft peaks form, 1 to 3 minutes.

BEFORE 7 grams sugar ⟶ **AFTER** 4 grams sugar (per ¼ cup)

half-batch maple whipped cream
This recipe will make 1 cup whipped cream.
Halve all ingredients; whipping times will not change.

Sweetener Substitutions

SUCANAT
2 tablespoons
Whipped cream will have slight molasses flavor; grind Sucanat in spice grinder until fine and powdery, about 1 minute.

COCONUT SUGAR
2 tablespoons
Whipped cream will be slightly darker in appearance and have mild nutty flavor; grind sugar in spice grinder until fine and powdery, about 1 minute.

HONEY
4 teaspoons
Whipped cream made with honey will taste sweeter and slightly floral.

GRANULATED SUGAR
1½ tablespoons
Whipped cream made with granulated sugar will taste mild and clean.

chocolate pound cake

Serves 8

WHY THIS RECIPE WORKS To make a low-sugar version of this crowd-pleasing cake, we needed to make some adjustments to our traditional recipe. First, we turned our attention to the chocolate, and found that we got the best chocolate flavor by using two types: Dutch-processed cocoa powder and a small amount of milk chocolate. By blooming both in hot water, we got bold chocolate flavor without the harshness that sometimes plagues plain cocoa powder. Sucanat's deep flavor complemented the chocolate nicely. To keep our cake from being greasy and overly tender, we dropped the amount of butter from 16 tablespoons to 12 tablespoons. Thoroughly creaming the chocolate, butter, and Sucanat together ensured ample rise and a perfect, velvety texture; the liquid-y melted chocolate helped ensure that the Sucanat dissolved fully, eliminating the need for grinding. Using three eggs gave the cake good structure without making it dense. For an accurate measurement of boiling water, bring a full kettle of water to a boil and then measure out the desired amount. The test kitchen's preferred loaf pan measures 8½ by 4½ inches; if you use a 9 by 5-inch loaf pan, start checking for doneness 5 minutes earlier than advised in the recipe. Our preferred brand of milk chocolate is Dove Silky Smooth Milk Chocolate (see page 21 for more information); other brands may contain different amounts of sugar.

1 cup (5 ounces) all-purpose flour
¾ teaspoons salt
¾ cup (2¼ ounces) Dutch-processed cocoa powder
2½ ounces milk chocolate, chopped fine
⅓ cup boiling water
12 tablespoons unsalted butter, softened
½ cup plus ⅓ cup (4⅓ ounces) Sucanat
1 tablespoon vanilla extract
3 large eggs

1. Adjust oven rack to lower-middle position and heat oven to 325 degrees. Grease and flour 8½ by 4½-inch loaf pan. Whisk flour and salt together in bowl. In separate bowl, combine cocoa and chocolate, pour boiling water over top, and stir until melted and smooth; let mixture cool for 5 minutes.

2. Using stand mixer fitted with paddle, beat cooled chocolate mixture, butter, Sucanat, and vanilla on medium-high speed until fluffy, 2 to 3 minutes. Add eggs, one at a time, and beat until thoroughly combined, about 1 minute, scraping down bowl as needed.

3. Reduce speed to low and add flour mixture in 3 additions, scraping down bowl as needed, until just combined. Give batter final stir by hand (it may look curdled). Scrape batter into prepared pan and bake until toothpick inserted in center comes out clean, 60 to 70 minutes, rotating pan halfway through baking.

4. Let cake cool in pan for 10 minutes. Remove cake from pan and let cool completely on wire rack, about 2 hours, before serving.

BEFORE 34 grams sugar ⟶ **AFTER** 19 grams sugar

Sweetener Substitutions

COCONUT SUGAR	⅔ plus ¼ cup (4⅓ ounces) Cake will have slight nutty flavor.
GRANULATED SUGAR	½ cup plus 2 tablespoons (4⅓ ounces) Cake will have slightly milder flavor.

Sweetener Substitutions

COCONUT SUGAR	¾ cup plus ⅓ cup (5 ounces) Cake will be darker in color and taste slightly less sweet; grind sugar as directed in step 1.
GRANULATED SUGAR	⅔ cup (5 ounces) Cake will be lighter in color and have milder flavor; do not grind sugar in step 1.

chai-spiced pound cake

Serves 8

WHY THIS RECIPE WORKS Traditionally made with a pound of each of four basic ingredients (sugar, flour, butter, and eggs), a perfect pound cake should have a fine, even crumb and a velvety texture. But significantly reducing the sugar meant that we needed to rethink the classic formula to maintain the integrity of this iconic dessert. First, we needed to work on the flavor. We chose Sucanat as our sweetener, since tasters enjoyed its nuanced molasses notes. But the cake still tasted a bit bland, so we turned to our spice cabinet. The right combination of warm spices gave our cake a bold, chai-inspired flavor profile that jazzed up the cake considerably. To fix the dense and dry texture, we first tested mixing methods: a bowl method using melted butter, a standard creaming method in which we combined softened butter with the Sucanat, and a reverse-creaming method, in which we combined the Sucanat with the dry ingredients and then added softened butter in small chunks. Tasters preferred the even texture and good rise produced by reverse creaming. To avoid a greasy cake, we reduced the amount of butter and added milk to make up for any lost richness. Traditional pound cake recipes contain no chemical leavener, but we found that adding just a small amount of baking powder provided much better and more reliable rise. But the leavener had a negative effect as well: The texture was now too light and delicate for a proper pound cake. Our original recipe called for cake flour, which had prevented the cake from becoming tough. But switching to all-purpose flour for our low-sugar pound cake worked like a charm, giving us just the plush, fine crumb we wanted. The test kitchen's preferred loaf pan measures 8½ by 4½ inches; if you use a 9 by 5-inch loaf pan, start checking for doneness 5 minutes earlier than advised in the recipe. You can skip grinding the Sucanat in step 1; however, the cake will have a speckled appearance.

⅔ cup plus ¼ cup (5 ounces) Sucanat

⅔ cup whole milk

3 large eggs

1 tablespoon vanilla extract

2¼ cups (11¼ ounces) all-purpose flour

1½ teaspoons baking powder

½ teaspoon salt

¼ teaspoon ground cardamom

¼ teaspoon ground cinnamon

¼ teaspoon ground cloves

¼ teaspoon ground ginger

12 tablespoons unsalted butter, cut into 12 pieces and softened

1. Adjust oven rack to middle position and heat oven to 325 degrees. Grease 8½ by 4½-inch loaf pan. Working in 3 batches, grind Sucanat in spice grinder until fine and powdery, about 1 minute. Whisk milk, eggs, and vanilla together in bowl.

2. Using stand mixer fitted with paddle, mix ground Sucanat, flour, baking powder, salt, cinnamon, cardamom, cloves, and ginger on low speed until combined. Add butter, 1 piece at a time, and mix until only pea-size pieces remain, about 2 minutes. Add half of milk mixture, increase speed to medium-high, and beat until light and fluffy, 30 to 45 seconds.

3. Scrape mixer bowl thoroughly with rubber spatula. Turn speed to medium-low, add remaining milk mixture, and beat until incorporated, about 30 seconds (batter will resemble soft-serve ice cream). Scrape down bowl again, transfer batter to prepared pan, and smooth top.

4. Bake until toothpick inserted in center comes out clean, 1 hour 5 minutes to 1 hour 10 minutes, rotating pan halfway through baking.

5. Let cake cool in pan for 10 minutes. Remove cake from pan and let cool completely on wire rack, about 2 hours, before serving.

BEFORE 32 grams sugar ⟶ **AFTER** 18 grams sugar

summer peach cake

Serves 10

WHY THIS RECIPE WORKS Sweet, juicy peaches are a treat on their own—but incorporating them into a tender cake elevates them to another level. We wanted a flavorful, peach-packed cake that we could pair with a simple, lightly sweetened dollop of whipped cream. Since peaches contain a lot of water, we knew that our biggest challenge would be keeping their moisture content under control while using less sugar. We started by making a thick cake batter with less liquid than normal, hoping that the peaches we folded in would provide the moisture our batter needed. But this cake turned out soggy and riddled with gummy spots. Moreover, we found that the peach flavor was muted and dull. To enhance the peaches' flavor and sweetness and reduce their moisture content, we roasted the peaches before incorporating them into the batter. We also added peach schnapps to both the roasted peaches and the batter. While this cake was less soggy and had an intense peach flavor that tasters loved, gummy spots still persisted. We needed something that would act as a barrier between the peaches and the cake. Coating the peaches in flour helped alleviate some of the gumminess, but we thought we could do better. We speculated that another pantry ingredient—bread crumbs—might be just the thing. We were happily surprised to find that tossing crushed panko crumbs with the roasted and strained peach chunks resulted in drastically fewer gummy spots, and the bread crumbs hydrated and incorporated seamlessly into the cake. To crush panko bread crumbs, place them in a zipper-lock bag and crush with a rolling pin. You can substitute frozen peaches for the fresh peaches; you do not need to thaw the fruit before roasting. You can skip grinding the Sucanat in step 1; however, the cake will be slightly speckled in appearance. If using a dark colored cake pan, start checking the cake for doneness 5 to 10 minutes earlier. This cake tastes best the same day it is made.

¾ cup (4 ounces) Sucanat

1 pound peaches, peeled, pitted, and cut into ½-inch pieces

3 tablespoons plus 1 teaspoon peach schnapps

2 teaspoons lemon juice

1 tablespoon vanilla extract

1 cup (5 ounces) all-purpose flour

1¼ teaspoons baking powder

¾ teaspoon salt

2 large eggs

8 tablespoons unsalted butter, melted and cooled

¼ cup sour cream

½ teaspoon almond extract

⅓ cup panko bread crumbs, crushed fine

1 recipe Half-Batch Maple Whipped Cream (page 143)

1. Adjust oven rack to middle position and heat oven to 425 degrees. Grease 9-inch round cake pan. Line rimmed baking sheet with aluminum foil and grease foil. Working in 3 batches, grind Sucanat in spice grinder until fine and powdery, about 1 minute.

2. Toss peaches with 2 tablespoons ground Sucanat, 3 tablespoons schnapps, lemon juice, and 1 teaspoon vanilla in bowl. Spread peaches in single layer on prepared sheet and roast until peaches release their juice and begin to caramelize, about 25 minutes. Let peaches cool on completely on sheet, about 30 minutes. Reduce oven temperature to 350 degrees.

3. Whisk flour, baking powder, and salt together in bowl. In separate bowl, whisk remaining ground Sucanat and eggs together until combined. Whisk in melted butter, sour cream, almond extract, remaining 2 teaspoons vanilla, and remaining 1 teaspoon peach schnapps until combined and smooth. Whisk in flour mixture until just combined.

4. Strain excess liquid from peaches. Toss peaches with crushed panko, then fold into batter. Scrape cake batter into prepared pan and smooth top.

5. Bake until cake is set and toothpick inserted into center comes out clean, 30 to 35 minutes, rotating pan halfway through baking. Let cake cool in pan for 5 minutes. Remove cake from pan and let cool completely on wire rack, about 1 hour. Serve with whipped cream.

BEFORE 33 grams sugar ⟶ **AFTER** 16 grams sugar

berry snack cake

Serves 9

WHY THIS RECIPE WORKS Looking for a flavorful, naturally sweetened cake that would be equally at home as an afternoon snack or dressed up with whipped cream for company, we decided to create a mixed berry snack cake. The warm, molasses notes from the Sucanat gave our cake a good flavor backbone, while lime zest gave the cake a bit of unexpected punch. Stirring the fruit right into the batter ensured that the bursts of flavor and sweetness were well distributed throughout the cake, allowing us to use less sugar in the batter itself. We found that the creaming method gave the cake the best texture, opening up the crumb and ensuring that the cake was perfectly tender, but still sturdy enough to support the berries. This cake can be served warm or at room temperature. You can substitute frozen berries for the fresh berries; do not thaw the fruit before adding it to the cake batter. This cake tastes best the same day it is made. You can skip grinding the Sucanat in step 2; however, the cake will have a speckled appearance.

1½ cups (7½ ounces) all-purpose flour

1½ teaspoons baking powder

½ teaspoon salt

½ cup plus 2 tablespoons (3½ ounces) Sucanat

8 tablespoons unsalted butter, softened

2 large eggs

1 tablespoon grated lime zest (2 limes)

1 teaspoon vanilla extract

⅓ cup whole milk

1½ cups (7½ ounces) blackberries, blueberries, and raspberries

1. Adjust oven rack to middle position and heat oven to 375 degrees. Make foil sling for 8-inch square baking pan by folding 2 long sheets of aluminum foil so each is 8 inches wide. Lay sheets of foil in pan perpendicular to each other, with extra foil hanging over edges of pan. Push foil into corners and up sides of pan, smoothing foil flush to pan. Grease foil.

2. Whisk flour, baking powder, and salt together in bowl. Working in 2 batches, grind Sucanat in spice grinder until fine and powdery, about 1 minute. Using stand mixer fitted with paddle, beat ground Sucanat and butter together on medium-high speed until pale and fluffy, about 3 minutes.

3. Add eggs, lime zest, and vanilla and beat until combined, about 30 seconds. Reduce speed to low and add flour mixture in 3 additions, alternating with milk in 2 additions, scraping down bowl as needed. Give batter final stir by hand, then gently fold in berries with rubber spatula.

4. Scrape batter into prepared pan and smooth top. Bake cake until light golden brown and toothpick inserted in center comes out with few moist crumbs attached, 25 to 35 minutes, rotating pan halfway through baking.

5. Let cake cool in pan for 30 minutes. Using foil overhang, remove cake from pan and transfer to wire rack. Discard foil and let cake cool completely, about 2 hours, before serving.

BEFORE 25 grams sugar ⟶ **AFTER** 13 grams sugar

Sweetener Substitutions

COCONUT SUGAR	¾ cup (3½ ounces) Cake will have slight nutty flavor; grind sugar as directed in step 2.
GRANULATED SUGAR	½ cup (3½ ounces) Cake will be pale in color and have milder flavor; do not grind sugar in step 2.

apple cake

Serves 8

WHY THIS RECIPE WORKS We wanted a moist and tender apple cake that actually tasted like its namesake. Our traditional recipe used applesauce to provide some flavor and moisture, but without any added sugar, the applesauce made our cake gummy. We took it out and added a couple of extra tablespoons of butter to compensate for the lost moisture. For deep apple flavor, we turned to two concentrated sources: dried apples and apple cider. Rehydrating the dried apples in the cider allowed us to easily puree them so they would seamlessly incorporate into the cake batter. As an added bonus, the dried apples and cider made our cake sweet enough all on their own, making additional sugar unnecessary. Cinnamon, nutmeg, cloves, and vanilla gave the cake a more nuanced flavor profile. A teaspoon of baking soda produced ample rise and a tender, rustic crumb. To make this delicious cake a display piece, we sliced up two whole apples, cooked them briefly in butter to drive off additional moisture, and shingled them on top of the cake before baking it. A coating of honey, melted butter, and lemon juice followed by a brief stint under the broiler gave the apples a pleasant sheen and appetizing golden appearance. You can substitute Jonagold, Braeburn, Pink Lady, or Gala apples for the Golden Delicious apples. If using a dark colored cake pan, start checking the cake for doneness 5 to 10 minutes earlier. This cake tastes best the same day it is made.

2 tablespoons unsalted butter, plus 10 tablespoons melted

2 Golden Delicious apples, cored, peeled, halved, and sliced ⅛ inch thick

2 cups apple cider

1 cup dried apples, cut into ½-inch pieces

1½ cups (7½ ounces) all-purpose flour

1 teaspoon baking soda

½ teaspoon salt

1 tablespoon vanilla extract

1½ teaspoons ground cinnamon

¼ teaspoon ground nutmeg

⅛ teaspoon ground cloves

1 large egg

2 teaspoons honey

1 teaspoon lemon juice

1. Melt 1 tablespoon butter in 12-inch skillet over medium-high heat. Add apples and cook, stirring often, until just translucent and slightly pliable, 3 to 5 minutes. Transfer to bowl and let cool.

2. Add cider and dried apples to now-empty skillet and simmer over medium heat until liquid evaporates and mixture appears dry, 15 to 20 minutes. Transfer to separate bowl and let cool.

3. Adjust oven rack to middle position and heat oven to 325 degrees. Grease 9-inch round cake pan. Whisk flour, baking soda, and salt together in large bowl. In food processor, process dried apple–cider mixture, vanilla, cinnamon, nutmeg, and cloves until smooth, about 30 seconds, scraping down bowl as needed. Add egg and process until combined, about 15 seconds. With processor running, slowly drizzle in 10 tablespoons melted butter. Using rubber spatula, fold pureed apple mixture into flour mixture until combined.

4. Scrape batter into prepared pan and smooth top. Shingle cooked apple slices around top in decorative circle. Bake until toothpick inserted in center of cake comes out clean, 32 to 35 minutes, rotating pan halfway through baking.

5. Remove cake from oven and heat broiler. Meanwhile, microwave remaining 1 tablespoon butter and honey until melted, 15 to 30 seconds. Stir in lemon juice and brush mixture over apples. Broil cake, checking often and turning as necessary, until apples are attractively caramelized, 4 to 6 minutes.

6. Let cake cool in pan for 10 minutes. Run knife around edge of cake to loosen. Invert cake onto plate, then invert again onto wire rack. Let cake cool completely, about 1½ hours, before serving.

BEFORE 27 grams sugar $\longrightarrow$ **AFTER** 18 grams sugar

pear upside-down cake

Serves 10

WHY THIS RECIPE WORKS Even though apples get a lot of the attention when it comes to fall fruit, pears are equally versatile for baking and pair well with warm spices and nutty flavors. We wanted to put this oft-overlooked fruit in the spotlight. A simple Sucanat-based faux-caramel, layered into the bottom of the pan, created a thick, luscious glaze that kept the flavor of the pears prominent. Next we focused on the cake itself. For a rustic, hearty feel and robust flavor, we decided to cut the all-purpose flour with ground walnuts. We settled on a 2:1 ratio of ground walnuts to all-purpose flour for a pleasantly coarse crumb. However, with so little flour, we couldn't rely on its protein for structure. To fix this problem, we looked at the other source of protein in our recipe: eggs. Since we didn't want our cake to be too fluffy or too dense, we needed to incorporate just the right amount of air into our eggs to achieve the right structure. Using a stand mixer to whip the batter resulted in a cake that was too light, while mixing the batter by hand made a cake that was too dense. Our solution: a food processor. The fast-moving, sharp blades incorporated just enough air into the batter to create a cake with a flat, even top and a nicely coarse crumb—a perfect vehicle for our caramel-coated pears. You can skip grinding the Sucanat in step 3; however, the cake will have a speckled appearance. If using a dark colored cake pan, start checking the cake for doneness 5 to 10 minutes earlier. This cake tastes best the same day it is made.

topping

- 2 tablespoons unsalted butter, melted
- 2 tablespoons Sucanat
- 2 teaspoons cornstarch
- ⅛ teaspoon salt
- 3 ripe but firm Bosc pears (8 ounces each)

cake

- ¾ cup (4 ounces) Sucanat
- 1 cup walnuts, toasted
- ½ cup (2½ ounces) all-purpose flour
- ¼ teaspoon salt
- ¼ teaspoon baking powder
- ⅛ teaspoon baking soda
- 3 large eggs
- 4 tablespoons unsalted butter, melted
- 3 tablespoons vegetable oil

1. FOR THE TOPPING Adjust oven rack to middle position and heat oven to 300 degrees. Grease 9-inch round cake pan and line bottom with parchment paper. Pour melted butter over bottom of pan and swirl to evenly coat. Combine Sucanat, cornstarch, and salt in small bowl and sprinkle evenly over melted butter.

2. Peel, halve, and core pears; reserve 1 pear half for another use. Cut remaining 5 pear halves into 4 wedges each. Arrange pears in circular pattern in cake pan with tapered ends pointing inward. Arrange smallest 2 pear wedges in center.

3. FOR THE CAKE Working in 3 batches, grind Sucanat in spice grinder until fine and powdery, about 1 minute. Pulse walnuts, flour, salt, baking powder, and baking soda in food processor until walnuts are finely ground, 8 to 10 pulses; transfer to bowl.

4. Process ground Sucanat and eggs and in now-empty processor until mixture doubles in volume, about 2 minutes. With processor running, add melted butter and oil in steady stream until incorporated. Add walnut-flour mixture and pulse to combine, 4 to 5 pulses.

5. Pour batter evenly over pears (some pear may show through). Bake until center of cake is set and toothpick inserted in center comes out clean, 1 hour to 1 hour 10 minutes, rotating pan after 40 minutes.

6. Let cake cool in pan for 15 minutes. Run knife around edge of cake to loosen. Invert cake onto plate, remove parchment, then transfer onto wire rack. Let cake cool completely, about 2 hours, before serving.

BEFORE 35 grams sugar ⟶ **AFTER** 19 grams sugar

Sweetener Substitutions

COCONUT SUGAR

Topping: 2 tablespoons
Cake: ½ cup plus ⅓ cup (4 ounces)
Cake will be darker in color and have milder flavor; grind sugar as directed in step 3.

GRANULATED SUGAR

Topping: 2 tablespoons
Cake: ⅓ cup plus ¼ cup (4 ounces)
Cake will be pale in color and have milder flavor; do not grind sugar in step 3.

honey-rosemary polenta cake with clementines

Serves 10

WHY THIS RECIPE WORKS A rustic, rosemary-scented polenta cake topped with a swath of honey whipped cream and clementines sounded like a perfect fit for a naturally sweetened dessert. But while tasters loved the flavor profile, swapping in a small amount of honey for the usual granulated sugar resulted in a dry, dense-textured cake. To fix this, we increased the amount of milk and the amount of leavener. Tasters weren't keen on having chewy, distracting bits of rosemary throughout the cake, so we simply infused the milk with a couple of sprigs of rosemary. A mere tablespoon of honey was enough to lightly sweeten the whipped cream, while sliced clementines gave the cake some citrusy freshness and an elegant finish. Do not substitute either regular or premade polenta for the instant polenta. Be sure to break up any large clumps of polenta with your fingers before adding it to the batter or the cake will have bits of hard polenta throughout. If using a dark colored cake pan, start checking the cake for doneness 5 to 10 minutes earlier.

cake

- 1½ cups whole milk
- 2 sprigs fresh rosemary
- 1½ cups (8¼ ounces) instant polenta
- 3 large eggs
- 5 tablespoons honey
- 2 teaspoons vanilla extract
- 1 cup (4 ounces) cake flour
- 1 teaspoon baking powder
- ½ teaspoon baking soda
- ½ teaspoon salt
- 8 tablespoons unsalted butter, cut into 8 pieces and softened

topping

- ½ cup heavy cream
- 1 tablespoon honey
- 4 clementines, peeled and sliced ⅛ inch thick

1. FOR THE CAKE Adjust oven rack to middle position and heat oven to 350 degrees. Grease 9-inch round cake pan and line bottom with parchment paper.

2. Bring milk and rosemary sprigs to simmer in medium saucepan over medium heat, then let steep off heat for 10 minutes; discard rosemary. Meanwhile, spread polenta onto rimmed baking sheet and toast in oven until fragrant, about 10 minutes. Stir polenta into milk until combined.

3. Whisk eggs, honey, and vanilla in bowl until combined. Using stand mixer fitted with paddle, mix flour, baking powder, baking soda, and salt on low speed until combined. Add butter, 1 piece at a time, and mix until only pea-size pieces remain, about 1 minute.

4. Add half of egg mixture, increase speed to medium-high, and beat until light and fluffy, about 1 minute. Reduce speed to medium-low, add remaining egg mixture, and beat until incorporated, about 30 seconds. Break up any large clumps of polenta, then beat into batter until combined and smooth, about 2 minutes. Give batter final stir by hand.

5. Scrape batter into prepared pan and smooth top. Bake until top is golden and toothpick inserted in center comes out clean, 30 to 35 minutes, rotating pan halfway through baking.

6. Let cake cool in pan for 10 minutes. Run knife around edge of cake to loosen. Invert cake onto plate, remove parchment, then invert cake onto wire rack. Let cake cool completely, about 2 hours. (Undecorated cake can be stored at room temperature for up to 3 days.)

7. FOR THE TOPPING Using stand mixer fitted with whisk attachment, whip cream and honey on medium-low speed until foamy, about 1 minute. Increase speed to high and whip until soft peaks form, 1 to 3 minutes. Spread whipped cream over top of cake, leaving ¼-inch border at edge. Shingle clementines over top and serve, using serrated knife to cut tidy slices.

BEFORE 29 grams sugar ⟶ **AFTER** 15 grams sugar

chocolate cherry almond torte

Serves 12

WHY THIS RECIPE WORKS Classic chocolate tortes are characterized by a rich, almost fudge-like texture. Knowing that we didn't want an airy crumb for this cake, we decided to sweeten it with date sugar; the denseness created by this superabsorbent sugar was a boon to our torte. But the date sugar's ability to absorb liquid was also problematic: Our cake was dry and a bit grainy because of the undissolved sugar. To impart more moisture, we created an almond "butter" using a food processor. The benefit of this was twofold: The fat from the nuts counteracted the dryness, and the food processor eliminated any residual grittiness. Chopped cherries brought some brightness to the rich chocolate. A simple ganache glaze made for a perfect refined finish. Our favorite brand of bittersweet chocolate is Ghirardelli 60% Cacao Bittersweet Chocolate Premium Baking Bar (see page 21 for more information); other brands may contain different amounts of sugar. If using a dark colored cake pan, start checking the cake for doneness 5 to 10 minutes earlier.

torte

- 8 ounces bittersweet chocolate, chopped fine
- 12 tablespoons unsalted butter, cut into ½-inch pieces
- 2 teaspoons vanilla extract
- ½ teaspoon instant espresso powder
- ¼ cup (1¼ ounces) all-purpose flour
- ½ teaspoon salt
- 1¼ cups blanched sliced almonds, lightly toasted
- 5 large eggs
- ⅓ cup (2 ounces) date sugar
- 8 ounces (1 cup) frozen cherries, thawed, drained, chopped coarse, and patted dry with paper towels

glaze and garnish

- 4 ounces bittersweet chocolate, chopped fine
- ½ cup heavy cream
- ¾ cup blanched sliced almonds, lightly toasted

1. FOR THE TORTE Adjust oven rack to middle position and heat oven to 325 degrees. Grease 9-inch round cake pan, line with parchment paper, and grease parchment. Microwave chocolate and butter in bowl at 50 percent power, stirring occasionally, until melted, about 4 minutes. Let cool completely, then stir in vanilla and espresso powder.

2. Combine flour and salt in bowl. Process almonds in food processor to smooth paste, 2 to 3 minutes; transfer to separate bowl. Add eggs to now-empty food processor and process until lightened in color and almost doubled in volume, about 3 minutes. With processor running, slowly add date sugar until incorporated, about 15 seconds.

3. Gently whisk processed egg mixture into cooled chocolate mixture until only few streaks of egg remain. Whisk in ground almond paste, followed by flour mixture, until combined. Using rubber spatula, fold in cherries. Scrape batter into prepared pan and smooth top. Bake until center is firm and toothpick inserted in center comes out with few moist crumbs attached, 25 to 30 minutes, rotating pan halfway through baking.

4. Let torte cool in pan for 15 minutes. Run knife around edge of torte to loosen. Invert torte onto plate, remove parchment, and transfer onto wire rack. Let cool completely, about 40 minutes.

5. FOR THE GLAZE AND GARNISH Place chocolate in medium bowl. Bring cream to simmer in small saucepan over medium-low heat, then pour over chocolate and let stand for 1 minute. Whisk mixture until smooth, then let cool slightly, about 3 minutes. Pour glaze onto center of torte. Use offset spatula to spread glaze evenly over top and sides of torte.

6. Pulse almonds in food processor until coarsely chopped, about 4 pulses. Using fine-mesh strainer, sift almonds to remove any fine bits. Press nuts onto side of torte to cover. Refrigerate torte on rack until glaze is set, at least 1 hour or up to 24 hours, before serving.

BEFORE 24 grams sugar ⟶ **AFTER** 15 grams sugar

honey-oat bundt cake

Serves 12

WHY THIS RECIPE WORKS We wanted a crowd-pleasing, low-sugar Bundt cake that highlighted the bold, floral flavor of honey. But the decrease in sugar created myriad issues. To achieve a cake that was moist, tender, and not greasy, we used a few tricks. First, we added some applesauce, which provided moisture without greasiness. Adding orange juice helped boost the leavening power of the baking soda (which is activated by an acidic ingredient), keeping the cake light. Another key to success: ground old-fashioned oats. They added a pleasant nutty depth that complemented the honey perfectly, as well as lending a soft and fluffy texture to the cake. To punch up the honey flavor, we made a simple soaking syrup of honey and vanilla, which we thinned out in the microwave so we could easily brush it over the finished cake. Do not substitute quick oats, instant oats, or steel-cut oats in this recipe.

cake

- ¾ cup old-fashioned rolled oats
- 2½ cups (12½ ounces) all-purpose flour
- 1¼ teaspoons salt
- 1 teaspoon baking powder
- ½ teaspoon baking soda
- ½ cup whole milk
- 8 tablespoons unsalted butter, melted
- 3 large eggs
- 6 tablespoons unsweetened applesauce
- ¼ cup orange juice
- 1 teaspoon vanilla extract
- ¾ cup honey

glaze

- ⅓ cup honey
- 1 teaspoon vanilla extract

Making Bundt Cake

1 To ensure cake comes out of pan easily, grease pan with baking spray with flour or mix 1 tablespoon melted unsalted butter with 1 tablespoon flour and brush paste evenly into pan with pastry brush.

2 To unmold cake, place wire rack on pan. Holding pan and rack tightly, flip cake over.

1. FOR THE CAKE Adjust oven rack to middle position and heat oven to 325 degrees. Coat 12-cup nonstick Bundt pan heavily with baking spray with flour. Process oats in food processor until finely ground, about 60 seconds.

2. Whisk ground oats, flour, salt, baking powder, and baking soda together in large bowl. In separate bowl, whisk milk, melted butter, eggs, applesauce, orange juice, and vanilla together, then whisk in honey until fully incorporated. Whisk egg mixture into flour mixture until combined. Scrape batter into prepared pan.

3. Bake until skewer inserted in middle of cake comes out clean, 45 to 55 minutes, rotating pan halfway through baking.

4. Let cake cool in pan for 30 minutes. Using paring knife, loosen cake from sides of pan and invert onto wire rack.

5. FOR THE GLAZE Microwave honey and vanilla until honey becomes fluid, about 30 seconds. Brush honey mixture over still-warm cake. Let cake cool completely, about 2 hours, before serving.

BEFORE 48 grams sugar → **AFTER** 25 grams sugar

Sweetener Substitutions

COCONUT SUGAR

Cake: 1½ cups (7 ounces)
Glaze: ¾ cup (3½ ounces)
Cake and glaze will be darker in color; glaze will take 6 hours to set. Grind sugar as directed in steps 2 and 5.

GRANULATED SUGAR AND CONFECTIONERS' SUGAR

Cake: 1 cup (7 ounces) granulated sugar
Glaze: ¾ cup plus 2 tablespoons (3½ ounces) confectioners' sugar
Cake and glaze will be paler in color and have milder flavor; omit cornstarch and do not grind sugars in steps 2 and 5.

spiced-citrus bundt cake

Serves 12

WHY THIS RECIPE WORKS With the height and tender crumb of a chiffon cake and the richness of a pound cake, Bundt cakes are win-win. We wanted a simple, low-sugar Bundt cake that would be bursting with citrus flavor. For a light and even crumb, we creamed the butter and sugar, which aerated the batter and contributed lightness to the final cake. Although our traditional recipe called for four eggs, we found that using only three kept the cake from being too rubbery. As for the citrus, we added a hefty amount of orange juice as well as a tablespoon of zest to the cake batter to create bold, unmistakable flavor. But while the orange flavor came through loud and clear, our cake was tasting one-dimensional. To round out the flavor profile, we added complementary spices: potent allspice, anise seeds, and ginger. Finally, we created a low-sugar glaze that incorporated even more orange juice and zest for a final hit of citrus. If you don't have baking spray with flour for greasing the Bundt pan, mix 1 tablespoon melted unsalted butter with 1 tablespoon flour to make a paste and brush it into the pan using a pastry brush. Do not skip grinding the Sucanat in steps 2 or 5, or the cake will contain large air pockets and the glaze will be gritty.

cake

- 3 cups (15 ounces) all-purpose flour
- 2 teaspoons ground allspice
- 1½ teaspoon ground anise seeds
- 1½ teaspoons ground ginger
- 1 teaspoon salt
- 1 teaspoon baking powder
- ½ teaspoon baking soda
- 1 tablespoon grated orange zest plus ¾ cup juice (2 oranges)
- 1 tablespoon vanilla extract
- 1¼ cups (7 ounces) Sucanat
- 16 tablespoons unsalted butter, softened
- 3 large eggs

glaze

- ½ cup plus 2 tablespoons (3½ ounces) Sucanat
- 1 ounce cream cheese, softened
- 4 teaspoons cornstarch
- 1 teaspoon grated orange zest plus 2 tablespoons juice

1. FOR THE CAKE Adjust oven rack to lower-middle position and heat oven to 350 degrees. Coat 12-cup nonstick Bundt pan heavily with baking spray with flour. Whisk flour, allspice, anise, ginger, salt, baking powder, and baking soda together in large bowl. In separate bowl, combine orange zest and juice and vanilla.

2. Working in 4 batches, grind Sucanat until fine and powdery, about 1 minute. Using stand mixer fitted with paddle, beat ground Sucanat and butter on medium-high speed until pale and fluffy, about 3 minutes. Add eggs, one at a time, and beat until combined. Reduce speed to low and add flour mixture in 3 additions, alternating with juice mixture in 2 additions, scraping down bowl as needed. Give batter final stir by hand.

3. Scrape batter into prepared pan. Bake until skewer inserted in middle of cake comes out clean, 45 to 55 minutes, rotating pan halfway through baking.

4. Let cake cool in pan for 30 minutes. Using paring knife, loosen cake from sides of pan and invert onto wire rack. Let cool completely, about 2 hours, before glazing.

5. FOR THE GLAZE Working in 2 batches, grind Sucanat until fine and powdery, about 1 minute. Whisk ground Sucanat, cream cheese, cornstarch, and orange zest and juice together in bowl until smooth. Pour glaze over top of cake, letting it drip down sides. Let glaze set, about 1 hour, before serving.

BEFORE 43 grams sugar ⟶ **AFTER** 25 grams sugar

chocolate pudding cake

Serves 6

WHY THIS RECIPE WORKS Most hot fudge pudding cakes end up looking rich and fudgy, but have very little chocolate flavor—and a hefty amount of sugar. For a low-sugar pudding cake with robust chocolate flavor, we ditched the granulated sugar entirely, so that the semisweet chocolate could shine. We decided to melt half the chocolate and incorporate it into the batter for a fudgy, chocolaty base; we chopped the other half and folded it into our batter, giving us plenty of gooey pockets of chocolate in the baked cake. We also bumped up the chocolate flavor further with Dutch-processed cocoa; because it is less acidic than natural cocoa powder, it produced a richer chocolate taste. Traditionally, pudding cake batter is baked with a layer of boiling water on the top, which hydrates the cake and sinks to the bottom during cooking, producing a chocolaty pudding layer. After some testing, we found that 1 cup of boiling water produced the perfect pudding cake consistency. We've had good luck using Ghirardelli Semi-Sweet Chocolate Premium Baking Bar in this recipe (see page 21 for more information); other brands may contain different amounts of sugar. For an accurate measurement of boiling water, bring a full kettle of water to a boil and then measure out the desired amount.

8 ounces semisweet chocolate, chopped fine
1 cup (5 ounces) all-purpose flour
¼ cup (¾ ounce) Dutch-processed cocoa powder
2 teaspoons baking powder
½ teaspoon salt
¾ cup whole milk
4 tablespoons unsalted butter, melted
1 large egg yolk
2 teaspoons vanilla extract
1 cup boiling water

1. Adjust oven rack to middle position and heat oven to 350 degrees. Grease 8-inch square baking pan. Microwave half of chocolate in bowl at 50 percent power, stirring occasionally, until melted, 2 to 4 minutes; let cool slightly.

2. Whisk flour, cocoa, baking powder, and salt together in large bowl. In separate bowl, whisk melted chocolate, milk, melted butter, egg yolk, and vanilla until smooth. Stir chocolate mixture into flour mixture until just combined. Fold in remaining chopped chocolate.

3. Scrape batter into prepared pan and smooth top. Gently pour boiling water over top; do not stir. Bake until top of cake looks cracked, sauce is bubbling, and toothpick inserted in cakey area comes out with few moist crumbs attached, about 25 minutes, rotating pan halfway through baking.

4. Let cake cool for 10 minutes before serving. To serve, scoop warm cake into individual serving bowls.

BEFORE 34 grams sugar ⟶ **AFTER** 23 grams sugar

Making Chocolate Pudding Cake

1 Scrape batter into prepared pan and smooth top.
2 Gently pour boiling water over top; do not stir.

mocha-mascarpone jelly roll cake

Serves 12

WHY THIS RECIPE WORKS A jelly roll—or Swiss roll—is perfect for any special occasion or holiday celebration. But these showpieces can be daunting to make: Too often, the cake breaks when rolled, the filling spills out, or the frosting doesn't set up properly; plus, the cake itself can be dry and rubbery. We wanted a moist, chocolaty cake that rolled well, with a flavorful, luscious filling. Knowing the filling would be the easier task, we started there. Mascarpone made a perfect base, since its richness and gentle tang paired nicely with the chocolate cake. We amped up the mascarpone's mild flavor with espresso powder and a small amount of almond extract. We tried sweetening the filling with Sucanat, honey, and maple syrup, and tasters far preferred the latter: While the bold flavors of Sucanat and honey overpowered the other flavors in the filling, the gentle sweetness of maple syrup worked perfectly. We decided that we could streamline our process by making the filling pull double duty: We reserved some of the filling mixture and folded in whipped cream to make a rich, creamy frosting for the outside of our jelly roll cake. Next, we turned our attention to the cake itself. Our traditional chocolate jelly roll cake called for whipping eggs and then gradually adding sugar, but since we were using maple syrup in the filling, we wanted to use it in the cake as well. We were happy to find that the syrup incorporated seamlessly into the whipped eggs, and a mere ½ cup provided plenty of sweetness without overpowering the chocolate. We also increased the amount of cocoa powder from ¼ cup to ⅓ cup to boost chocolate flavor and make up for the structure that the extra sugar would normally provide. Finally, our rich, flavorful jelly roll cake came together into a dessert worth sharing.

filling and frosting

- ½ cup maple syrup
- 2 teaspoons instant espresso powder
- 1 teaspoon almond extract
- ⅛ teaspoon salt
- 1 pound (2 cups) mascarpone cheese
- 1 cup heavy cream

cake

- ¾ cup (3¾ ounces) all-purpose flour
- ⅓ cup (1 ounce) unsweetened cocoa powder
- 1 teaspoon baking powder
- ¼ teaspoon salt
- 5 large eggs
- ½ cup maple syrup
- 1 teaspoon vanilla extract

1. FOR THE FILLING AND FROSTING Whisk maple syrup, espresso powder, almond extract, and salt together in bowl. In large bowl, stir mascarpone with rubber spatula until softened and smooth, then whisk in maple mixture. Measure out ½ cup and set aside.

2. Using stand mixer fitted with whisk attachment, whip cream on medium-low speed until foamy, about 1 minute. Increase speed to high and whip until soft peaks form, 1 to 2 minutes. Using rubber spatula, fold in ½ cup reserved mascarpone mixture until combined. Refrigerate mascarpone-maple mixture and whipped cream–mascarpone mixture separately until needed or for up to 2 days.

3. FOR THE CAKE Adjust oven rack to lower-middle position and heat oven to 325 degrees. Grease 18 by 13-inch rimmed baking sheet, line with parchment paper, and grease parchment. Whisk flour, cocoa, baking powder, and salt together in bowl.

4. Using stand mixer fitted with whisk attachment, whip eggs on medium-low speed until foamy, about 1 minute. Gradually add maple syrup in steady stream. Increase speed to high and whip until mixture has tripled in volume, is pale yellow color, and ribbons fall from whisk, 5 to 7 minutes. Beat in vanilla.

5. Remove bowl from stand mixer. Sift flour mixture over top of whipped eggs. Using rubber spatula, fold flour mixture into eggs until incorporated and no traces of flour remain.

6. Scrape batter into prepared sheet and spread into even layer. Bake until cake is firm to touch and springs back when pressed lightly, about 15 minutes, rotating sheet halfway through baking.

7. Invert second baking sheet, grease bottom lightly, and line with parchment. Remove cake from oven and run knife around edge of cake to loosen. Working quickly while cake is warm, place second baking sheet on top, parchment side down, and gently flip pans over. Remove sheet and parchment now on top. Starting from short side, roll cake and bottom parchment into log. Let cake cool, seam side down, for 15 minutes.

8. Gently unroll cake. Stir mascarpone-maple mixture to loosen, then spread evenly over cake, leaving 1-inch border along bottom edge. Re-roll cake around filling, leaving parchment behind as you roll. Transfer cake to serving platter. Spread whipped cream–mascarpone mixture over top and sides of cake and refrigerate for at least 30 minutes or up to 2 days. Serve.

BEFORE 37 grams sugar $\longrightarrow$ **AFTER** 17 grams sugar

Making Jelly Roll Cake

1 Invert second baking sheet, grease bottom lightly, and line bottom of upside-down pan with parchment.

2 Remove cake from oven and run knife around edge of cake to loosen.

3 Working quickly, place second baking sheet on top, parchment side down, and gently flip pans over. Remove sheet and parchment now on top.

4 Starting from short side, roll warm cake with parchment on bottom into log. Let cake cool, seam side down, for 15 minutes.

5 Gently unroll cake and spread filling evenly over cake, leaving 1-inch border along bottom edge.

6 Re-roll cake around filling, leaving parchment behind as you roll.

blueberry cheesecake

Serves 12

WHY THIS RECIPE WORKS For a low-sugar version of this company-worthy classic, we wanted a flavorful, silky cheesecake bursting with flavor. We knew we wanted to incorporate blueberries; we hoped that their natural sweetness and beautiful color would complement the tangy cream cheese. We tested incorporating the berries in two ways: pureeing the berries and stirring them into the filling and folding them into the filling as whole berries. Tasters loved the flavor of the blueberries, but in test after test, our cheesecake came out a wan lavender color with spots from the berry skins or pockets of tough blueberries punctuating our silky cream cheese filling. We decided instead to take the blueberries out of the filling and make them into a topping. We made a simple compote, cooking down the blueberries with a little Sucanat to create a topping that would slowly run down the sides of our cake without being too wet. We then focused on the filling itself. Lemon zest seemed like the perfect counterpoint to the cream cheese and blueberries; grinding it with the Sucanat ensured that we didn't end up with chewy strands of zest in the cake. We strained the filling to get rid of any grainy bits and cooked the cake in a water bath to ensure an even silkier texture. Cooking the cheesecake to 150 degrees instead of waiting for visual cues made our recipe more foolproof. You can use fresh blueberries in the topping if desired; crush one-third of the fresh berries after adding them to the pot. For neat, professional-looking pieces of cake, clean the knife thoroughly between slices. Do not skip grinding the Sucanat in steps 1 and 3, or the crust will be crumbly and the filling will taste gritty.

crust

- 3 tablespoons (1 ounce) Sucanat
- 6 whole graham crackers, broken into pieces
- 2 tablespoons unsalted butter, melted and cooled

filling

- ⅓ cup plus ¼ cup (3 ounces) Sucanat
- 1 tablespoon grated lemon zest plus 2 tablespoons juice
- 1½ pounds cream cheese, softened
- ¼ teaspoon salt
- 1 tablespoon vanilla extract
- 4 large eggs
- ½ cup heavy cream

topping

- 1 tablespoon unsalted butter
- 10 ounces (2 cups) frozen blueberries
- 2 tablespoons Sucanat
- Pinch salt
- ½ teaspoon lemon juice

1. FOR THE CRUST Adjust oven rack to middle position and heat oven to 325 degrees. Grease 9-inch springform pan. Grind Sucanat in spice grinder until fine and powdery, about 1 minute. Process cracker pieces in food processor until finely ground, about 30 seconds. Add ground Sucanat and melted butter and pulse until crumbs are evenly moistened, about 10 pulses.

2. Transfer mixture to prepared pan and press into even layer with bottom of dry measuring cup. Bake crust until fragrant and beginning to brown, about 10 minutes. Let crust cool to room temperature, about 30 minutes. Do not turn off oven. Once cool, wrap bottom and sides of pan with 2 sheets of foil and set in large roasting pan lined with dish towel. Bring kettle of water to boil.

3. FOR THE FILLING Working in 2 batches, grind Sucanat and lemon zest in spice grinder until Sucanat is fine and powdery, about 1 minute. Using stand mixer fitted with paddle, beat ground Sucanat mixture, cream cheese, and salt on medium speed until combined, 1 to 3 minutes. Add lemon juice and vanilla and beat until combined, about 1 minute, scraping down bowl as needed. Add eggs, one at a time, and beat until combined, about 3 minutes. Add heavy cream and beat until incorporated, about 1 minute.

4. Strain filling through fine-mesh strainer into large bowl, using rubber spatula to help push filling through strainer. Carefully pour filling over crust. Set roasting pan on oven rack and pour enough boiling water into roasting pan to come about halfway up sides of springform pan. Bake until cake registers 150 degrees, about 1 hour.

5. Transfer roasting pan to wire rack, run paring knife around cake, and let cool for 45 minutes. Remove cake from roasting pan, discard foil, and let cool on wire rack until barely warm, about 3 hours, running knife around edge of cake every hour or so. Cover cake with plastic wrap and refrigerate until chilled, at least 3 hours or up to 3 days.

6. FOR THE TOPPING Melt butter in small saucepan over medium heat. Add blueberries, Sucanat, and salt and bring to boil. Reduce heat to medium-low and simmer, stirring occasionally, until thickened, about 10 minutes. Off heat, stir in lemon juice and let cool to room temperature for at least 30 minutes or up to 2 hours.

7. To unmold cheesecake, wrap hot dish towel around pan and let sit for 1 minute. Remove sides of pan. Slide thin metal spatula between crust and pan bottom to loosen, then slide cake onto serving platter. Let cheesecake sit at room temperature for 30 minutes. Before serving, spoon topping over top of cheesecake.

BEFORE 35 grams sugar → **AFTER** 16 grams sugar

Making Cheesecake

1 Wrap bottom and sides of pan with 2 sheets of foil and set in large roasting pan lined with dish towel.
2 Place roasting pan with cheesecake in oven, and pour enough boiling water into roasting pan to come about halfway up sides of springform pan.

Sweetener Substitutions

COCONUT SUGAR	Crust: 3 tablespoons Filling: ½ cup plus 2 tablespoons (3 ounces) Topping: 2 tablespoons Filling will have slight nutty flavor and topping will taste slightly bitter. Grind sugar as directed in steps 1 and 3.
GRANULATED SUGAR	Crust: 2 tablespoons Filling: 7 tablespoons (3 ounces) Topping: 2 tablespoons Filling and topping will have milder flavor. Do not grind sugar in steps 1 and 3.

pies and tarts

apple-pear pie

Serves 8

WHY THIS RECIPE WORKS Apple pie is a classic favorite, but most recipes call for copious amounts of sugar along with the apples. We found that we could scale down the sugar in our traditional recipe by about 75 percent and still achieve a filling that was plenty sweet, but tasters found this pie a bit one-dimensional and bland. Adding extra spices helped, but with the amount needed to give the pie enough flavor, the apples were completely overpowered. We decided to take a different approach, hoping to give our pie nuanced flavor while still allowing the fruit to shine. Surprisingly, we found our answer in another fall staple: pears. An equal amount of apples and pears provided the best balance of flavor, while just ¼ teaspoon of cinnamon and a whole vanilla bean rounded out the flavor of the filling. To keep the pie from being a soggy mess of unevenly cooked fruit, we partially cooked the pears and apples together, along with a small amount of Sucanat, lemon zest, cinnamon, and the vanilla bean, then strained away all but ¼ cup of liquid. A squeeze of lemon juice, added to the reserved liquid, provided brightness and brought the flavors into focus. We found that it was important to bake the pie at two different temperatures: We started it in a hotter, 425-degree oven, which allowed the crust to set and develop good color and then dropped it to 375 degrees to allow the crust and filling to gently finish cooking. You can use Fuji, Jonagolds, or Braeburns in place of the Golden Delicious apples. You can substitute 2 teaspoons vanilla extract for the vanilla bean if desired.

1 vanilla bean

2½ pounds Golden Delicious apples, peeled, halved, cored, and sliced ¼ inch thick

2½ pounds ripe but firm Bartlett or Bosc pears, peeled, halved, cored, and sliced ¼ inch thick

⅓ cup (1¾ ounces) Sucanat

½ teaspoon grated lemon zest plus 1 tablespoon juice

¼ teaspoon salt

¼ teaspoon ground cinnamon

1 recipe All-Butter Double-Crust Pie Dough (page 216), bottom crust fitted into 9-inch pie plate and chilled and top crust rolled into 12-inch circle and chilled

1 large egg white, lightly beaten

1. Cut vanilla bean in half lengthwise and scrape out seeds using tip of paring knife. Toss apples, pears, Sucanat, lemon zest, salt, cinnamon, and vanilla seeds and bean together in Dutch oven. Cover and cook over medium heat, stirring often, until fruit is tender but still holds its shape, 15 to 20 minutes. Transfer fruit mixture and any juices to rimmed baking sheet and let cool to room temperature, about 30 minutes. Discard vanilla bean.

2. Adjust oven rack to lowest position and heat oven to 425 degrees. Drain cooled apple mixture in colander set over bowl. Measure out ¼ cup drained juice, discarding extra, and stir in lemon juice.

3. Spread apple mixture into chilled dough-lined pie plate, mounding fruit slightly in middle, and drizzle with juice mixture. Loosely roll dough circle around rolling pin and gently unroll it onto filling.

4. Trim any overhanging dough to ½ inch beyond lip of plate, then pinch edges of top and bottom crusts firmly together. Tuck overhang under itself; folded edge should be flush with edge of plate. Crimp dough evenly around edge of plate using your fingers. Cut four 2-inch slits in top of dough and brush surface with beaten egg white.

5. Set pie on aluminum foil–lined baking sheet and bake until crust is light golden brown, about 25 minutes. Reduce oven temperature to 375 degrees, rotate sheet, and continue to bake until juices are bubbling and crust is deep golden brown, 40 to 50 minutes. Let pie cool on wire rack until juices have thickened, about 2 hours. Serve.

BEFORE 50 grams sugar ⟶ **AFTER** 34 grams sugar

Sweetener Substitutions

COCONUT SUGAR	**6 tablespoons (1¾ ounces)** Pie will have nutty, bold flavor.
GRANULATED SUGAR	**¼ cup (1¾ ounces)** Pie will taste slightly less sweet.

peach pie

Serves 8

WHY THIS RECIPE WORKS Perfectly ripe, juicy peaches lend themselves beautifully to pie; gently sweetened and cradled in a buttery crust, there are few desserts better suited for the end of a summer meal. But too often, the peaches' delicate flavor is masked by too much sugar, and the juiciness of the fruit turns against you, making for a soupy, leaky pie. We decided to omit the usual granulated sugar in favor of a mere ¼ cup of Sucanat, letting the natural sweetness of the peaches do most of the heavy lifting. Our traditional recipe called for only ¼ teaspoon of cinnamon and a pinch of nutmeg, but reducing the amount of sugar meant that these small amounts barely came through. We upped both spices and added cardamom, which contributed another layer of aromatic flavor to the pie filling. We also found that the lemon juice in our traditional recipe was no longer necessary—its tartness became overpowering. We omitted it, but kept the lemon zest for citrusy backbone. To make sure the juicy peaches didn't turn our filling soupy, we needed to corral the moisture that the peaches gave off during cooking. To draw out some of their moisture, we mixed them with the Sucanat, let them sit for 30 minutes, and strained out the peach juice, reserving a measured amount to stir into the filling. Using two different thickeners—pectin and cornstarch—produced a clear, silky texture without any of the gumminess that larger amounts of either one produced. Mashing some of the peaches helped to create a cohesive filling. A simplified lattice crust made for a beautiful, buttery finish to our pie. For fruit pectin we recommend both Sure-Jell for Less or No Sugar Needed Recipes and Ball RealFruit Low or No-Sugar Needed Pectin. For more information on peeling peaches, see page 209.

3 pounds ripe but firm peaches, peeled, quartered, pitted, and sliced ½ inch thick

¼ cup (1½ ounces) Sucanat

1 teaspoon grated lemon zest

⅛ teaspoon salt

2 tablespoons low- or no-sugar-needed fruit pectin

½ teaspoon ground cinnamon

¼ teaspoon ground nutmeg

¼ teaspoon ground cardamom

1 tablespoon cornstarch

1 recipe All-Butter Double-Crust Pie Dough (page 216), bottom crust fitted into 9-inch pie plate and chilled and top crust cut into 10 strips and frozen until firm

1 large egg white, lightly beaten

1. Toss peaches, 2 tablespoons Sucanat, lemon zest, and salt together in bowl and let sit at room temperature for 30 minutes to 1 hour. In separate bowl, combine remaining 2 tablespoons Sucanat, pectin, cinnamon, nutmeg, and cardamom.

2. Adjust oven rack to lowest position and heat oven to 425 degrees. Transfer 1 cup peaches to small bowl and mash with fork until coarse paste forms. Drain remaining peach mixture in colander set over bowl; reserve ½ cup drained juice and discard extra. Return peaches to bowl and toss with cornstarch and mashed peaches.

3. Whisk ½ cup drained juice and pectin mixture together in 12-inch skillet. Cook over medium heat, stirring occasionally, until slightly thickened and pectin is dissolved, 3 to 5 minutes. Add to peaches and toss to combine. Spread peach mixture into chilled dough-lined pie plate.

4. Remove lattice strips from freezer; if too stiff to be workable, let stand at room temperature for several minutes. Lay 2 strips across center of pie, perpendicular to each other. Arrange 4 strips around edge of pie in shape of square. Lay remaining 4 strips between strips in center and around edge to make lattice design.

5. Trim any overhanging dough to ½ inch beyond lip of plate, then pinch edges of lattice strips and bottom crust firmly together. Tuck overhang under itself; folded edge should be flush with edge of plate. Crimp dough evenly around edge of plate using your fingers. Brush lattice with beaten egg white.

6. Set pie on aluminum foil-lined baking sheet and bake until crust is light golden brown, about 25 minutes. Reduce oven temperature to 375 degrees, rotate sheet, and continue to bake until juices are bubbling and crust is deep golden brown, 25 to 30 minutes. Let pie cool on wire rack until juices have thickened, about 2 hours. Serve.

BEFORE 33 grams sugar $\longrightarrow$ **AFTER** 19 grams sugar

Making Faux Lattice Top

1 Lay 2 strips across center of pie, perpendicular to each other.
2 Arrange 4 strips around edge of pie in shape of square.
3 Lay remaining 4 strips between strips in center and around edge to make lattice design.
4 Trim any overhanging dough to ½ inch beyond lip of plate, then pinch edges of lattice strips and bottom crust firmly together.
5 Tuck overhang under itself; folded edge should be flush with edge of plate.
6 Crimp dough evenly around edge of plate using your fingers.

Sweetener Substitutions

COCONUT SUGAR	⅓ cup (1½ ounces) Pie will have slightly nutty, caramel flavor.
GRANULATED SUGAR	3 tablespoons Pie will have milder flavor.

blueberry pie

Serves 8

WHY THIS RECIPE WORKS We wanted a blueberry pie filling that put the focus squarely on an abundance of plump, juicy blueberries—without relying on any added sugar at all. A full 6 cups of fresh blueberries made up the base of our filling, but we still needed to figure out how to thicken the filling so that it was neither soupy nor gluey. We tested cornstarch, flour, and tapioca starch, and found that cornstarch and flour consistently produced pasty, starchy fillings. Tapioca worked slightly better, but by the time we had added enough to get the pie to slice neatly, the filling turned gluey and dull. Our traditional recipe took advantage of the natural pectin present in apples to thicken the pie, a trick which also worked well here. One grated Granny Smith apple (squeezed to remove excess moisture), along with a small amount of tapioca, provided enough thickening power to set the pie beautifully. The apple nearly disappeared into the filling, enhancing the blueberries' flavor without adding any of its own. We cooked half of the berries to create a jammy, concentrated base for our filling and then folded in the remaining berries to create a satisfying balance of intensely flavorful cooked fruit and bright-tasting fresh fruit. A little lemon zest rounded out the flavor of the filling. To encourage the excess juice to evaporate, we cut out small round steam vents in our top crust. We recommend placing a baking sheet underneath while baking to catch any juice that might bubble out.

30 ounces (6 cups) blueberries

1 Granny Smith apple, peeled, cored, and shredded

2 tablespoons instant tapioca, ground

2 teaspoons grated lemon zest

⅛ teaspoon salt

1 recipe All-Butter Double-Crust Pie Dough (page 216), bottom crust fitted into 9-inch pie plate and chilled and top crust rolled into 12-inch circle and chilled

2 tablespoons unsalted butter, cut into ¼-inch pieces

1 large egg white, lightly beaten

1. Place 3 cups blueberries in medium saucepan. Cook over medium heat, stirring and mashing occasionally with potato masher, until half of blueberries are broken down and mixture measures 1½ cups, about 12 minutes. Let cool to room temperature, about 20 minutes.

2. Adjust oven rack to lowest position and heat oven to 400 degrees. Place shredded apple in center of dish towel. Gather ends together and twist tightly to drain as much liquid as possible. Transfer apple to large bowl and stir in cooked blueberry mixture, remaining 3 cups uncooked blueberries, tapioca, lemon zest, and salt until combined. Transfer blueberry mixture to chilled dough-lined pie plate and scatter butter over top.

3. Using 1¼-inch round cookie cutter, cut out single round in center of 12-inch dough circle. Cut out 6 more rounds from dough, 1½ inches from edge of center hole and equally spaced around center hole. Loosely roll dough circle around rolling pin and gently unroll it onto filling.

4. Trim any overhanging dough to ½ inch beyond lip of plate, then pinch edges of top and bottom crusts firmly together. Tuck overhang under itself; folded edge should be flush with edge of plate. Crimp dough evenly around edge of plate using your fingers. Brush surface with beaten egg white.

5. Set pie on aluminum foil–lined baking sheet and bake until crust is light golden brown, about 25 minutes. Reduce oven temperature to 350 degrees, rotate sheet, and continue to bake until juices are bubbling and crust is deep golden brown, 30 to 40 minutes longer. Let pie cool on wire rack until juices have thickened, about 2 hours. Serve.

BEFORE 33 grams sugar ⟶ **AFTER** 13 grams sugar

Making Blueberry Pie

1 Cook 3 cups blueberries, stirring and mashing occasionally with potato masher, until half of blueberries are broken down and mixture measures 1½ cups.

2 Using clean dish towel, wring as much liquid as possible from shredded apple.

3 Transfer blueberry-apple mixture to chilled dough-lined pie plate and scatter butter over top.

4 Using 1¼-inch round cookie cutter, cut out single round in center of dough circle. Cut out 6 more rounds from dough, 1½ inches from edge of center hole and equally spaced around center hole.

5 Loosely roll dough circle around rolling pin and gently unroll it onto filling. Trim any overhanging dough to ½ inch.

6 Tuck overhang under itself; folded edge should be flush with edge of plate. Crimp dough evenly around edge of plate using your fingers.

roasted sweet potato pie

Serves 8

WHY THIS RECIPE WORKS We set out to create a luscious, silky-smooth sweet potato pie that would be naturally sweetened and contain much less sugar than our traditional recipe. We wondered whether the sweetness of the potatoes alone would be enough to carry our pie. We tested a variety of potato preparation methods and techniques, from deeply roasting the potatoes in the oven, both whole and in slices, to simply steaming them in the microwave, and found that tasters preferred the richness of the whole roasted potatoes. But even with the best cooking method figured out, we couldn't overcome the potatoes' inherent savory qualities. We still wanted our pie to be a sweet and decadent treat, so we decided to add a small amount of honey to the filling. Wanting to complement but not overwhelm the flavor of the roasted potatoes, we tested varying amounts of honey and found that a mere 5 tablespoons was enough to create a satisfyingly sweet filling. To boost the filling's flavor further, we used cinnamon and nutmeg, which we bloomed in butter to bring out their flavors. A hefty amount of vanilla and bit of bourbon gave our pie a beautifully nuanced flavor profile. Some sour cream provided subtle tang, and combining all of our ingredients in the food processor ensured an ultrasmooth filling. Rich with warm spice notes, creamy and custardy, sweet but not over the top, this pie was perfectly balanced.

1¾ pounds sweet potatoes (about 3 potatoes), scrubbed
4 tablespoons unsalted butter
¾ teaspoon ground cinnamon
¼ teaspoon ground nutmeg
½ teaspoon salt
1 cup sour cream
3 large eggs plus 2 large yolks
5 tablespoons honey
2 tablespoons bourbon
1 tablespoon vanilla extract
1 recipe All-Butter Pie Crust (page 214), baked and cooled

1. Adjust oven rack to middle position and heat oven to 425 degrees. Arrange potatoes on aluminum foil–lined baking sheet and bake until tip of knife slips easily into potato center, 40 to 50 minutes. Halve potatoes lengthwise to expose flesh and let cool slightly, about 15 minutes. Reduce oven temperature to 350 degrees.

2. Melt butter with cinnamon and nutmeg in microwave, 15 to 30 seconds. Scoop flesh from baked potatoes into bowl of food processor. Add salt and process until smooth, about 1 minute, scraping down bowl as needed. Add spiced butter, sour cream, eggs and yolks, honey, bourbon, and vanilla and process until smooth, about 1 minute, scraping down bowl as needed.

3. Pour potato mixture into cooled pie crust. Set pie on baking sheet and bake until filling is set around edges but center registers 165 degrees and jiggles slightly when pie is shaken, 40 to 45 minutes, rotating sheet halfway through baking. Let pie cool completely on wire rack, about 2 hours. Serve.

BEFORE 37 grams sugar ⟶ **AFTER** 16 grams sugar

summer berry pie

Serves 8

WHY THIS RECIPE WORKS We wanted to develop a naturally sweetened berry pie with bright, vibrant flavor. A mix of raspberries, blackberries, and blueberries struck the perfect balance of sweetness and brightness. The filling did not require much additional flavoring beyond a small amount of Sucanat, which rounded out the sweetness of the berries, but we still needed a way to thicken the filling. We knew that the berries contained natural pectin, so we pureed a portion of them and cooked them with the Sucanat, which helped create a more cohesive pie. Tasters liked the consistency, but still wanted neater slices. To achieve this, we found that we needed a small amount of cornstarch to supplement the natural pectin in the fruit. To give the remaining berries a beautiful, glossy appearance before using them to top the pie, we tossed them with a small amount of the pureed filling. A dollop of whipped cream offered a rich counterpoint to the sweet-tart brightness of this delicious summery treat.

10 ounces (2 cups) raspberries
10 ounces (2 cups) blackberries
10 ounces (2 cups) blueberries
½ cup plus 2 tablespoons (3½ ounces) Sucanat
3 tablespoons cornstarch
⅛ teaspoon salt
1 tablespoon lemon juice
1 recipe Graham Cracker Pie Crust (page 221), baked and cooled
1 cup Maple Whipped Cream (page 143)

1. Gently toss berries together in large bowl. Process 2½ cups berries in food processor until very smooth, about 1 minute. Strain processed berries through fine-mesh strainer into small saucepan, pressing on solids to extract as much puree as possible (you should have about 1½ cups puree); discard solids.

2. Whisk Sucanat, cornstarch, and salt together in bowl, then whisk into strained puree. Bring puree mixture to boil over medium heat, stirring constantly, and cook until thick and pudding-like, about 7 minutes. Off heat, stir in lemon juice and let cool slightly, about 5 minutes.

3. Add 2 tablespoons cooked puree to remaining berries in bowl and toss gently to coat. Pour remaining warm berry puree into cooled pie crust. Spread berries evenly over top. Cover pie loosely with plastic wrap and refrigerate until filling is chilled and set, at least 3 hours or up to 24 hours. Serve with whipped cream.

BEFORE 38 grams sugar ⟶ **AFTER** 24 grams sugar

Sweetener Substitutions	
COCONUT SUGAR	¾ cup (3½ ounces) Pie will taste similar.
GRANULATED SUGAR	½ cup (3½ ounces) Pie will have milder flavor.

dark chocolate cream pie

Serves 8

WHY THIS RECIPE WORKS Our ideal chocolate cream pie has a silky-smooth filling with intense but well-balanced chocolate flavor. To make our low-sugar version, we started by replacing the Oreo crust with a crust made from chocolate graham crackers. The graham crackers contained much less sugar than the traditional cream-filled cookies, and as long as we firmly pressed the crust into the dish, it held up perfectly when sliced. For the chocolate filling, initial tests with decreasing amounts of Sucanat revealed surprising results: Just a few tablespoons of Sucanat were enough to sweeten the filling. We decreased the sugar content even further by switching from semisweet to bittersweet chocolate. Along with the bittersweet chocolate, a small amount of unsweetened chocolate produced the most complex, up-front chocolate flavor. For a creamy, rich custard base, we used half-and-half (which tasters preferred over milk or heavy cream) and whisked in some butter after the custard had cooked. To ensure that no bits of overcooked egg made it into our pie, we strained the filling into the crust. A topping of lightly sweetened whipped cream served as the perfect finishing touch on this decadent dessert. Our favorite brand of bittersweet chocolate is Ghirardelli 60% Cacao Bittersweet Chocolate Premium Baking Bar (see page 21 for more information); other brands may contain different amounts of sugar. Our favorite brand of unsweetened chocolate is Hershey's Unsweetened Baking Bar (see page 21 for more information). Do not skip grinding the Sucanat in step 4, or the whipped cream will be gritty.

pie

- 6 large egg yolks
- 3 tablespoons Sucanat
- 2 tablespoons cornstarch
- 2½ cups half-and-half
- ¼ teaspoon salt
- 6 tablespoons unsalted butter, cut into ½-inch pieces and chilled
- 6 ounces bittersweet chocolate, chopped fine
- 1 ounce unsweetened chocolate, chopped fine
- 1 teaspoon vanilla extract
- 1 recipe Chocolate Graham Cracker Pie Crust (page 221), baked and cooled

topping

- 1 tablespoon Sucanat
- 1½ cups heavy cream
- 1 tablespoon vanilla extract
  Pinch salt

1. FOR THE PIE Whisk egg yolks, Sucanat, and cornstarch in medium bowl until well combined. Bring half-and-half and salt to simmer in medium saucepan over medium heat. Slowly whisk ½ cup half-and-half mixture into yolk mixture to temper, then slowly whisk tempered yolk mixture into pot. Cook, whisking constantly, until thick and glossy, 2 to 3 minutes.

2. Off heat, whisk in chilled butter until incorporated. Whisk in bittersweet chocolate, unsweetened chocolate, and vanilla until chocolate is melted; make sure to scrape bottom and corners of pan with rubber spatula.

3. Strain filling through fine-mesh strainer into cooled pie crust. Lay sheet of plastic wrap directly on surface of pudding and refrigerate until firm, about 2 hours.

4. FOR THE TOPPING Grind Sucanat in spice grinder until fine and powdery, about 1 minute. Using stand mixer fitted with whisk attachment, whip cream, ground Sucanat, vanilla, and salt on medium-low speed until foamy, about 1 minute. Increase speed to high and whip until soft peaks form, 1 to 3 minutes. Spread whipped cream over pie and serve.

BEFORE 37 grams sugar ⟶ **AFTER** 24 grams sugar

Sweetener Substitutions

COCONUT SUGAR	Pie: 3 tablespoons **Topping: 1 tablespoon** Pie will taste similar; grind sugar as directed in step 4.
GRANULATED SUGAR	Pie: 2 tablespoons **Topping: 1 tablespoon** Pie will have milder chocolate flavor; do not grind sugar in step 4.

lemon cream pie

Serves 8

WHY THIS RECIPE WORKS Making a great lemon cream pie is all about creating balance—the tart lemon curd contrasting with sweet whipped cream; the luscious, satiny filling inside a crisp, delicate crust. But to achieve that, we first needed to perfect each element on its own. We started with the curd. Our original recipe relied on sweetened condensed milk to sweeten the curd and achieve a thick, decadent consistency. But for our low-sugar version, we knew the sweetened condensed milk was a nonstarter; the recipe called for two cans, and each can contained 22 grams of sugar. Instead, we created a more traditional cooked curd, using a combination of two whole eggs and seven egg yolks to achieve a creamy, dense texture. We used a hefty amount of lemon zest and juice and balanced the sharp tanginess with honey. To ensure a perfectly smooth texture, we strained the curd before stirring in heavy cream, which tempered the tartness that additional sugar would usually tame. Once the curd was complete, we poured it into our graham cracker crust and baked it. For a lightly sweet and flavorful whipped cream topping, we quickly whipped heavy cream with honey, vanilla, and salt in a stand mixer until soft peaks formed and then slathered it over the top of the cooled pie. Even with less than half the sugar of the traditional recipe, this pie was plenty sweet, with every element coming together in perfect harmony.

pie

- 2 large eggs plus 7 large yolks
- ½ cup honey
- ¼ cup grated lemon zest plus ⅔ cup juice (4 lemons)
- ⅛ teaspoon salt
- 4 tablespoons unsalted butter, cut into 4 pieces
- 3 tablespoons heavy cream
- 1 recipe Graham Cracker Pie Crust (page 221), baked and cooled

topping

- 1½ cups heavy cream
- 2 tablespoons honey
- 1 teaspoon vanilla
- ⅛ teaspoon salt

1. FOR THE PIE Adjust oven rack to middle position and heat oven to 375 degrees. Whisk eggs and yolks, honey, lemon zest and juice, and salt in medium saucepan until smooth. Cook over medium-low heat, stirring constantly with rubber spatula, until mixture thickens slightly and registers 165 degrees, 5 to 7 minutes.

2. Off heat, whisk in butter and cream until incorporated. Strain filling through fine-mesh strainer into cooled pie crust. Bake until filling is shiny and opaque and center jiggles slightly when shaken, 8 to 10 minutes, rotating pan halfway through baking. Let pie cool completely, about 2 hours.

3. FOR THE TOPPING Using stand mixer fitted with whisk attachment, whip cream, honey, vanilla, and salt on medium-low speed until foamy, about 1 minute. Increase speed to high and whip until soft peaks form, 1 to 3 minutes. Spread whipped cream over pie and serve.

BEFORE 64 grams sugar ⟶ **AFTER** 26 grams sugar

Sweetener Substitutions

COCONUT SUGAR	Pie: ⅓ cup (1½ ounces) Topping: 1 tablespoon Pie will be darker in color; grind sugar as directed in step 5.
GRANULATED SUGAR	Pie: 3 tablespoons Topping: 1 tablespoon Pie will be lighter in color and have clean banana flavor; do not grind sugar in step 5.

banana cream pie

Serves 8

WHY THIS RECIPE WORKS Banana cream pie should spark visions of tropical decadence, but so often the filling disappoints: It usually veers to overly mushy or criminally rubbery, and the banana flavor itself is bland. We wanted a silky-smooth low-sugar filling that would be packed with tons of banana flavor. We tried simply slicing all of our bananas and layering them into low-sugar vanilla pastry cream, but tasters complained that the pastry cream wasn't sweet enough on its own, and the banana flavor (even with five whole bananas) was barely noticeable. To boost the pastry cream's flavor, we pureed a couple of the bananas and incorporated the puree into the cream. But while tasters appreciated the intense banana flavor, the starchy fruit had marred the smooth texture of the pastry cream. To avoid this, we roasted the bananas unpeeled before pureeing them, which alleviated some of their starchiness without turning them watery. Processing the bananas into the cooked pastry cream was easy, and straining the cream before spreading it into the crust ensured an ultra-smooth texture. As for the remaining bananas, we simply sliced them and layered them with the pastry cream to reinforce the banana flavor. A small amount of whipped cream was enough to top the pie without washing out the banana flavor we had worked so hard to create. Do not skip grinding the Sucanat in step 5 or the whipped cream will taste gritty. Be sure to use very ripe, heavily speckled (or even black) bananas in this recipe.

pie

- 5 very ripe bananas
- ¼ cup (1½ ounces) Sucanat
- 6 large egg yolks
- 3 tablespoons cornstarch
- 2½ cups half-and-half
- ¼ teaspoon salt
- 4 tablespoons unsalted butter, cut into 4 pieces and chilled
- 2 teaspoons vanilla extract
- 1 tablespoon lemon juice
- 1 recipe Graham Cracker Pie Crust (page 221), baked and cooled

topping

- 1 tablespoon Sucanat
- ¾ cup heavy cream
- 1 teaspoon vanilla extract
  Pinch salt

1. FOR THE PIE Adjust oven rack to upper-middle position and heat oven to 350 degrees. Place 2 unpeeled bananas on baking sheet and bake until skins are completely black, about 20 minutes. Let cool for about 5 minutes, then peel.

2. Whisk Sucanat, egg yolks, and cornstarch in medium bowl until well combined. Bring half-and-half and salt to simmer in medium saucepan over medium heat. Slowly whisk ½ cup half-and-half mixture into yolk mixture to temper, then slowly whisk tempered yolk mixture into pot. Cook, whisking constantly, until thick and glossy, 2 to 3 minutes.

3. Off heat, whisk in chilled butter and vanilla until incorporated. Transfer filling to food processor, add warm roasted bananas and lemon juice, and process until smooth, about 1 minute. Strain filling through fine-mesh strainer into bowl.

4. Peel remaining 3 bananas and cut crosswise into ¼-inch slices. Spread half of filling evenly into cooled pie crust. Arrange banana slices in single layer over top, then spread remaining filling over bananas. Lay sheet of plastic wrap directly on surface of pudding and refrigerate until firm, about 2 hours.

5. FOR THE TOPPING Grind Sucanat in spice grinder until fine and powdery, about 1 minute. Using stand mixer fitted with whisk attachment, whip ground Sucanat, cream, vanilla, and salt on medium-low speed until foamy, about 1 minute. Increase speed to high and whip until soft peaks form, 1 to 3 minutes. Spread whipped cream over pie and serve.

BEFORE 40 grams sugar ⟶ **AFTER** 24 grams sugar

coconut-lime cream pie

Serves 8

WHY THIS RECIPE WORKS A great coconut cream pie ought to highlight the unique flavor of its namesake, yet most recipes for this diner staple are nothing more than a vanilla cream pie decorated with coconut. Working from the ground up, we opted for a low-sugar graham cracker crust, hoping its delicate texture would complement the coconut filling rather than overshadow it with too much sweetness. For our filling, we started by creating a custard using a combination of milk, coconut milk, and egg yolks. We found that reducing the amount of sugar in our custard really allowed the coconut flavor to shine through, and using coconut sugar in place of the usual granulated sugar gave the custard an even fuller flavor. A little butter helped achieve a velvety smooth texture, while cornstarch added some stability when slicing through the thick filling. Lime zest offered a fresh, citrusy backbone to the filling. In the hopes of further boosting the coconut flavor in the custard, we tried incorporating unsweetened shredded coconut. However, the shredded coconut didn't offer much in the way of flavor, and tasters found the texture distracting. We decided instead to toast the coconut to bring out its flavor and then sprinkle it on top of our pie. As for the classic whipped cream topping, we flavored it with a bit of coconut sugar, vanilla extract, and lime zest so that it would mirror the flavors of the luscious custard beneath. Do not use light coconut milk in this recipe. Do not skip grinding the coconut sugar in step 3, or the whipped cream will taste gritty. Our favorite brand of coconut milk is Chaokoh; other brands may contain different amounts of sugar. You will need two limes for this recipe.

pie

- ½ cup (2½ ounces) coconut sugar
- 5 large egg yolks
- 3 tablespoons cornstarch
- 1 (13.5-ounce) can coconut milk
- 1 cup milk
- ¼ teaspoon salt
- 2 tablespoons unsalted butter, cut into 2 pieces and chilled
- 2 teaspoons vanilla extract
- 2 teaspoons grated lime zest, plus 2 tablespoons juice
- 1 recipe Graham Cracker Pie Crust (page 221), baked and cooled

topping

- 1 tablespoon coconut sugar
- 1½ cups heavy cream
- 1 teaspoon vanilla
- ¼ teaspoon grated lime zest
  Pinch salt
- 1 tablespoon unsweetened shredded coconut, toasted

1. FOR THE PIE Whisk sugar, egg yolks, and cornstarch in large bowl until well combined. Bring coconut milk, milk, and salt to simmer in medium saucepan over medium heat. Slowly whisk 1 cup coconut milk mixture into yolk mixture to temper, then slowly whisk tempered yolk mixture into pot. Cook, whisking constantly, until thick and glossy, 1 to 2 minutes.

2. Off heat, whisk in chilled butter, vanilla, and lime zest and juice. Pour filling into cooled pie crust. Lay sheet of plastic wrap directly on surface of pudding and refrigerate until firm, about 2 hours.

3. FOR THE TOPPING Before serving, grind sugar in spice grinder until fine and powdery, about 1 minute. Using stand mixer fitted with whisk attachment, whip cream, ground coconut sugar, vanilla, lime zest, and salt on medium-low speed until foamy, about 1 minute. Increase speed to high and whip until stiff peaks form, 1 to 3 minutes. Spread whipped cream over pie, sprinkle with toasted coconut, and serve.

BEFORE 31 grams sugar ⟶ **AFTER** 18 grams sugar

Sweetener Substitutions

SUCANAT

Pie: **7 tablespoons (2½ ounces)**
Topping: **1 tablespoon**
Pie will be lighter in color and taste slightly earthy; grind Sucanat as directed in step 3.

GRANULATED SUGAR

Pie: **6 tablespoons (2½ ounces)**
Topping: **1 tablespoon**
Pie will have yellow hue and strong lime flavor; do not grind sugar in step 3.

blueberry–lemon curd tart

Serves 8

WHY THIS RECIPE WORKS We set our sights on a low-sugar lemon tart—but we didn't want to end up with a puckery, one-note dessert. Our low-sugar, honey-sweetened lemon curd was a good starting point, but we quickly realized that we would need to balance out the curd with another, complementary flavor element. We thought that blueberry would be a perfect candidate, providing complementary brightness and a little warmth. A simple blueberry compote was a welcome addition, but to keep the total sugar content down we could use only a small amount of blueberries, and tasters lamented that the compote did not cover the entirety of the tart. Instead, we tried a different approach: We pureed the blueberries, strained them, added some cornstarch, cooked the mixture until it was thick and glossy, and poured it over our set lemon curd layer. The resulting tart was visually stunning—the blueberry layer had a beautiful satiny shine, and the two distinct layers made for a striking cross-section when sliced. But tasters felt the lemon overpowered the blueberries' delicate flavor, so we scaled down the lemon filling and increased the amount of blueberries. This version was delicious, but the blueberry layer was a bit runny despite its nice sheen. To ensure sliceability without diminishing the shine, we tried increasing the amount of cornstarch. Unfortunately, the mixture quickly became too thick, gummy, and opaque. After rigorous testing with varying cooking times, temperatures, and concentrations, we realized that the answer lay in temperature: Cooking the mixture to about 170 degrees produced a shiny, sliceable, and velvety blueberry layer. If using frozen blueberries, be sure to thaw them fully before cooking.

¼ cup lemon zest plus ½ cup juice
   (4 lemons)
1 large egg plus 5 large yolks
⅓ cup plus ¼ cup honey
   Salt
4 tablespoons unsalted butter, cut into
   4 pieces and chilled
2 tablespoons heavy cream
1 recipe Classic Tart Crust (page 218),
   partially baked and cooled
10 ounces (2 cups) blueberries
2 tablespoons cornstarch
2 tablespoons water

1. Adjust oven rack to middle position and heat oven to 350 degrees. Measure out and 1 tablespoon lemon juice and set aside. Whisk remaining lemon juice, lemon zest, egg and yolks, ⅓ cup honey, and pinch salt in medium saucepan until smooth. Cook over medium-low heat, stirring constantly with rubber spatula, until mixture thickens slightly and registers 165 degrees, about 5 minutes.

2. Off heat, whisk in chilled butter until melted. Strain lemon curd through fine-mesh strainer into bowl, then gently stir in cream with rubber spatula.

3. Pour warm lemon curd into cooled tart crust. Set tart on baking sheet and bake until filling is shiny and opaque and center jiggles slightly when shaken, 10 to 12 minutes, rotating pan halfway through baking. Transfer tart with baking sheet to wire rack and let cool slightly.

4. Meanwhile, process blueberries in food processor until smooth, about 2 minutes. Strain puree through clean fine-mesh strainer into medium saucepan, pressing on solids to extract as much liquid as possible (you should have about ¾ cup); discard solids.

5. Whisk in remaining ¼ cup honey and ⅛ teaspoon salt. Whisk cornstarch and water together in small bowl, then whisk into strained blueberry mixture. Bring to simmer over medium-low heat, stirring constantly, and cook until thickened slightly and registers 170 degrees, about 4 minutes.

6. Off heat, whisk in reserved 1 tablespoon lemon juice. Pour blueberry mixture evenly over cooled lemon filling. Tap pan lightly on counter to release any air bubbles, then refrigerate until blueberry mixture is set and shiny, about 2 hours. To serve, remove outer ring of tart pan, slide thin metal spatula between tart and tart pan bottom, and carefully slide tart onto serving platter or cutting board.

BEFORE 42 grams sugar ⟶ **AFTER** 27 grams sugar

Making Blueberry–Lemon Curd Tart

1 Cook lemon curd mixture over medium-low heat, stirring constantly with rubber spatula, until mixture thickens slightly and registers 165 degrees, about 5 minutes.

2 After straining cooked lemon curd and finishing it with butter and cream, pour it into cooled tart crust.

3 Bake tart until filling is shiny and opaque and center jiggles slightly when shaken, 10 to 12 minutes.

4 Meanwhile, simmer pureed blueberry mixture until thickened slightly and registers 170 degrees, about 4 minutes.

5 Pour blueberry mixture evenly over cooled lemon filling and tap pan lightly on counter to release any air bubbles.

6 Refrigerate tart until blueberry mixture is set and shiny, about 2 hours.

pear and almond tart

Serves 8

WHY THIS RECIPE WORKS This classic French dessert consists of satiny slices of tender, fragrant poached pears embedded in an almond-based custard-cake filling (known as frangipane), all contained in a crisp, buttery tart crust. We wanted to develop a low-sugar, naturally sweetened version. First, we poached pears in spiced wine to infuse them with flavor, happily realizing that we didn't need any sweetener in the poaching liquid. As for the filling, we decided to use honey in place of the traditional granulated sugar; its bold, floral notes worked beautifully with the other flavors. Rather than grinding almonds in a food processor, we opted for more convenient (and even-textured) almond flour. A quick glaze with honey, lemon, and cornstarch provided a glossy sheen to the tart. We like the bright, crisp flavor of pears poached in Sauvignon Blanc, but you can use Chardonnay to give the poached pears a deeper, oakier flavor.

poached pears

- ½ vanilla bean
- 1 (750-ml) bottle white wine
- 4 (2-inch) strips lemon zest plus 2 tablespoons juice
- 1 cinnamon stick
- 3 whole cloves
- ¼ teaspoon salt
- 4 Bosc or Bartlett pears (8 ounces each), peeled, halved, and cored

almond filling

- 1⅓ cups (6 ounces) almond flour
- 2 tablespoons cornstarch
- ⅛ teaspoon salt
- 1 large egg
- ½ teaspoon almond extract
- ½ teaspoon vanilla extract
- 6 tablespoons unsalted butter, softened
- 6 tablespoons honey
- 1 recipe Classic Tart Crust (page 218), partially baked and cooled

glaze and almonds

- 2 tablespoons honey
- 1 tablespoon lemon juice
- 1 teaspoon cornstarch
- ⅛ teaspoon salt
- ¼ cup sliced almonds, toasted

1. FOR THE POACHED PEARS Cut vanilla bean in half lengthwise and scrape out seeds using tip of paring knife. Combine vanilla bean and seeds, wine, lemon zest and juice, cinnamon, cloves, and salt in medium saucepan and bring to boil over medium-high heat. Add pears, return to simmer, then reduce heat to low. Cover and poach pears, turning occasionally, until tender, 15 to 20 minutes. Off heat, let pears cool in liquid until translucent and cool enough to handle, about 1 hour.

2. FOR THE ALMOND FILLING Adjust oven rack to middle position and heat oven to 325 degrees. Whisk almond flour, cornstarch, and salt together in bowl. In separate small bowl, whisk egg, almond extract, and vanilla together.

3. Using stand mixer fitted with paddle, beat butter and honey on medium-high speed until pale and fluffy, about 1½ minutes. Slowly add egg mixture and beat until combined, about 3 minutes (batter may look slightly curdled). Reduce speed to low and add almond flour mixture, beating until combined, about 1 minute, scraping down bowl as needed. Give batter final stir by hand. Spread batter evenly into cooled tart crust.

4. Remove cooled pears from poaching liquid and pat dry with paper towels. Slice 1 pear in half crosswise into ¼-inch-thick slices (do not separate slices). Pat pear dry again, discard first 4 slices from narrow end, and place in center of tart using spatula.

5. Working with remaining pear halves, one at a time, slice crosswise into ¼-inch-thick slices (do not separate slices); pat dry, pressing to fan slices toward narrow end. Using spatula, arrange fanned pears evenly around tart, with narrow end pointing towards center.

6. Set tart on baking sheet and bake until crust is deep golden brown and almond filling is puffed, browned, and firm to touch, about 1 hour, rotating sheet halfway through baking. Transfer tart with sheet to wire rack and let cool for 10 minutes.

7. FOR THE GLAZE AND ALMONDS Whisk honey, lemon juice, cornstarch, and salt together in small saucepan. Simmer over medium-low heat until slightly thickened and translucent, about 1 minute. Brush glaze over pears, sprinkle with almonds and let tart cool completely, about 2 hours. To serve, remove outer ring of tart pan, slide thin metal spatula between tart and tart pan bottom, and carefully slide tart onto serving platter or cutting board.

BEFORE 44 grams sugar ⟶ **AFTER** 25 grams sugar

Making Pear and Almond Tart

1 Slice 1 pear half crosswise into ¼-inch-thick slices, being careful to keep slices together.
2 Discard first 4 slices from narrow end and place pear in center of tart using spatula.
3 Working with remaining pear halves, one at a time, slice crosswise into ¼-inch-thick slices.
4 Pat sliced pears dry and press to fan slices toward narrow end.
5 Using spatula, arrange fanned pears evenly around tart, with narrow end pointing towards center.
6 Bake tart until crust is deep golden brown and almond filling is puffed, browned, and firm to touch, about 1 hour, before glazing.

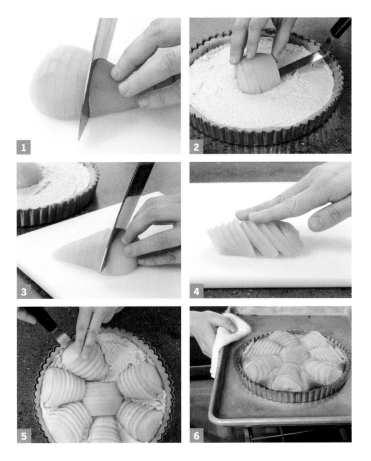

caramel-nut tart

Serves 8

WHY THIS RECIPE WORKS Stunning, decadent, and rich, caramel-nut tarts are usually made with hefty amounts of sugar and corn syrup, and are often drizzled with chocolate. We wanted our version to be just as impressive but a bit more restrained and sophisticated, allowing the deeply flavorful caramel and crunchy, buttery nuts to shine through. To that end, we decided to use Sucanat to make our caramel, since its rounded molasses notes would give the caramel enough flavor that we could achieve big impact with a relatively small amount. We were surprised to find that the Sucanat thickened to just the right consistency at only 260 degrees—about 100 degrees less than caramel made with granulated sugar. A small hit of bourbon and vanilla rounded out the flavor, while cream and butter ensured that our caramel was rich and perfectly gooey. We stirred a generous amount of mixed nuts into the caramel to give the tart visual and textural interest. A sprinkling of sea salt really brought the tart up a notch, amplifying the salty-sweet flavors. We like a mix of pecans, walnuts, hazelnuts, pistachios, almonds, and macadamia nuts in this tart. If using macadamia nuts, be sure to cut them in half. For safety, be sure to use a tall-sided saucepan to cook the caramel in step 1.

1 cup (5⅓ ounces) Sucanat

½ cup water

¼ teaspoon salt

⅓ cup heavy cream

3 tablespoons unsalted butter

1 tablespoon bourbon

1 tablespoon vanilla extract

2 cups unsalted mixed almonds, hazelnuts, pecans, walnuts, pistachios, and halved macadamia nuts

1 recipe Classic Tart Crust (page 218), partially baked and cooled

½ teaspoon flake sea salt

1. Adjust oven rack to middle position and heat oven to 350 degrees. Bring Sucanat, water, and salt to boil in large saucepan over medium-high heat, stirring occasionally to dissolve Sucanat.

2. Reduce heat to medium and simmer, stirring frequently, until mixture is dark brown, has thickened slightly, and registers 260 degrees, 10 to 13 minutes (caramel will have slightly bitter smell).

3. Off heat, carefully pour cream into caramel mixture and swirl to incorporate (mixture will bubble and steam); let bubbling subside. Stir in butter, bourbon, and vanilla until melted and well combined. Stir in nuts.

4. Pour warm filling into cooled tart crust. Set tart on aluminum foil–lined baking sheet and bake until caramel is vigorously bubbling, about 10 minutes.

5. Let tart cool on baking sheet to room temperature, about 2 hours, then sprinkle with sea salt. To serve, remove outer ring of tart pan, slide thin metal spatula between tart and tart pan bottom, and carefully slide tart onto serving platter or cutting board.

BEFORE 52 grams sugar ⟶ **AFTER** 26 grams sugar

Sweetener Substitutions

COCONUT SUGAR	1 cup plus 2 tablespoons (5⅓ ounces) Tart will have looser consistency and slight bitter flavor.
GRANULATED SUGAR	¾ cup (5⅓ ounces) Tart will be lighter in color and taste slightly sweeter and chewier; cook sugar until caramelized and registers 360 degrees in step 2, about 15 minutes.

fresh fruit tart with mascarpone and honey

Serves 8

WHY THIS RECIPE WORKS Fresh fruit tarts usually offer little substance beyond their dazzling beauty, with rubbery, overly sweet pudding fillings and cloying glazes. To create a tart that was just as beautiful but highlighted the juicy fruit as the source of sweetness, we had to be creative. We started by trying to make a pastry cream with half the amount of sugar but found it eggy and bland. No matter what flavors we added to it, we were dissatisfied with the result. In search of a rich, great-tasting base for our fresh fruit, we landed on whipped cream. We enriched the cream with mascarpone for a luxurious texture, and added a small amount of unflavored gelatin to ensure that the mixture wouldn't turn soupy under the fruit. We found that a small amount of honey was all that was needed to sweeten the cream mixture. A small dab of apple jelly to glaze our fruit made for a beautiful, satiny finish without adding unnecessary extra sweetness. We like a combination of kiwis, strawberries, and blueberries in this tart. Do not allow the mascarpone to warm to room temperature before using it or it may break when mixed with the other ingredients.

½ teaspoon unflavored gelatin

2 teaspoons water

½ cup heavy cream

2 tablespoons honey

1 tablespoon vanilla extract

4 ounces (½ cup) mascarpone, chilled

1 recipe Classic Tart Crust (page 218), fully baked and cooled

5 ounces (1 cup) blueberries

7½ ounces (1½ cups) strawberries, hulled and halved lengthwise

2 large kiwis, peeled and sliced crosswise ¼ inch thick

1 tablespoon apple jelly

1. Sprinkle gelatin over water in bowl and let sit until softened, about 5 minutes. Microwave mixture until bubbling around edges and gelatin dissolves, 10 to 15 seconds.

2. Using stand mixer fitted with whisk attachment, whip cream, honey, vanilla, and gelatin mixture on medium-low speed until foamy, about 1 minute. Increase speed to medium-high and whip until soft peaks form, 1 to 3 minutes. Gently fold in mascarpone. Spread mixture evenly into cooled tart crust.

3. Arrange blueberries around edge of tart. Arrange strawberries, cut side down, inside blueberries. Shingle kiwi slices, slightly overlapping them, in floral pattern inside strawberries.

4. Microwave jelly until fluid, about 10 seconds. Using pastry brush, dab melted jelly over fruit. Chill assembled tart in fridge for at least 1 hour or up to 4 hours. To serve, remove outer ring of tart pan, slide thin metal spatula between tart and tart pan bottom, and carefully slide tart onto serving platter or cutting board.

BEFORE 28 grams sugar → **AFTER** 16 grams sugar

apple, goat cheese, and honey tart

Serves 8

WHY THIS RECIPE WORKS Taking inspiration from a dessert cheese course, we set out to create an elegant tart that combined typical cheese board elements—goat cheese, apples, and honey. We started by sautéing the apples in a little butter, which boosted flavor, drove off excess moisture, and lightly browned the apples. We then combined fresh goat cheese with a little honey for sweetness and lemon juice for brightness, as well as a bit of cream and an egg yolk to add richness and help hold everything together. We processed the goat cheese mixture until it was as smooth as pastry cream and poured it into our baked and cooled tart crust. For a beautiful presentation, we arranged the apples attractively on top. Typically, these types of tarts are slathered with apricot jelly for extra sweetness and an attractive sheen, but this often overwhelms the other flavors. Wanting to keep the flavor profile more streamlined, we ditched the jelly and reached for honey instead, which we thinned out with a bit of lemon juice. After briefly baking the tart, we finished the tart off with a quick stint under the broiler, which caramelized the apples on top. This recipe works best with Honeycrisp, Golden Delicious, Fuji, Jonagold, and Braeburn apples.

2 tablespoons unsalted butter

1¼ pounds apples, peeled, cored, halved, and sliced ¼ inch thick

¼ cup honey

2 teaspoons lemon juice

8 ounces goat cheese

2 tablespoons heavy cream

1 large egg yolk

1 recipe Classic Tart Crust (page 218), partially baked and cooled

1. Adjust oven rack to middle position and heat oven to 375 degrees. Melt butter in 12-inch skillet over medium-high heat. Add apples and cook, stirring occasionally, until pliable and lightly browned, 5 to 7 minutes. Transfer to bowl and let cool.

2. In separate bowl, combine honey and lemon juice. In food processor, process 2 tablespoons honey-lemon mixture, goat cheese, cream, and egg yolk until mixture is smooth, about 60 seconds, scraping down bowl as needed.

3. Spread goat cheese mixture evenly into cooled tart crust. Starting at outer edge of tart, shingle cooked apple slices around top in decorative circle. Drizzle apples with remaining honey-lemon mixture. Set tart on baking sheet and bake tart until apples are tender and goat cheese is just starting to set (center should jiggle when shaken), about 10 minutes, rotating sheet halfway through baking.

4. Remove tart from oven and heat broiler. Cover crust edge with aluminum foil to prevent burning. Broil tart, checking often and turning as necessary, until apples are attractively caramelized, 4 to 5 minutes.

5. Let tart cool on baking sheet to room temperature, about 2 hours. To serve, remove outer ring of tart pan, slide thin metal spatula between tart and tart pan bottom, and carefully slide tart onto serving platter or cutting board.

BEFORE 29 grams sugar ⟶ **AFTER** 20 grams sugar

fig, cherry, and walnut tart

Serves 8

WHY THIS RECIPE WORKS Fig-walnut tart is a classic Italian dessert that features fresh figs in a flaky, tender pastry crust. But sweet, delicate figs can be hard to come by in supermarkets due to their perishable nature and their relatively short growing season. To re-create this sophisticated tart using less sugar and more accessible ingredients, we started in the dried fruit aisle, since dried figs are far more common than fresh. We knew we would have to rehydrate them before baking or they would end up tough and leathery, so we took the opportunity to add depth of flavor at the same time in the form of brandy and orange zest. Traditionally, halved or quartered figs are arranged attractively in a tart crust before baking, but since we were using dried figs we opted to process the whole mixture to a smooth puree before adding toasted chopped walnuts. We were happily surprised to find that we didn't need to add any sugar to the recipe thanks to the inherent sweetness of the figs. The texture, on the other hand, was a little one-dimensional. The processed figs wound up feeling pasty and heavy in our delicate tart shell, and while the walnuts broke up the texture, we needed to add something bright and juicy to our filling. Cherries and figs are a winning combination, so we thawed, drained, and chopped frozen cherries (a perfect match for our dried figs in convenience and year-round availability) and stirred them into the processed figs with the walnuts. This was the change we were looking for; not only did the cherries break up the texture of our filling, they also added juiciness and bright flavor. You can use Black Mission figs in this recipe; however, the sugar content will be different.

6 ounces dried Turkish or Calimyrna figs, stemmed and quartered

1 cup water

½ cup brandy

1 tablespoon grated orange zest

12 ounces frozen sweet cherries, thawed, drained, and chopped

1 cup walnuts, toasted and chopped

1 recipe Classic Tart Crust (page 218), partially baked and cooled

1 cup Maple Whipped Cream (page 143)

1. Adjust oven rack to middle position and heat oven to 375 degrees. Combine figs, water, brandy, and orange zest in small saucepan and simmer over medium-low heat until figs are softened and beginning to break down, 15 to 20 minutes. Transfer mixture to food processor and process until smooth, about 15 seconds. Transfer fig puree to large bowl and stir in chopped cherries and walnuts.

2. Spread fig mixture evenly into cooled tart crust. Set tart on baking sheet and bake until crust is golden brown and filling is set, 25 to 30 minutes, rotating pan halfway through baking.

3. Transfer tart with baking sheet to wire rack and let cool to room temperature, about 2 hours. To serve, remove outer ring of tart pan, slide thin metal spatula between tart and tart pan bottom, and carefully slide tart onto serving platter or cutting board. Serve with whipped cream.

BEFORE 44 grams sugar $\longrightarrow$ **AFTER** 23 grams sugar

Removing a Tart from a Pan

1 Holding tart steady on your hand, gently remove outer metal ring from tart.

2 Slide thin metal spatula between tart and tart pan bottom and carefully slide tart onto serving platter or cutting board.

peach-blackberry free-form tart

Serves 6

WHY THIS RECIPE WORKS To create a rustic and flavorful free-form tart, we started with a buttery, flaky, yet sturdy tart dough. For the filling, we decided to use peaches and blackberries, which tasters found to be both visually and texturally appealing. Our traditional recipe called for just 6 tablespoons of sugar—five in the filling to sweeten the fruit, and one sprinkled on top—but we wondered if the fruit could carry the tart without any sweetener at all. However, tasters felt the fruit was a little too tart, even when perfectly ripe. After a few tests, we discovered that just 3 tablespoons of Sucanat in the filling was enough to offset the tartness and coax out the natural sweetness in the fruit, and we were able to eliminate the final sprinkle of sugar in favor of an egg white wash to encourage browning. We placed the fruit in the center of the rolled out tart dough, being sure to leave enough of a border so we could fold the dough around our filling. Because the fruit is exposed to the heat of the oven, we found that baking the tart at too low a temperature resulted in leathery, dried-out fruit and a pale crust. But if the temperature was too high, the fruit became overly charred and the crust darkened only on the folds but remained pale and underdone in the creases. A 375-degree oven worked best, producing an evenly baked, flaky crust and juicy, warm fruit. For more information on making a free-form tart, see page 213.

1 recipe Free-Form Tart Dough (page 220)

1 pound ripe but firm peaches, peeled, halved, pitted and cut into ½-inch wedges

5 ounces (1 cup) blackberries

3 tablespoons Sucanat

1 large egg white, lightly beaten

1. Roll dough into 12-inch circle between 2 large sheets of parchment paper (if dough sticks to parchment, dust lightly with flour). Slide dough, still between parchment, onto baking sheet and refrigerate until firm, about 15 minutes.

2. Adjust oven rack to middle position and heat oven to 375 degrees. Gently toss peaches, blackberries and Sucanat in bowl to combine. Remove top sheet parchment from dough. Mound peach mixture in center of dough, leaving 3–inch border around edge. Fold outer 3 inches of dough over filling, pleating dough every 2 to 3 inches as needed. Gently pinch pleated dough to secure, but do not press dough into fruit. Brush tart dough with beaten egg white.

3. Bake tart until golden brown and peaches are tender, about 1 hour, rotating sheet halfway through baking.

4. Let tart cool on baking sheet for 10 minutes. Using parchment, slide tart onto wire rack, then discard parchment. Let tart cool until juices have thickened, about 25 minutes. Serve warm or at room temperature.

BEFORE 20 grams sugar ⟶ **AFTER** 12 grams sugar

Peeling Peaches

1 Score small X at base of each peach with paring knife.

2 Lower peaches into boiling water and simmer until skins loosen, 30 to 60 seconds.

3 Transfer peaches immediately to ice water and let cool for 1 minute.

4 Using paring knife, remove strips of loosened peel, starting at X on base of each peach.

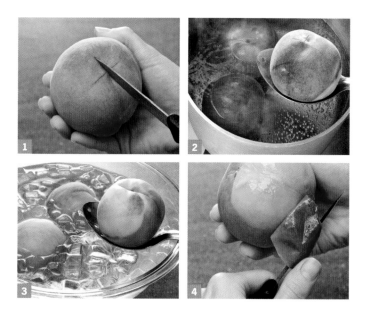

Sweetener Substitutions

COCONUT SUGAR	**3 tablespoons** Tart will have toasted, nutty flavor.
GRANULATED SUGAR	**2 tablespoons** Tart will have sharp, flat flavor.

pear-ginger free-form tart

Serves 6

WHY THIS RECIPE WORKS Thanks to their fruit-based fillings, free-form tarts are a great choice for naturally sweetened desserts. Since we had already developed a free-form tart recipe that highlighted the best fruit of the summer months (see page 208), we turned our attention to the sweet flavor of one of our favorite fall fruits: pears. Since they're hardier than summer stone fruits, pears require a longer cooking time, so simply pouring raw fruit into dough and baking it wasn't an option: The crust was scorched by the time the pears were tender. For perfectly cooked pears and crust, we precooked the pears (and drained away any excess liquid) before filling the raw dough. This allowed the fruit and the crust to finish cooking at the same time, resulting in tender pears and a golden-brown crust. Without any added flavorings our tart seemed a little dull, and we decided that ginger would be just the thing we needed to spice up our dessert. A combination of ground and fresh ginger gave our tart a balanced backbone, while just a dash of lemon juice kept the ginger from overwhelming the delicate flavor of the pears.

1 recipe Free-Form Tart Dough (page 220)

2 pounds ripe but firm Bartlett or Bosc pears, peeled, halved, cored, and sliced ½ inch thick

⅓ cup (1¾ ounces) Sucanat

1½ tablespoons lemon juice

1 teaspoon grated fresh ginger

¼ teaspoon ground ginger

⅛ teaspoon salt

1 large egg white, lightly beaten

1. Roll dough into 12-inch circle between 2 large sheets of parchment paper (if dough sticks to parchment, dust lightly with flour). Slide dough, still between parchment, onto baking sheet and refrigerate until firm, about 15 minutes.

2. Adjust oven rack to middle position and heat oven to 375 degrees. Microwave pears in covered bowl, stirring occasionally, until pears are translucent and slightly pliable, 7 to 10 minutes. Transfer to colander and let pears drain for about 20 minutes, stirring occasionally.

3. Gently combine cooled pears, Sucanat, lemon juice, grated ginger, ground ginger, and salt in bowl. Remove top sheet parchment from dough. Mound pear mixture in center of dough, leaving 3-inch border around edge. Fold outer 3 inches of dough over filling, pleating dough every 2 to 3 inches as needed. Gently pinch pleated dough to secure, but do not press dough into fruit. Brush tart dough with beaten egg white.

4. Bake tart until golden brown and pears are tender, about 1 hour, rotating sheet halfway through baking.

5. Let tart cool on baking sheet for 10 minutes. Using parchment, slide tart onto wire rack, then discard parchment. Let tart cool until juices have thickened, about 25 minutes. Serve warm or at room temperature.

BEFORE 34 grams sugar ⟶ **AFTER** 23 grams sugar

Making Free-Form Tart

1 Roll dough into 12-inch circle between
   2 large sheets of parchment paper (if dough
   sticks to parchment, dust lightly with flour).
2 Slide dough, still between parchment,
   onto baking sheet and refrigerate until firm,
   about 15 minutes.
3 Remove top sheet parchment from dough.
4 Mound fruit in center of dough, leaving
   3-inch border around edge. Fold outer
   3 inches of dough over filling, pleating
   dough every 2 to 3 inches as needed.
5 Gently pinch pleated dough to secure,
   but do not press dough into fruit.
6 Brush tart dough with beaten egg white
   before baking.

Sweetener Substitutions

COCONUT SUGAR	6 tablespoons (1¾ ounces) Tart will taste nutty and slightly bitter.
GRANULATED SUGAR	¼ cup (1¾ ounces) Tart will taste slightly bland.

all-butter pie crust

Makes one 9-inch pie crust

WHY THIS RECIPE WORKS We wanted to come up with a single-crust pie dough that would complement any pie recipe. We tested our way through a plethora of pie dough recipes and decided to go with a version that relied on butter for most of its fat content; the butter gave the crust richer, fuller flavor than shortening. To supplement the butter, we used a small amount of sour cream, since the acid in sour cream slows down the development of gluten and ensures a tender, flaky crust. Although the original recipe called for just a tablespoon of sugar, tasters agreed that sweetener was unnecessary, especially when paired with our flavorful, naturally sweetened fillings. However, without the sugar to help absorb moisture, the dough turned out a bit greasy—a problem easily fixed by decreasing the butter by a tablespoon. A food processor made quick work of mixing the dough.

3 tablespoons ice water, plus extra as needed

4 teaspoons sour cream

1¼ cups (6¼ ounces) all-purpose flour

½ teaspoon salt

7 tablespoons unsalted butter, cut into ¼-inch pieces and chilled

1. Whisk ice water and sour cream together in bowl. Process flour and salt in food processor until combined, about 5 seconds. Scatter chilled butter over top and pulse until butter is size of small lentils, about 10 pulses. Drizzle half of sour cream mixture over top and pulse until incorporated, about 3 pulses; repeat with remaining sour cream mixture.

2. Pinch dough with your fingers; if dough feels dry and does not hold together, add 1 to 2 tablespoons more ice water and pulse until dough forms large clumps and no dry flour remains, 3 to 5 pulses.

3. Form dough into 4-inch disk, wrap tightly in plastic wrap, and refrigerate for 1 hour. (Dough can be refrigerated for up to 2 days or frozen for up to 2 months. If frozen, let dough thaw completely on counter before rolling.)

4. Adjust oven rack to middle position and heat oven to 375 degrees. Let chilled dough sit on counter to soften slightly, about 10 minutes. Roll dough into 12-inch circle on lightly floured counter. Loosely roll dough around rolling pin and gently unroll it onto 9-inch pie plate, letting excess dough hang over edge. Ease dough into plate by gently lifting edge of dough with your hand while pressing into plate bottom with your other hand. Trim overhang to ½ inch beyond lip of plate. Tuck overhang under itself; folded edge should be flush with edge of plate. Crimp dough evenly around edge of plate using your fingers. Wrap dough-lined plate loosely in plastic and freeze until dough is firm, about 15 minutes.

5. Line chilled pie crust with double layer of aluminum foil, covering edges to prevent burning, and fill with pie weights. Bake until dough looks dry and is pale in color, 25 to 30 minutes, rotating plate halfway through baking. Transfer plate to wire rack, remove weights and foil, and let cool completely, about 30 minutes.

BEFORE 1 gram sugar ⟶ **AFTER** 0 grams sugar

Making Pie Crust

1 Form dough into 4-inch disk, wrap tightly
   in plastic wrap, and refrigerate for 1 hour.
2 Roll dough into 12-inch circle on lightly
   floured counter.
3 Loosely roll dough around rolling pin
   and gently unroll it onto 9-inch pie plate,
   letting excess dough hang over edge.
4 Ease dough into plate by gently lifting edge
   of dough with your hand while pressing into
   plate bottom with your other hand.
5 Trim overhang to ½ inch beyond lip of
   plate and tuck overhang under itself; folded
   edge should be flush with edge of plate.
6 Crimp dough evenly around edge of plate
   using your fingers.
7 Line chilled pie crust with double layer of
   aluminum foil, covering edges to prevent
   burning, and fill with pie weights. Bake
   crust for 25 to 30 minutes.
8 Transfer plate to wire rack, remove
   weights and foil, and let cool completely,
   about 30 minutes.

all-butter double-crust pie dough

Makes enough for one double-crust 9-inch pie

WHY THIS RECIPE WORKS A beautifully browned, perfectly flaky pie crust is the crowning glory of any double-crust pie; with the success of our single crust pie dough, our task was as simple as scaling up our ingredients to create a perfect double crust dough. Mixing the sour cream with the water ensured that it was evenly distributed throughout the dough. We found that it was essential to make sure our dough was divided into two even pieces so that our bottom and top crusts were of equal size and could be properly crimped together. When making a lattice crust, we found that it was helpful to freeze the strips of dough briefly to make them easier to handle.

⅓ cup ice water, plus extra as needed
3 tablespoons sour cream
2½ cups (12½ ounces) all-purpose flour
1 teaspoon salt
14 tablespoons unsalted butter, cut into ¼-inch pieces and chilled

1. Whisk ice water and sour cream together in bowl. Process flour and salt in food processor until combined, about 5 seconds. Scatter chilled butter over top and pulse until butter is size of small lentils, about 10 pulses. Drizzle half of sour cream mixture over top and pulse until incorporated, about 3 pulses; repeat with remaining sour cream mixture.

2. Pinch dough with your fingers; if dough feels dry and does not hold together, add 1 to 2 tablespoons more ice water and pulse until dough forms large clumps and no dry flour remains, 3 to 5 pulses

3. Divide dough into 2 even pieces. Form each piece into 4-inch disk, wrap tightly in plastic wrap, and refrigerate for 1 hour. Before rolling dough out, let it sit on counter to soften slightly, about 10 minutes. (Dough can be refrigerated for up to 2 days or frozen for up to 2 months. If frozen, let dough thaw completely on counter before rolling.)

4. Roll 1 piece dough into 12-inch circle on lightly floured counter. Loosely roll dough around rolling pin and gently unroll it onto 9-inch pie plate, letting excess dough hang over edge. Ease dough into plate by gently lifting edge of dough with your hand while pressing into plate bottom with your other hand. Wrap loosely in plastic wrap and refrigerate until dough is firm, about 30 minutes.

5A. FOR A TRADITIONAL TOP CRUST Roll second piece of dough into 12-inch circle on lightly floured counter, transfer to parchment paper–lined baking sheet and cover with plastic; refrigerate for 30 minutes.

5B. FOR A LATTICE TOP CRUST Roll second piece of dough into 13½ by 10½-inch rectangle on generously floured counter, then transfer to parchment paper–lined baking sheet. Trim dough to 13 by 10-inch rectangle and slice lengthwise into ten 13-inch-long strips. Separate strips slightly, cover with plastic, and freeze until very firm, about 30 minutes.

BEFORE 2 grams sugar ⟶ **AFTER** 0 grams sugar

Making Double-Crust Pie

1 Pinch dough with your fingers until dough holds together; if dough does not hold together, add extra ice water and pulse until dough forms large clumps and no dry flour remains, 3 to 5 pulses.

2 Divide dough into 2 even pieces. Form each piece into 4-inch disk, wrap tightly in plastic wrap, and refrigerate for 1 hour.

3 For bottom crust, lay 1 piece of dough on lightly floured counter and roll dough outward from its center into 12-inch circle.

4 Loosely roll dough around rolling pin and gently unroll it onto 9-inch pie plate.

5 Lift dough and gently press it into pie plate, letting excess hang over plate's edge.

6 Wrap loosely in plastic wrap and refrigerate until dough is firm, about 30 minutes.

7A For traditional top crust, roll second piece of dough into 12- inch circle, transfer to parchment paper–lined baking sheet, and refrigerate for 30 minutes.

7B For lattice crust, roll and trim dough into 13 by 10-inch rectangle and slice lengthwise into ten 13-inch-long strips. Separate strips slightly, cover with plastic, and freeze until very firm, about 30 minutes.

classic tart crust

Makes one 9-inch tart crust

WHY THIS RECIPE WORKS While pie crusts are tender and flaky, classic tart crusts should be fine-textured, crisp, and just a bit crumbly; more like shortbread than pie crust. We set out to achieve the perfect naturally sweetened tart dough that could act as a base for any number of tart recipes. We found that a single egg yolk and 1 tablespoon of cream gave the dough the necessary richness. A stick of butter provided great flavor and made for a delicate crumb—any more and the dough became difficult to handle. In place of the confectioners' sugar in our traditional recipe, we used Sucanat, which we ground to give it a fine texture that prevented the tart crust from turning out speckled. Rolling the dough and fitting it into the tart pan was easy, and we used the extra dough to patch any holes. Do not skip grinding the Sucanat in step 1 or the dough will look speckled and be difficult to roll out. If the dough is soft or sticky, slide onto a baking sheet and refrigerate until firm.

1 large egg yolk
1 tablespoon heavy cream
½ teaspoon vanilla extract
¼ cup (1⅓ ounces) Sucanat
1¼ cups (6¼ ounces) all-purpose flour
¼ teaspoon salt
8 tablespoons unsalted butter, cut into ¼-inch pieces and chilled

1. Whisk egg yolk, cream, and vanilla together in bowl. Grind Sucanat in spice grinder until fine and powdery, about 1 minute. Process flour, ground Sucanat, and salt in food processor until combined, about 5 seconds. Scatter chilled butter over top and pulse until mixture resembles coarse cornmeal, about 15 pulses. With processor running, add egg yolk mixture and process until dough just comes together, about 12 seconds.

2. Form dough into 6-inch disk, wrap tightly in plastic wrap, and refrigerate for 1 hour. (Dough can be wrapped tightly in plastic and refrigerated for up to 2 days or frozen for up to 1 month. If frozen, let dough thaw completely on counter before rolling.)

3. Let chilled dough sit on counter to soften slightly, about 10 minutes. Roll dough into 11-inch circle on lightly floured counter. Loosely roll dough around rolling pin and gently unroll it onto 9-inch tart pan with removable bottom, letting excess dough hang over edge. Ease dough into pan by gently lifting edge of dough with your hand while pressing into corners and fluted sides of pan with your other hand. Run rolling pin over top of pan to remove any excess dough. Wrap dough-lined pan loosely in plastic, place on large plate, and freeze until dough is chilled and firm, about 30 minutes. (Dough-lined tart pan can be wrapped tightly in plastic and refrigerated for up to 2 days or frozen for up to 1 month.)

4. Adjust oven rack to middle position and heat oven to 375 degrees. Set dough-lined tart pan on baking sheet, line with double layer of aluminum foil, covering edges to prevent burning, and fill with pie weights.

5A. FOR A PARTIALLY BAKED TART CRUST Bake until crust is golden brown and set, about 30 minutes, rotating pan halfway through baking. Remove weights and foil and let crust cool.

5B. FOR A FULLY BAKED TART CRUST Bake until crust is golden brown and set, about 30 minutes, rotating pan halfway through baking. Carefully remove weights and foil and continue to bake until deep golden brown, 5 to 10 minutes longer. Let crust cool completely, about 1 hour.

BEFORE 9 grams sugar $\longrightarrow$ **AFTER** 5 grams sugar

Making Tart Crust

1 With processor running, add egg yolk mixture and process until dough just comes together, about 12 seconds.

2 Form dough into 6-inch disk, wrap tightly in plastic wrap, and refrigerate for 1 hour.

3 Roll dough into 11-inch circle on lightly floured counter.

4 Loosely roll dough around rolling pin and gently unroll it onto 9-inch tart pan with removable bottom, letting excess dough hang over edge.

5 Ease dough into pan by gently lifting edge of dough with your hand while pressing into corners and fluted sides of pan with your other hand.

6 Run rolling pin over top of pan to remove any excess dough.

7 Set dough-lined tart pan on baking sheet, line with double layer of aluminum foil, covering edges to prevent burning, and fill with pie weights.

8 For partially baked tart crust, bake until crust is golden brown and set, about 30 minutes. For fully baked tart crust, remove foil after baking for 30 minutes and bake for 5 to 10 minutes longer.

Sweetener Substitutions

COCONUT SUGAR	¼ cup (1⅓ ounces) Crust will look darker; grind sugar as directed in step 1.
CONFECTIONERS' SUGAR	⅓ cup (1⅓ ounces) Crust will look pale and have mild flavor.

free-form tart dough

Makes enough for one 9-inch tart

WHY THIS RECIPE WORKS We found that the best free-form tart dough relied on the simplest list of ingredients—just butter, flour, and water. We knew that without the support of a pie plate, this dough would need to be sturdier than pie crust without being tough. To achieve this, we started by testing various ratios of flour to butter until we had the best balance of buttery flavor and structure. To maximize the flakiness of the crust, we employed a French technique known as *fraisage*, in which the dough is smeared against the counter with the heel of your hand. This created paper-thin streaks of butter and flour that baked up into delicate, flaky layers. Testing revealed that not only was sweetener unnecessary, but the tenderizing power of the sugar also made the crust more brittle. In the end, this dough needed nothing more than a bit of salt to make it taste great.

1½ cups (7½ ounces) all-purpose flour
½ teaspoon salt
10 tablespoons unsalted butter, cut into ½-inch pieces and chilled
4-6 tablespoons ice water

1. Process flour and salt in food processor until combined, about 5 seconds. Scatter chilled butter over top and pulse until mixture resembles coarse sand and butter pieces are size of small lentils, about 10 pulses. Continue to pulse, adding water 1 tablespoon at a time, until dough begins to form small curds that hold together when pinched with your fingers, about 10 pulses.

2. Turn mixture onto lightly floured counter and gather into rectangular pile. Starting at farthest end, use heel of your hand to smear small amount of dough against counter. Continue to smear dough until all crumbs have been worked. Gather smeared crumbs together in another rectangular pile and repeat process.

3. Form dough into 4-inch disk, wrap tightly in plastic wrap, and refrigerate for 1 hour. Before rolling dough out, let it sit on counter to soften slightly, about 10 minutes. (Dough can be refrigerated for up to 2 days or frozen for up to 1 month. If frozen, let dough thaw completely on counter before rolling.)

BEFORE 0 grams sugar ⟶ **AFTER** 0 grams sugar

Making Free-Form Tart Dough

1 Turn processed mixture onto lightly floured counter and gather into rectangular pile.
2 Starting at farthest end, use heel of your hand to smear small amount of dough against counter.

graham cracker pie crust

Makes one 9-inch pie crust

WHY THIS RECIPE WORKS We wanted to create a crisp, sturdy graham cracker crust to act as a base for a variety of pies. To start, we ground graham crackers to fine crumbs in the food processor, then bound the crumbs together using softened butter. We thought that the warm, molasses flavor of Sucanat would be perfect here, and tested various amounts until we discovered we didn't need any added sweetener at all; the graham crackers were sweet and flavorful enough on their own. However, without any additional sugar, the final crust was a bit crumbly and delicate. To fix this, we simply packed the crust very tightly in the pie plate before baking. The easiest way to accomplish this was using the back of a measuring cup: We could evenly press the crumbs using the flat bottom of the cup, while the curved edge helped with pressing the crumbs into the corners. Tightly packing the crumbs ensured perfectly clean slices every time. We don't recommend using store-bought graham cracker crumbs here, as they can often be stale.

9 whole graham crackers, broken into 1-inch pieces

5 tablespoons unsalted butter, cut into 5 pieces and softened

1. Adjust oven rack to middle position and heat oven to 325 degrees. Process graham crackers in food processor to fine, even crumbs, 30 to 60 seconds. Scatter butter over top and pulse until mixture resemble coarse sand, 15 to 20 pulses.

2. Sprinkle mixture into 9-inch pie plate. Using bottom of measuring cup, press crumbs firmly into even layer on bottom and sides of pie plate. Bake until crust is fragrant and set, 20 to 22 minutes, rotating plate halfway through baking. Let crust cool completely, about 30 minutes.

BEFORE 8 grams sugar $\longrightarrow$ **AFTER** 4 grams sugar

chocolate graham cracker pie crust
Substitute chocolate graham crackers for graham crackers.
BEFORE 9 grams sugar $\longrightarrow$ **AFTER** 5 grams sugar

Making Graham Cracker Crust

Sprinkle crumb mixture into 9-inch pie plate. Using bottom of measuring cup, press crumbs firmly into even layer on bottom and sides of pie plate.

fruit desserts

apple crisp

Serves 6

WHY THIS RECIPE WORKS Apple crisp should be a simple pleasure, but too often the topping is sandy or soggy and the filling ends up mushy and flavorless. We wanted a topping just as crisp and crunchy as its name implied, and a naturally sweetened filling that allowed the apples to shine. We started by tossing sliced apples with a small amount of Sucanat, as well as cornstarch to encourage the apples' exuded juices to thicken into a luxurious sauce. While many recipes call for baking the topping and filling together, we decided to first bake the apple filling covered, which allowed the apples to steam slightly and become tender. We added the topping at the end so that it wouldn't have enough time to get soggy. Chopped toasted almonds added extra crunch, and refrigerating the topping mixture while the apples baked ensured that it stayed together in cohesive chunks when baked. We recommend using Golden Delicious, Jonagold, or Braeburn apples in this recipe. Do not substitute quick oats, instant oats, or steel-cut oats in this recipe. Do not skip grinding the Sucanat in step 1 or the topping will taste dry and dusty.

topping

- ⅓ cup plus ¼ cup (3 ounces) Sucanat
- 6 tablespoons unsalted butter, melted
- ½ teaspoon ground cinnamon
- ¼ teaspoon ground nutmeg
- ⅛ teaspoon salt
- ½ cup (2½ ounces) all-purpose flour
- ½ cup (1½ ounces) old-fashioned rolled oats
- ½ cup slivered almonds, toasted and chopped

filling

- 3 pounds apples, peeled, cored, and sliced into ½-inch wedges
- 2 tablespoons Sucanat
- 2 teaspoons lemon juice
- 2 teaspoons cornstarch
- ¾ teaspoon ground cinnamon
- ⅛ teaspoon salt

1. FOR THE TOPPING Working in 2 batches, grind Sucanat in spice grinder until fine and powdery, about 1 minute. Whisk ground Sucanat, melted butter, cinnamon, nutmeg, and salt together in large bowl. Using rubber spatula, fold in flour, oats, and almonds until combined and mixture resembles thick, cohesive dough. Cover with plastic wrap and refrigerate until needed.

2. FOR THE FILLING Adjust oven rack to middle position and heat oven to 400 degrees. Toss apples, Sucanat, lemon juice, cornstarch, cinnamon, and salt together in bowl. Transfer to 8-inch square baking dish, cover with aluminum foil, and set on foil-lined rimmed baking sheet. Bake until apples are juicy and tender, 1 hour 5 minutes to 1¼ hours, rotating sheet halfway through baking.

3. Carefully stir fruit to redistribute juices, then crumble topping into ½-inch pieces (with some smaller loose bits) over top. Bake uncovered until fruit is bubbling and topping is deep golden brown, about 15 minutes, rotating sheet halfway through baking. Transfer to wire rack and let crisp cool for 20 minutes before serving.

BEFORE 61 grams sugar ⟶ **AFTER** 41 grams sugar

Making Crisp

Pinch topping into ½-inch pieces (with some smaller loose bits) and sprinkle over partially baked filling.

Sweetener Substitutions

COCONUT SUGAR
Topping: ½ cup plus 2 tablespoons (3 ounces)
Filling: 2 tablespoons
Crisp will have darker color and taste slightly tart; grind sugar as directed in step 1.

GRANULATED SUGAR
Topping: 7 tablespoons (3 ounces)
Filling: 2 tablespoons
Crisp will have lighter color and taste less sweet; do not grind sugar in step 1.

Sweetener Substitutions

| COCONUT SUGAR | Topping: ¼ cup (1¼ ounces)
Filling: 1 tablespoon
Crisp will taste similar; grind sugar as directed in step 1. |
| GRANULATED SUGAR | Topping: 3 tablespoons
Filling: 1 tablespoon
Crisp will taste similar; do not grind sugar in step 1. |

cherry-hazelnut crisp

Serves 6

WHY THIS RECIPE WORKS We wanted an exemplary cherry crisp—a lush, sweet-tart cherry filling covered with truly crisp morsels of topping—and we wanted it with much less sugar. Because of the cherries' naturally intense sweetness, we needed only a tablespoon of Sucanat in our filling. But our first few crisps were somewhat dull and flat in flavor, and the excess liquid from the cherries swallowed up the crumble topping. To solve this, we first drained the juice from the cherries and reduced it on the stovetop along with some red wine. This drove off some moisture and enhanced the sweetness and flavor of the filling. A bit of cornstarch gave the sauce a rich, spoon-clinging consistency, while butter offered richness and a squeeze of lemon juice balanced out the other flavors. With our filling down, we turned to the topping. We started with our core ingredients—Sucanat, flour, and butter—and added cinnamon, nutmeg, and vanilla extract for a solid flavor backbone. But with the decreased sugar content, the topping didn't crisp as much as we would have liked. We solved this by swapping out some flour for hazelnuts, which gave the topping richness, character, and crunch. You can substitute 2 pounds fresh cherries, halved and pitted, for the frozen cherries; skip microwaving and draining the cherries in step 2, and substitute ½ cup water for juice in step 3. Do not skip grinding the Sucanat in step 1 or the topping will taste dry and dusty.

topping

- ¼ cup (1¼ ounces) Sucanat
- 1 cup hazelnuts, toasted, skinned, and chopped
- ½ cup (2½ ounces) all-purpose flour
- ¼ teaspoon ground cinnamon
- ⅛ teaspoon ground nutmeg
- ⅛ teaspoon salt
- 5 tablespoons unsalted butter, melted
- ½ teaspoon vanilla extract

filling

- 2 pounds frozen sweet cherries
- ½ cup red wine
- 1 teaspoon vanilla extract
- ½ teaspoon salt
- ¼ teaspoon ground cinnamon
- 2 tablespoons unsalted butter, cut into 2 pieces
- 2 teaspoons lemon juice
- 1 tablespoon Sucanat
- 1 tablespoon cornstarch

1. FOR THE TOPPING Grind Sucanat in spice grinder until fine and powdery, about 1 minute. Pulse ground Sucanat, hazelnuts, flour, cinnamon, nutmeg, and salt in food processor until nuts are finely chopped, about 9 pulses. Drizzle melted butter and vanilla over top and pulse until mixture resembles crumbly, wet sand, about 5 pulses.

2. FOR THE FILLING Adjust oven rack to middle position and heat oven to 400 degrees. Microwave frozen cherries in covered bowl, stirring occasionally, until thawed, about 6 minutes. Drain cherries in colander set over bowl. Measure out and reserve ½ cup drained juice in separate bowl; supplement juice with water if necessary.

3. Combine ½ cup reserved cherry juice, red wine, vanilla, salt, and cinnamon in 12-inch skillet and cook over medium heat until mixture measures ½ cup, 6 to 10 minutes. Stir in butter and lemon juice and cook until butter is melted about 1 minute. Add drained cherries and Sucanat and cook, stirring occasionally, until cherries are warmed through and Sucanat is dissolved, about 5 minutes.

4. Stir in cornstarch and simmer, stirring constantly, until liquid is thickened, about 1 minute. Transfer mixture to 8-inch square baking dish and set on aluminum foil–lined rimmed baking sheet.

5. Pinch topping into ½-inch pieces (with some smaller loose bits) and sprinkle over filling. Bake until fruit is bubbling and topping is deep golden brown, about 15 minutes, rotating sheet halfway through baking. Transfer to wire rack and let crisp cool for 20 minutes before serving.

BEFORE 55 grams sugar ⟶ **AFTER** 28 grams sugar

peach-raspberry crumble

Serves 6

WHY THIS RECIPE WORKS For a peach-raspberry crumble bursting with summer fruit flavor and crowned with a buttery-crisp topping, we started by perfecting the filling. Letting the peaches macerate with a little bit of Sucanat and salt and draining away all but 2 tablespoons of the exuded liquid was a simple and effective way to rein in the peaches' moisture and ensure that our filling wasn't watery. We then tossed the peaches with cornstarch to further thicken the filling. A small amount of orange zest offered complexity without giving itself away. To make sure the delicate raspberries didn't turn to mush, we simply sprinkled them over the top of the peaches. With the filling set, we turned our attention to the crumble topping. A small amount of Sucanat was enough to create a sweet dough. Cinnamon and nutmeg offered warm spice notes, while pecans and oats provided nutty flavor and crunch. A splash of milk helped loosen up the dough so that it would be easy to crumble into pea-size pieces. As the crumble baked, the peaches and raspberries became soft and tender, and the topping crisped up and turned a perfect golden brown. Do not substitute quick oats, instant oats, or steel-cut oats in this recipe. Although we prefer the flavor of fresh peaches here, you can substitute 1¾ pounds of thawed frozen peaches; toss the peaches with Sucanat and salt and drain as directed in step 1. Do not skip grinding the Sucanat in step 3 or the topping will taste dry and dusty. For more information on how to peel peaches, see page 209.

filling

- 2½ pounds ripe but firm peaches, peeled, halved, pitted, and sliced into ½-inch wedges
- 2 tablespoons Sucanat
- ⅛ teaspoon salt
- 2 teaspoons cornstarch
- 1 teaspoon grated orange zest
- 1 teaspoon vanilla extract
- 10 ounces (2 cups) raspberries

topping

- ¼ cup (1¼ ounces) Sucanat
- 6 tablespoons unsalted butter, melted
- 2 tablespoons milk
- ½ teaspoon ground cinnamon
- ¼ teaspoon salt
- ⅛ teaspoon ground nutmeg
- ¾ cup (3¾ ounces) all-purpose flour
- ½ cup (1½ ounces) old-fashioned rolled oats
- ½ cup pecans, chopped fine

1. FOR THE FILLING Gently toss peaches with Sucanat and salt in bowl and let sit, stirring occasionally, for 30 minutes. Drain peaches in colander set over bowl; reserve 2 tablespoons juice and discard extra.

2. Return drained peaches to bowl and toss with reserved peach juice, cornstarch, orange zest, and vanilla. Transfer to 8-inch square baking dish and top with raspberries. Set dish on aluminum foil–lined rimmed baking sheet.

3. FOR THE TOPPING Meanwhile, adjust oven rack to middle position and heat oven to 375 degrees. Grind Sucanat in spice grinder until fine and powdery, about 1 minute. Whisk ground Sucanat, melted butter, milk, cinnamon, salt, and nutmeg together in large bowl. Using rubber spatula, fold in flour, oats, and pecans until combined and mixture resembles thick, cohesive dough.

4. Pinch topping into ½-inch pieces (with some smaller loose bits) and sprinkle over filling. Bake until fruit is bubbling and topping is well browned, 25 to 30 minutes, rotating sheet halfway through baking. Transfer to wire rack and let crumble cool for 20 minutes before serving.

BEFORE 56 grams sugar ⟶ **AFTER** 28 grams sugar

peach cobbler

Serves 8

WHY THIS RECIPE WORKS Peach cobbler's greatest asset—an abundance of fresh, ripe peaches—can also be its biggest liability. The peach juice can turn the filling watery and the biscuits soggy; plus, the filling is often too sweet. We wanted a recipe for a low-sugar peach cobbler that lived up to its full potential. To create a pleasantly thick filling, we cooked peeled, sliced peaches on the stovetop—first covered so they would release their juices and then uncovered so that the excess moisture could evaporate. Allowing the peaches to lightly caramelize concentrated their flavor and sweetness; the generous amount of peaches offered 23 grams of sugar per serving and tasted plenty sweet even without any added sugar. For balanced fruit flavor and a texture that wasn't overly mushy, we reserved a portion of the peaches to stir in just before baking. For the buttermilk biscuit topping, we created a light and airy dough using both baking soda and baking powder. Cinnamon gave the biscuits a rounded flavor and made them less pale. To keep things simple, we used a spoon to dollop the dough across the top of the peaches and then put the whole skillet in the oven. Our lightly browned and tender biscuits perfectly complemented our sweet and just-juicy-enough peach filling. Although we prefer the flavor of fresh peaches here, you can substitute 4 pounds of thawed frozen peaches. Do not skip grinding the Sucanat in step 3 or the biscuits will be tough and speckled. For more information on how to peel peaches, see page 209.

filling

- 4 tablespoons unsalted butter, cut into 4 pieces
- 5 pounds peaches, peeled, halved, pitted and sliced into ½-inch wedges (10 cups)
- 1 teaspoon grated orange zest plus 2 tablespoons juice
- 1 teaspoon ground ginger
- ¼ teaspoon ground cinnamon
- ¼ teaspoon salt
- 1 tablespoon water
- 1½ teaspoons cornstarch

topping

- ⅓ cup (1¾ ounces) Sucanat
- 1½ cups (7½ ounces) all-purpose flour
- 1½ teaspoons baking powder
- ¼ teaspoon baking soda
- ¾ teaspoon ground cinnamon
- ½ teaspoon salt
- ¾ cup buttermilk
- 6 tablespoons unsalted butter, melted and cooled
- 1 teaspoon vanilla extract

1. FOR THE FILLING Adjust oven rack to middle position and heat oven to 425 degrees. Melt butter in 12-inch ovensafe skillet over medium-high heat. Add 6 cups peaches, orange zest and juice, ginger, cinnamon, and salt, cover, and cook until peaches begin to release their juices, about 5 minutes.

2. Uncover and continue to simmer, stirring often, until all liquid has evaporated and peaches begin to caramelize, 15 to 20 minutes. Add remaining 4 cups peaches and cook until warmed through, about 5 minutes. Whisk water and cornstarch together in small bowl, then stir mixture into peaches. Cover skillet and remove from heat.

3. FOR THE TOPPING Meanwhile, grind Sucanat in spice grinder until fine and powdery, about 1 minute. Whisk ground Sucanat, flour, baking powder, baking soda, cinnamon, and salt together in large bowl. In separate bowl whisk buttermilk, melted butter, and vanilla together. Using rubber spatula, stir buttermilk mixture into flour mixture until just combined.

4. Using spoon, scoop out and drop 1-inch pieces of dough onto filling, spaced about ½ inch apart. Bake until filling is bubbling and thickened and topping is golden brown, 18 to 22 minutes, rotating skillet halfway through baking. Transfer to wire rack and let cobbler cool for 20 minutes before serving.

BEFORE 43 grams sugar ⟶ **AFTER** 30 grams sugar

Sweetener Substitutions

COCONUT SUGAR	**7 tablespoons (2 ounces)** Shortcakes will taste similar but have darker color; grind sugar as directed in step 2.
GRANULATED SUGAR	**⅓ cup (2 ounces)** Shortcakes will be slightly more crumbly; do not grind sugar in step 2.

strawberry shortcakes

Serves 6

WHY THIS RECIPE WORKS Strawberry shortcakes can easily go astray, with overly sweet, gloppy fillings and tough biscuits. To make the strawberries shine, we replaced the typical granulated sugar with a small amount of Sucanat. To find the balance between a juicy, jammy filling and dry berries that wouldn't stay on the biscuits, we crushed a portion of the berries and preserved the shape of the rest by quartering them. As for the shortcakes, we included an egg in the dough, as well as some milk and sour cream, which produced moist and buttery biscuits with a delicate, slightly cakey crumb—the perfect complement to the sweet berries and cream. Although our traditional shortcake recipe called for sprinkling the tops of the biscuits with sugar before baking, we found that brushing them with butter offered plenty of rich flavor and eliminated the need for extra sugar. We prefer whole milk in this recipe, but 1 or 2 percent low-fat milk may be substituted. Do not skip grinding the Sucanat in step 2 or the biscuits will be dry, crumbly, and speckled.

30 ounces strawberries, hulled and quartered (6 cups)

6 tablespoons (2 ounces) Sucanat

2 cups (10 ounces) all-purpose flour

1 tablespoon baking powder

½ teaspoon salt

8 tablespoons unsalted butter, cut into ½-inch pieces and chilled, plus 2 tablespoons melted

½ cup sour cream

¼ cup whole milk

1 large egg

2 cups Maple Whipped Cream (page 143)

1. Using potato masher, crush 2 cups strawberries in large bowl until coarsely mashed and juicy. Fold in remaining 4 cups strawberries and ¼ cup Sucanat, cover, and let sit, stirring occasionally, for 30 minutes.

2. Meanwhile, adjust oven rack to upper-middle position and heat oven to 375 degrees. Line rimmed baking sheet with parchment paper. Grind remaining 2 tablespoons Sucanat in spice grinder until fine and powdery, about 1 minute. Process ground Sucanat, flour, baking powder, and salt in food processor until combined, about 5 seconds. Scatter chilled butter pieces over top and pulse until mixture resembles coarse meal, about 7 pulses. Transfer to large bowl.

3. Whisk sour cream, milk, and egg together in bowl, then stir into flour mixture with rubber spatula until large clumps form. Using your hands, knead lightly until dough comes together and no dry flecks of flour remain.

4. Using ½-cup dry measuring cup, scoop 6 dough rounds onto baking sheet. Brush tops evenly with melted butter. Bake until golden brown, 25 to 30 minutes, rotating sheet halfway through baking. Transfer to wire rack and let cool on sheet for 10 minutes. (Baked and cooled biscuits can be stored at room temperature for up to 24 hours.)

5. Split each biscuit in half and place bottoms on individual serving plates. Spoon portion of fruit over each bottom, then top with dollop of whipped cream. Cap with biscuit tops and serve immediately.

BEFORE 32 grams sugar ⟶ **AFTER** 22 grams sugar

Sweetener Substitutions

COCONUT SUGAR	½ cup (2½ ounces)	
	Buckles will have deeper flavor and taste slightly bitter.	
GRANULATED SUGAR	6 tablespoons (2½ ounces)	
	Buckles will taste similar.	

blueberry-walnut buckles

Serves 8

WHY THIS RECIPE WORKS Buckles are a distinctly American-style dessert in which fresh fruit is enrobed in a sweet and buttery cake batter, topped with crunchy streusel, and sprinkled with nuts. Our traditional recipe called for ⅔ cup of granulated sugar in the cake batter, but we found that a mere 7 tablespoons of Sucanat provided plenty of flavor and sweetness. Since we couldn't rely on the small amount of Sucanat for structure, we needed to adjust the consistency of the batter in other ways. Eggs and heavy cream helped with richness and stability, while baking powder ensured that it wasn't too dense. Although our traditional recipe called for simply sprinkling nuts on top of the buckles, tasters wanted more nut flavor throughout. Making the batter in a food processor instead of a stand mixer allowed us to grind some nuts right into the batter, boosting flavor as well as structure. A bit of lime zest and vanilla rounded out the flavor of the batter, which now cradled the berries beautifully. With a sprinkling of crunchy toasted walnuts on top, our buckles were so flavorful that tasters didn't miss the usual sugar-laden streusel topping—a change that allowed us to cut the sugar content by more than half.

¾ cup walnuts, toasted and chopped coarse

7 tablespoons (2½ ounces) Sucanat

5 tablespoons unsalted butter, softened

½ teaspoon salt

½ cup heavy cream

2 large eggs

1 tablespoon vanilla extract

1 tablespoon grated lime zest (2 limes)

1 cup (5 ounces) all-purpose flour

¾ teaspoon baking powder

15 ounces (3 cups) blueberries

1. Adjust oven rack to middle position and heat oven to 375 degrees. Spray eight 6-ounce ramekins with vegetable oil spray and place on rimmed baking sheet.

2. Process ½ cup walnuts, Sucanat, butter, and salt in food processor until finely ground, about 20 seconds. With processor running, add cream, eggs, vanilla, and lime zest and process until smooth, about 15 seconds. Add flour and baking powder and pulse until just combined, about 5 pulses.

3. Transfer batter to large bowl and gently fold in blueberries. Spoon batter evenly into prepared ramekins and sprinkle with remaining ¼ cup walnuts.

4. Bake buckles until golden and beginning to pull away from sides of ramekins, 25 to 30 minutes, rotating sheet halfway through baking. Let buckles cool on wire rack for 10 minutes before serving.

BEFORE 39 grams sugar ⟶ **AFTER** 15 grams sugar

raspberry-pistachio buckles
Substitute shelled pistachios for walnuts, lemon zest for lime zest, and fresh raspberries for blueberries.

BEFORE 22 grams sugar ⟶ **AFTER** 12 grams sugar

blackberry-hazelnut buckles
Omit lime zest. Substitute skinned hazelnuts for walnuts and fresh blackberries for blueberries. Add ¼ teaspoon hazelnut extract to processor with vanilla.

BEFORE 22 grams sugar ⟶ **AFTER** 12 grams sugar

fruit desserts

235

pear strudel

Serves 6

WHY THIS RECIPE WORKS For the ultimate low-sugar pear strudel, we set our sights on a flavorful, moist filling wrapped in a flaky, golden crust. We started with the pear filling. Deeply flavorful Sucanat complemented the pears nicely, and ¼ cup was all we needed to supplement the natural sweetness of the pears. We added a little pear brandy for additional pear flavor; cinnamon offered warm background notes while lemon juice kept the flavors in balance. Although the flavor of this strudel was good, tasters wanted more textural contrast; chopped walnuts fit the bill and added a pleasant nutty flavor to the strudel. To avoid a soggy crust, we parcooked the pears in the microwave and drained away the excess liquid. Next, we turned our attention to the phyllo dough. Traditional strudel recipes often call for brushing every layer of dough with butter and then sprinkling with sugar. We wanted to eliminate the sugar from this step, and tried using just butter, but this made the dough greasy and overly rich. Instead, we decided to put the drained pear juice to work: We stirred a small amount into the melted butter, which reinforced the pear flavor and helped achieve the perfectly crisp and golden crust we were after. However, we found that when we sliced into our finished strudel, the crisp crust we had worked so hard for tended to split and crack along the top and disintegrate into the filling, leaving us with a mess. We found that the air vents, traditionally called for to prevent the inner layers of phyllo from becoming mushy, were weakening the structure of the dough. To solve this, we simply skipped cutting the air vents and instead sliced the strudel almost immediately after it came out of the oven. Phyllo dough is also available in larger 18 by 14–inch sheets; if using, cut them in half to make 14 by 9–inch sheets. To thaw the phyllo, let it sit in the refrigerator overnight or on the counter for 4 to 5 hours; do not microwave the phyllo.

1½ pounds ripe but firm Bosc or Bartlett pears, peeled, quartered, cored, and sliced ¼ inch thick

¼ cup (1½ ounces) Sucanat

2 tablespoons pear brandy

1 teaspoon lemon juice

¼ teaspoon ground cinnamon
Salt

½ cup walnuts, toasted and chopped fine

1½ teaspoons flour

4 tablespoons unsalted butter, melted

12 (14 by 9-inch) phyllo sheets, thawed

1. Adjust oven rack to upper-middle position and heat oven to 375 degrees. Combine pears, Sucanat, brandy, lemon juice, cinnamon, and ⅛ teaspoon salt in large bowl, cover, and microwave, stirring occasionally, until pears are slightly pliable, about 3 minutes. Drain pears in colander set over bowl for 5 minutes. Measure out and reserve ¼ cup drained juice in separate bowl; supplement juice with water if necessary. Return pears to bowl and stir in walnuts and flour.

2. Spray baking sheet with vegetable oil spray. Combine ¼ cup drained juice, melted butter, and ⅛ teaspoon salt in bowl. Place 16½ by 12-inch sheet parchment on counter, long side facing you.

3. With short sides facing you, place 1 phyllo sheet on left side of parchment and another on right side of parchment, overlapping them in center by 1 inch. Brush phyllo with butter mixture. With long side facing you, place third phyllo sheet so that it extends 6 inches beyond top edge of other phyllo sheets and overlaps them by about 3 inches; brush it with ½ tablespoon butter mixture. Repeat this step 3 more times with remaining 9 phyllo sheets and 4½ tablespoons butter mixture.

4. Arrange pears into 11 by 4-inch rectangle on bottom third of phyllo, leaving 2-inch border along bottom and 2½-inch border along sides. Using parchment to lift, fold sides and then bottom of phyllo sheets over filling, leaving parchment behind as you fold. Loosely but firmly roll phyllo around filling, leaving parchment behind as you roll.

5. Gently transfer strudel to prepared baking sheet, seam side down and brush with remaining butter mixture. Bake until golden brown, 27 to 35 minutes, rotating sheet halfway through baking.

6. Let strudel cool on baking sheet for 3 minutes, then transfer to serving platter or cutting board and slice into 6 pieces. Let sliced strudel cool for 20 minutes longer before serving.

BEFORE 34 grams sugar $\longrightarrow$ **AFTER** 19 grams sugar

Making Strudel

1 Place 1 phyllo sheet on left side of parchment, short side facing you.

2 Place second piece phyllo on right side of parchment, overlapping them in center by 1 inch.

3 Brush phyllo with melted butter–juice mixture.

4 Place third phyllo sheet, long side facing you, so that it extends 6 inches beyond top edge of other phyllo sheets and overlaps them by about 3 inches; brush it with ½ tablespoon melted butter–juice mixture. Repeat with remaining phyllo sheets.

5 Arrange pears into 11 by 4-inch rectangle on bottom third of phyllo, leaving 2-inch border along bottom and 2½-inch border along sides.

6 Using parchment to lift, fold sides and then bottom of phyllo sheets over filling, leaving parchment behind as you fold.

Sweetener Substitutions

COCONUT SUGAR	⅓ cup (1½ ounces) Strudel will have sweet, toffee-nut flavor and darker color.
GRANULATED SUGAR	3 tablespoons Strudel will have milder flavor.

fruit desserts

apple turnovers

Serves 8

WHY THIS RECIPE WORKS The perfect apple turnover should have a crisp, golden brown puff pastry crust that is chock-full of tender apples—not sugar. To streamline the process, we used a food processor to coarsely chop the apples and then tossed them with a bit of Sucanat and cinnamon before spooning the mixture right into our puff pastry. These turnovers were plenty sweet, but tasters found the filling far too wet, runny, and unevenly cooked. To get rid of excess moisture, we let the processed apples macerate with the Sucanat and then we drained the exuded juices. The results were better: The filling was slightly more set and the apples were more evenly cooked. But the filling was now too dry. Not wanting to muddy the flavor of our filling, we decided to enhance the apple flavor by tossing the macerated apples with a bit of unsweetened applesauce. These turnovers were the best yet, and tasters loved the intense apple flavor and saucier texture of the filling. While turnovers are often finished with a sugary glaze or sprinkled with sugar before baking, we opted to skip this step to keep the sugar content down. But tasters still wanted a bit of sweetness in the pastry itself. We realized that the answer was in an ingredient we had been tossing down the drain: the juice from the macerated apples. Brushing the tops of the turnovers with some of the reserved juice gave them just enough sweetness and enhanced the apple flavor even more. Right before baking, we gave the turnovers a final brush with egg white to give them even more color and a glossy sheen. These final turnovers were perfect: deep golden brown, crisp, and bubbling with a thick, saucy apple filling. We recommend using Golden Delicious, Jonagold or Braeburn apples in this recipe. To thaw frozen puff pastry, let it sit in the refrigerator for 24 hours or on the counter for 30 minutes to 1 hour; do not microwave the pastry.

1 pound apples, peeled, cored, and chopped

¼ cup (1½ ounces) Sucanat

1 tablespoon lemon juice

¼ teaspoon ground cinnamon

⅛ teaspoon salt

½ cup unsweetened applesauce

2 (9½ by 9-inch) sheets puff pastry, thawed

1 large egg white, lightly beaten

1. Adjust oven rack to middle position and heat oven to 400 degrees. Line rimmed baking sheet with parchment paper. Pulse apples in food processor until most pieces are ¼ to ½ inch thick, about 6 pulses. Toss apples, Sucanat, lemon juice, cinnamon, and salt together in bowl and let stand for 5 minutes. Drain apple mixture in fine-mesh strainer set over bowl, reserving 3 tablespoons juice. In separate bowl, combine drained apples and applesauce.

2. On lightly floured counter, roll each pastry sheet into 10-inch square, then cut each into four 5-inch squares, for a total of 8 squares. Place 2 heaping tablespoons apple mixture in center of each square. Brush edges of dough with half of reserved apple juice, then fold dough over filling to form triangle. Crimp edges with fork to seal.

3. Using paring knife, cut two ½-inch slits in tops of turnovers. Transfer turnovers to prepared sheet and brush with remaining reserved apple juice. Freeze turnovers until firm, about 20 minutes. (Once frozen, turnovers can be transferred to airtight container and frozen for up to 1 month.)

4. Brush frozen turnovers with beaten egg white and bake until well browned, 20 to 26 minutes, rotating sheet halfway through baking. Transfer turnovers to wire rack and let cool slightly, about 20 minutes. Serve warm or at room temperature.

BEFORE 25 grams sugar ⟶ **AFTER** 13 grams sugar

Making Turnovers

1 On lightly floured counter, roll each pastry sheet into 10-inch square, then cut each into four 5-inch squares (for a total of 8 squares).

2 Place 2 heaping tablespoons filling in center of dough, brush edges with juice, then fold dough over filling to form triangle.

3 Crimp edges of each triangle with fork to seal turnovers.

4 Using paring knife, cut two ½-inch slits in tops of turnovers and brush with juice.

Sweetener Substitutions

COCONUT SUGAR	⅓ cup (1½ ounces) Turnovers will have darker-colored filling and taste less sweet.
GRANULATED SUGAR	3 tablespoons (1½ ounces) Turnovers will have lighter-colored filling and taste less sweet.

fruit desserts

blueberry turnovers

Serves 8

WHY THIS RECIPE WORKS We wanted a turnover with a bright, floral blueberry filling and a crisp, slightly caramelized exterior. We knew that the blueberries needed to be cooked to drive off any excess moisture before we filled our pastries. For our first test, we made a filling without any sweetener and just a touch of lemon juice, since the acid would help to activate the natural pectin in the berries and encourage the filling to thicken. But tasters found this filling a bit too runny, and they wanted more sweetness and complexity. We decided to sweeten the filling with maple syrup, which tasters preferred over honey—the maple's subtler flavor didn't interfere with the brightness of the blueberry filling. Reserving some extra syrup to brush on the tops of the turnovers provided extra sweetness and encouraged browning. To fix the filling's texture, we tried cooking the filling down until it resembled jam, but the longer cooking time eliminated much of the fresh berry flavor, and the blueberries tasted a bit flat. We decided instead to add some cornstarch to the blueberries toward the end of cooking; this reduced the overall cooking time and preserved the subtle flavors of the blueberries. Freezing the turnovers briefly before baking ensured that the puff pastry baked into perfectly flaky layers. Finally, our turnovers were packed with intense blueberry flavor and the filling had the perfect consistency. To thaw frozen puff pastry, let it sit in the refrigerator for 24 hours or on the counter for 30 minutes to 1 hour; do not microwave the pastry.

1¼ pounds (4 cups) blueberries
¼ cup maple syrup
½ teaspoon grated lemon zest plus 1 tablespoon juice
⅛ teaspoon salt
Pinch ground cinnamon
1 tablespoon cornstarch
1 tablespoon water
2 (9½ by 9-inch) sheets puff pastry, thawed
1 large egg white, lightly beaten

1. Adjust oven rack to middle position and heat oven to 400 degrees. Line rimmed baking sheet with parchment paper. Combine blueberries, 2 tablespoons maple syrup, lemon zest and juice, salt, and cinnamon in medium saucepan. Cook over medium heat, stirring occasionally, until blueberries begin to break down, release their juices, and mixture begins to thicken, 18 to 20 minutes.

2. Whisk cornstarch and water together in bowl, then add to blueberries and cook until mixture has thickened to jam-like consistency, about 1 minute. Remove from heat and let cool to room temperature, about 20 minutes.

3. On lightly floured counter, roll each pastry sheet into 10-inch square, then cut each into four 5-inch squares, for a total of 8 squares. Place 2 tablespoons blueberry mixture in center of each square. Brush edges of dough with 1 teaspoon of remaining maple syrup, then fold dough over filling to form rectangle. Crimp edges with fork to seal.

4. Using paring knife, cut two ½-inch slits in tops of turnovers. Transfer turnovers to prepared sheet and brush with remaining 5 teaspoons maple syrup. Freeze turnovers until firm, about 20 minutes. (Once frozen, turnovers can be transferred to airtight container and frozen for up to 1 month)

5. Brush frozen turnovers with beaten egg white and bake until well browned, 20 to 26 minutes, rotating sheet halfway through baking. Transfer turnovers to wire rack and let cool slightly, about 20 minutes. Serve warm or at room temperature.

BEFORE 25 grams sugar → **AFTER** 13 grams sugar

cherry clafouti

Serves 8

WHY THIS RECIPE WORKS Cherry clafouti is a classic French dessert consisting of dark, sweet cherries enveloped in a rich, custardy batter. We set our sights on a naturally sweetened, low-sugar version of this dessert. To concentrate the flavor and natural sweetness of the cherries, we roasted them in a hot oven for 15 minutes. Tossing them with a small amount of flour absorbed excess liquid and ensured that our batter didn't turn runny. A bit of cinnamon rounded out the flavor of our clafouti while switching from a casserole dish to a preheated 12-inch skillet encouraged more flavorful browning and helped to set the custard. We prefer whole milk in this recipe, but 1 or 2 percent low-fat milk may be substituted. You can substitute 1½ pounds frozen cherries, thawed and patted dry, for the fresh cherries. You can skip grinding the Sucanat in step 3; however, the clafouti will have a speckled appearance.

1½ pounds fresh sweet cherries, pitted and halved
1 teaspoon lemon juice
2 teaspoons all-purpose flour, plus ½ cup (2½ ounces)
¼ teaspoon ground cinnamon
7 tablespoons (2½ ounces) Sucanat
4 large eggs
1 tablespoon vanilla extract
¼ teaspoon salt
1 cup heavy cream
⅔ cup whole milk
1 tablespoon unsalted butter

1. Adjust oven racks to lowest and upper-middle positions, place 12-inch ovensafe skillet on lower rack, and heat oven to 425 degrees. Line rimmed baking sheet with aluminum foil and place cherries, cut side up, on sheet. Roast cherries on upper rack until just tender and cut sides look dry, about 15 minutes.

2. Transfer cherries to medium bowl, toss with lemon juice, and let cool for 5 minutes. Combine 2 teaspoons flour and cinnamon in bowl, then sprinkle over cherries and toss to coat.

3. Meanwhile, grind Sucanat in two batches in spice grinder until fine and powdery, about 1 minute. Whisk ground Sucanat, eggs, vanilla, and salt in large bowl until smooth and pale, about 1 minute. Whisk in remaining ½ cup flour until smooth. Whisk in cream and milk until incorporated.

4. Carefully remove skillet from oven (skillet handle will be hot) and set on wire rack. Add butter and swirl to coat bottom and sides of skillet (butter will melt and brown quickly). Pour batter into skillet and arrange cherries evenly on top (some will sink).

5. Transfer skillet to lower rack and bake until clafouti puffs and turns golden brown (edges will be dark brown) and center registers 195 degrees, 18 to 22 minutes, rotating skillet halfway through baking. Transfer skillet to wire rack and let cool for 25 minutes. Slice into wedges and serve.

BEFORE 31 grams sugar ⟶ **AFTER** 21 grams sugar

Making Clafouti

1 Roast pitted and halved cherries until just tender and cut sides look dry, about 15 minutes.
2 Arrange cherries evenly over top of batter in skillet (some will sink).

Sweetener Substitutions

COCONUT SUGAR   ½ cup (2½ ounces)
                       Clafouti will have mild toffee flavor; grind sugar as directed in step 3.

GRANULATED SUGAR   6 tablespoons (2½ ounces)
                       Clafouti will taste less sweet; do not grind sugar in step 3.

summer berry gratin

Serves 6

WHY THIS RECIPE WORKS Often served over fresh berries, sabayon is a creamy, sugar-forward dessert sauce that makes for a simple, elegant treat. To create a low-sugar version with all the custardy appeal of the original, we decided to use honey as our sweetener, which we knew would keep the color clean and would be easy to incorporate with the other ingredients. Although many classic recipes call for wine, we found its flavor overpowering with so little sugar to balance it out. Instead, we opted to flavor our sabayon with just lemon juice and a little zest. Two egg yolks and a small amount of water produced just the light, airy consistency we were after. A moderate amount of honey sweetened the sabayon, tempering the lemon's tart bite without overwhelming it. For additional richness without unwanted eggy flavor, we made a quick whipped cream and folded it in to the sabayon. For the berries, we selected a mixture of raspberries, blueberries, and blackberries and dressed them up with some honey and fresh tarragon, whose sweet anise notes complemented the berries nicely and gave the dessert a sophisticated and distinctive flavor. We then baked the berries briefly—just long enough for them to start releasing their juices. To finish, we dolloped the sabayon on top of the berries before broiling, which browned the sabayon and offered pleasant caramel notes to our simple dessert. You will need six shallow 6-ounce broiler-safe gratin dishes for this recipe. Make sure to keep an eye on the sabayon while broiling as it can burn quickly.

¼ cup honey

2 tablespoons water

2 large egg yolks

½ teaspoon grated lemon zest plus 2 tablespoons juice

Salt

5 ounces (1 cup) raspberries

5 ounces (1 cup) blackberries

5 ounces (1 cup) blueberries

1 tablespoon minced fresh tarragon

3 tablespoons heavy cream

1. Adjust oven rack to upper-middle position and heat oven to 400 degrees. Line rimmed baking sheet with aluminum foil. Combine 3 tablespoons honey, water, egg yolks, lemon zest and juice, and ⅛ teaspoon salt together in medium bowl and set over saucepan filled with 1 inch of barely simmering water. Cook, whisking gently but constantly, until mixture is slightly thickened, creamy, and glossy, 5 to 10 minutes (mixture will form loose mounds when dripped from whisk).

2. Remove bowl from saucepan and whisk constantly for 30 seconds to cool slightly. Transfer bowl to refrigerator and chill until mixture is completely cool, about 10 minutes.

3. Meanwhile, gently combine raspberries, blackberries, blueberries, tarragon, and ⅛ teaspoon salt in bowl. Microwave remaining 1 tablespoon honey until loose, about 20 seconds. Drizzle warm honey over berry mixture and toss gently to coat evenly. Divide berry mixture evenly among six shallow 6-ounce gratin dishes set on prepared sheet. Bake berries until warm and just beginning to release their juices, about 8 minutes.

4. Transfer sheet to wire rack and heat broiler. Whisk heavy cream in medium bowl until it holds soft peaks, 30 to 90 seconds. Using rubber spatula, gently fold whipped cream into cooled egg mixture, then spoon mixture evenly over berries. Broil until topping is golden brown, 1 to 2 minutes, rotating sheet halfway through broiling. Serve immediately.

BEFORE 22 grams sugar ⟶ **AFTER** 16 grams sugar

pineapple-mango fools

Serves 8

WHY THIS RECIPE WORKS A fool is an old-fashioned dessert in which a flavorful, refreshing fruit puree gets layered with lightly sweetened whipped cream in convenient, single-serving cups. To allow the fruit flavor to shine, we decided not to add any sweetener to our fruit puree. We caramelized the pineapple and mango in a skillet to concentrate their sweetness and flavor; flambéing some rum in the pan gave the mixture complex flavor without any harshness from the alcohol. Pulsing the mixture a few times in a food processor gave it just the right texture—not completely smooth, but not overly chunky either. Thai basil and lime juice offered nuanced, sophisticated flavor. We added a small amount of honey to our whipped cream for complementary sweetness, and we topped the layered desserts with toasted macadamia nuts for crunch and buttery, nutty flavor. If you can't find Thai basil, regular basil will work. Before flambéing, be sure to roll up long shirtsleeves, tie back long hair, and turn off the exhaust fan and any lit burners.

2 tablespoons unsalted butter

1 pineapple, peeled, cored, and cut into ½-inch pieces (4 cups)

1 mango, peeled, pitted, and cut into ½-inch pieces

¼ teaspoon salt

¼ cup dark rum

2 tablespoons shredded fresh Thai basil

2 teaspoons lime juice

2 cups heavy cream

2 tablespoons honey

½ cup macadamia nuts, toasted and chopped

1. Melt butter in 12-inch skillet over medium-high heat. Add pineapple, mango, and salt and cook, stirring occasionally, until golden brown, 15 to 20 minutes. Off heat, add rum and let warm through, about 5 seconds. Wave lit match over pan until rum ignites, then shake pan to distribute flames. When flames subside, scrape up any browned bits and transfer to large bowl. Refrigerate until chilled, about 45 minutes.

2. Pulse chilled pineapple mixture in food processor until finely chopped and no pieces larger than ¼ inch remain, about 5 pulses. Transfer to bowl and stir in basil and lime juice.

3. Using stand mixer fitted with whisk attachment, whip cream and honey on medium-low speed until foamy, about 1 minute. Increase speed to high and whip until soft peaks form, 1 to 3 minutes. Spoon ¼ cup pineapple mixture into bottoms of eight 8-ounce glasses or jars, then top evenly with ¼ cup whipped cream. Spoon remaining pineapple mixture into glasses and dollop remaining whipped cream over top. Sprinkle with macadamia nuts and serve immediately.

BEFORE 53 grams sugar ⟶ **AFTER** 29 grams sugar

Flambéing Rum

1 Off heat, add rum and let warm through, about 5 seconds.

2 Wave lit match over pan until rum ignites, then shake pan to distribute flames.

chilled maple-glazed oranges

Serves 6

WHY THIS RECIPE WORKS Many Italian cookbooks offer recipes for glazed or macerated oranges, but all of them use white sugar, and most of them are bland, cloyingly sweet, and lack complexity. We wanted to use an alternative sweetener to our advantage to create a deeply complex and intensely fragrant dessert. We thought that maple syrup might provide the perfect bittersweet, caramel-y counterpoint to the bright, juicy oranges. We started by macerating sliced oranges in a cooked maple caramel and then poaching them in the oven. But poaching rendered the oranges mushy and soft, and they all but disintegrated at the push of a fork. We ditched the poaching step and decided to develop more orange flavor by searing the orange halves before slicing them. We used the fond that had developed from searing the oranges to flavor the maple caramel, and we added some cloves for a subtle spicy note. These oranges were firmer, but tasters wanted even more orange aroma and deeper caramel flavor. Our thoughts turned to the orange peels: Packed with essential oils, the peels promised an incredible source of flavor if we could somehow bring those oils out. We decided to char the peels to draw out their intense citrus notes and steeped the peels in the caramel sauce. The results were unbelievable: The charred peels gave the caramel a potent orange flavor, bittersweet undertones, and a vibrant complexity that tasters could not resist. A sprinkle of pine nuts gave just enough textural contrast to this perfect, light, and aromatic end to any hearty meal. You can substitute Cara Cara or blood oranges for the navel oranges in this recipe, though the sugar content will vary slightly.

7 navel oranges (6 whole, scrubbed and dried, 1 juiced to yield ⅓ cup juice)
1 tablespoon unsalted butter
6 tablespoons maple syrup
4 whole cloves
¼ teaspoon salt
¼ cup pine nuts, toasted

1. Using vegetable peeler, remove twenty 2-inch strips orange zest from whole oranges, avoiding pith. Using paring knife, cut away remaining peel and pith from oranges and cut each orange in half lengthwise.

2. Melt half of butter in 12-inch nonstick skillet over medium-high heat. Add peels and cook, stirring occasionally, until well browned, 3 to 5 minutes. Transfer peels to small bowl. Melt remaining butter in now-empty skillet over medium heat. Add orange halves, curved side down, and cook until dark golden brown, 3 to 5 minutes. Transfer oranges to cutting board and cut crosswise into ½-inch-thick slices; transfer to large bowl.

3. Add maple syrup to now-empty skillet and bring to boil over medium heat. Reduce heat to medium-low and cook until mixture thickens and registers 270 degrees, 3 to 4 minutes (syrup will smell slightly burnt). Off heat, carefully stir in browned peels, orange juice, cloves, and salt. Return skillet to medium-low heat and cook, swirling occasionally, until mixture thickens slightly and registers 220 degrees, about 2 minutes.

4. Strain mixture through fine-mesh strainer into bowl with orange slices. Add some of peels and cloves from strainer to oranges and stir gently to combine. Cover with plastic wrap and refrigerate, stirring occasionally, for at least 2 hours or up to 2 days.

5. To serve, portion oranges and syrup into serving bowls, discarding peels and cloves. Sprinkle with pine nuts and serve.

BEFORE 57 grams sugar ⟶ **AFTER** 26 grams sugar

maple-caramel apples with cinnamon cream

Serves 8

WHY THIS RECIPE WORKS Caramelizing apples until satiny and tender, then topping them with a warm, decadent caramel sauce is a perfect treatment for this often-humble fruit. But in many recipes, the apples turn out barely browned and anemic, or, by the time they're beautifully browned, they are mealy and fall apart. We wanted to find a foolproof method for cooking the apples and make a flavorful sauce without relying on granulated sugar. After several tests with different sweeteners, we found that maple syrup was the perfect candidate. Because maple syrup browns, caramelizes, and thickens the same way white sugar does, it makes a flavorful, luscious caramel. By cooking the apples in butter and a small amount of maple syrup, we could quickly achieve browning without risking overcooking the apples. In fact, the browning occurred a little too quickly: Tasters found these apples a bit underdone. We decided to introduce the maple syrup at a later stage in cooking to allow the apples more time to cook through. This produced perfectly tender apples with burnished amber exteriors. We made a caramel with some extra maple syrup and finished it with heavy cream and Calvados to create a rich, velvety sauce. With a dollop of cinnamon whipped cream and some toasted almonds, this dessert is sure to satisfy any sweet tooth. We recommend using firm apples, such as Jonagold, Fuji, or Braeburn, in this recipe. Note that soft apples will cook more quickly; if using soft apples, begin checking for doneness about 5 minutes early.

whipped cream

- ½ cup heavy cream
- 1 tablespoon maple syrup
- ¼ teaspoon vanilla extract
- ⅛ teaspoon ground cinnamon
  Pinch salt

apples

- 2 tablespoons unsalted butter
- 4 crisp apples (6½ ounces each), peeled, cored, and halved
- 6 tablespoons maple syrup
- ¼ cup heavy cream
- 1 tablespoon Calvados or apple brandy
- ¼ teaspoon salt
- ½ cup sliced almonds, toasted

1. FOR THE WHIPPED CREAM Using stand mixer fitted with whisk attachment, whip all ingredients on medium-low speed until foamy, about 1 minute. Increase speed to high and whip until stiff peaks form, 1 to 3 minutes. Cover and refrigerate until ready to serve.

2. FOR THE APPLES Melt butter in 12-inch nonstick skillet over medium heat. Place apples cut side down in skillet and cook until beginning to brown, 8 to 10 minutes. Flip apples cut side up, add 2 tablespoons maple syrup to skillet, and cook until apples are just tender, 4 to 6 minutes, adjusting heat as needed to prevent syrup from getting too dark. Off heat, turn apples to coat with caramel, then transfer, cut side up, to platter.

3. Add remaining ¼ cup maple syrup to now-empty skillet and bring to boil over medium heat. Reduce heat to medium-low and cook until mixture thickens slightly and registers 260 degrees, 3 to 4 minutes. Off heat, carefully whisk in cream, Calvados, and salt. Return skillet to medium-low heat and simmer until alcohol has evaporated and mixture thickens again, about 1 minute.

4. Drizzle caramel evenly over apples and sprinkle with almonds. Serve, passing whipped cream separately.

BEFORE 35 grams sugar → **AFTER** 21 grams sugar

roasted pears with cider-caramel sauce

Serves 8

WHY THIS RECIPE WORKS Roasted pears can easily become a raft for a sticky-sweet caramel sauce that over-powers the flavor of the pears. Plus, the pears are often either colorless and mushy or burned and crunchy. We knew we had our work cut out for us if we wanted to achieve our goal: a low-sugar recipe for crisp-tender, beautifully caramelized roasted pears. By starting our fruit over the direct heat of the stovetop we were able to evaporate some of the juices that would otherwise inhibit proper browning. We finished the pears in the oven so that the gentle, ambient heat would cook the pears while continuing to brown the outsides. Once the pears were cooked through, we made a simple, flavorful sauce for them using apple cider. The cider picked up the flavorful browned bits left behind by the pears, and we boosted flavor further using ginger, cinnamon, and star anise—no extra sugar needed. Finally, a sprinkling of dried cranberries added a tart-sweet element, while chopped hazelnuts provided welcome crunch and nuttiness. We recommend using firm pears, such as Bartlett or Bosc, in this recipe. Other nuts, such as almonds, pecans, or walnuts, can be substituted for the hazelnuts.

3 tablespoons unsalted butter

4 firm but ripe pears (7 ounces each), peeled, halved, and cored

1 cup apple cider

½ teaspoon cornstarch

¼ cup dried cranberries, chopped

1 cinnamon stick

2 star anise pods

1 (2-inch) piece ginger, peeled and lightly crushed

⅛ teaspoon salt

2 tablespoons chopped toasted and skinned hazelnuts

1. Adjust oven rack to middle position and heat oven to 450 degrees. Melt 2 tablespoons butter in 12-inch ovensafe skillet over medium-high heat. Place pear halves cut side down in skillet and cook until pears just begin to brown, about 3 minutes.

2. Transfer skillet to oven and roast pears for 15 minutes. Using tongs, carefully flip pears cut side up and continue to roast until tip of paring knife easily pierces fruit, about 10 minutes.

3. Carefully remove skillet from oven (skillet handle will be hot) and transfer pears to platter. Whisk cider and cornstarch together in bowl. Return skillet to medium-high heat and add cider mixture, cranberries, cinnamon, star anise, ginger, and salt. Simmer vigorously, scraping up any browned bits with spoon, until sauce is thickened slightly and measures ¾ cup, 5 to 7 minutes.

4. Off heat, discard cinnamon, star anise, and ginger and stir in remaining 1 tablespoon butter. Spoon sauce over pears, sprinkle with hazelnuts, and serve.

BEFORE 24 grams sugar ⟶ **AFTER** 14 grams sugar

puddings, custards, and frozen treats

dark chocolate pudding

Serves 6

WHY THIS RECIPE WORKS Homemade chocolate pudding too often turns out gritty, with a lackluster chocolate flavor. We were after a low-sugar chocolate pudding that tasted deeply of chocolate and was thickened to a perfectly silky, creamy texture. Four ounces of bittersweet chocolate was the most our pudding could handle—any less and the rich chocolate flavor was lost, any more and the texture was compromised. To enhance the chocolate flavor, we added a small amount of cocoa powder, and we replaced the usual granulated sugar with more flavorful Sucanat. However, with the decreased sweetness, the espresso powder called for in our traditional recipe became overpoweringly bitter, so we omitted it. To thicken the pudding without leaving any chalky, gritty residue, we used a combination of egg yolks and cornstarch; finishing the custard with butter ensured a velvety texture. Our favorite brand of bittersweet chocolate is Ghirardelli 60% Cacao Bittersweet Chocolate Premium Baking Bar (see page 21 for more information); other brands may contain different amounts of sugar. You can use either Dutch-processed or natural cocoa powder in this recipe; our favorite brand of Dutch-processed cocoa is Droste Cocoa and our favorite brand of natural cocoa is Hershey's Natural Unsweetened Cocoa (see page 21 for more information).

¼ cup (1¼ ounces) Sucanat

2 tablespoons unsweetened cocoa powder

2 tablespoons cornstarch

¼ teaspoon salt

½ cup heavy cream

3 large egg yolks

2½ cups whole milk

4 ounces bittersweet chocolate, chopped fine

5 tablespoons unsalted butter, softened

2 teaspoons vanilla extract

1. Whisk Sucanat, cocoa, cornstarch, and salt together in large saucepan. Add cream and egg yolks and whisk until fully incorporated, making sure to scrape corners of pan. Whisk in milk until well combined and smooth.

2. Cook over medium heat, whisking constantly, until mixture is thickened and bubbling over entire surface, 5 to 8 minutes. Off heat, add chocolate, butter, and vanilla and whisk until melted and smooth.

3. Strain pudding through fine mesh strainer into bowl. Place lightly greased parchment paper against surface of pudding and refrigerate until cold, at least 4 hours or up to 2 days. Whisk pudding until smooth before serving.

BEFORE 31 grams sugar $\longrightarrow$ **AFTER** 20 grams sugar

---

Sweetener Substitutions

COCONUT SUGAR	¼ cup (1¼ ounces) Pudding will taste similar.
GRANULATED SUGAR	3 tablespoons Pudding will have milder, less intense chocolate flavor.

SUCANAT	7 tablespoons (2⅓ ounces)
	Pudding will be lighter in color, less sweet, and have milder flavor.
GRANULATED SUGAR	⅓ cup (2⅓ ounces)
	Pudding will be lighter in color, less sweet, and have milder flavor.

toasted coconut–banana pudding

Serves 6

WHY THIS RECIPE WORKS While banana pudding often conjures images of whipped cream and wafer cookies layered with vanilla pudding and bananas, we wanted to come up with a true banana pudding that would put all the banana flavor in the pudding itself—without any of the usual sugar-laden distractions. Roasting very ripe bananas concentrated their flavor by eliminating excess liquid and helped to break down the banana fibers so we could incorporate them more easily into the pudding. Tasters preferred the richer, creamier consistency of pudding made with half-and-half to pudding made with milk. Adding just a teaspoon of lemon juice prevented browning in the refrigerator. Although our pudding now had good banana flavor, tasters felt it was a bit one-dimensional. We decided to add coconut to the mix, hoping that the tropical flavors would pair well together. Replacing some of the half-and-half with coconut milk was an easy and effective swap, and we settled on coconut sugar as our sweetener to provide rich, toasty undertones. A sprinkling of toasted coconut flakes was the perfect finish to this decadent, tropical dessert. Although we prefer the creamy, rich flavor of regular coconut milk in this recipe, low-fat coconut milk can be substituted; low-fat coconut milk will have a mild coconut flavor and the pudding will be thinner. Our favorite brand of coconut milk is Chaokoh; other brands may contain different amounts of sugar and fat, which will affect the overall flavor and texture of the pudding.

2 very ripe bananas
½ cup (2⅓ ounces) coconut sugar
2 tablespoons cornstarch
¼ teaspoon salt
1 cup canned coconut milk
4 large egg yolks
2 cups half-and-half
2 tablespoons unsalted butter, softened
1 tablespoon vanilla extract
1 teaspoon lemon juice
½ cup (1 ounce) unsweetened flaked coconut, toasted

1. Adjust oven rack to upper-middle position and heat oven to 350 degrees. Place unpeeled bananas on aluminum foil–lined rimmed baking sheet and bake until skins are completely black, bananas have split open, and juices are starting to bubble, about 30 minutes; let cool slightly.

2. Meanwhile, whisk coconut sugar, cornstarch, and salt together in large saucepan. Add coconut milk and egg yolks and whisk until fully incorporated, making sure to scrape corners of pan. Whisk in half-and-half until well combined and smooth.

3. Cook over medium heat, whisking constantly, until mixture is thickened and bubbling over entire surface, 5 to 8 minutes. Off heat, add butter and vanilla and whisk until melted and smooth.

4. Transfer pudding to food processor, add peeled roasted bananas and lemon juice, and process until smooth, about 1 minute. Strain pudding through fine-mesh strainer into bowl. Place lightly greased parchment paper against surface of pudding and refrigerate until cold, at least 4 hours or up to 2 days. Whisk pudding until smooth and sprinkle with toasted coconut before serving.

BEFORE 39 grams sugar $\longrightarrow$ **AFTER** 21 grams sugar

puddings, custards, and frozen treats

maple rice pudding

Serves 8

WHY THIS RECIPE WORKS With perfectly tender grains of rice bound loosely in a subtly sweet, creamy base, old-fashioned rice pudding has a lot of appeal. But our traditional recipe relied on just as much sugar as rice. We set out to develop a low-sugar, naturally sweetened rice pudding without losing sight of what makes this dessert great. First, we turned our attention to perfecting the rice's flavor and texture. Tasters liked rice that was parcooked in water rather than milk or cream, since the dairy masked the rice's delicate flavor. When it came time to make the pudding, we found that whole milk alone made the pudding too thin; adding some half-and-half upped the richness without putting it over the top. Once the pudding had simmered to just the right consistency, we added cinnamon and vanilla for depth. While our traditional rice pudding recipe called for granulated sugar, we opted for maple syrup instead. The syrup was easy to incorporate, and its subtle sweetness and well-rounded flavor were a perfect fit for our pudding. Stirring in ½ cup of milk just before serving ensured a pleasantly thick—but not stodgy—consistency. We prefer the richer flavor and creamier texture of whole milk in this recipe; however, 2 percent low-fat milk can be substituted; do not substitute 1 percent low-fat or skim milk. Use a heavy-bottomed saucepan to prevent scorching.

2   cups water
1   cup long-grain white rice
½   teaspoon salt
2½   cups half-and-half
2½   cups whole milk
½   cup maple syrup
2   teaspoons vanilla extract
1½   teaspoons ground cinnamon

1. Bring water to boil in large saucepan over medium-high heat. Reduce heat to low and stir in rice and salt. Cover and simmer until water is almost fully absorbed, 15 to 20 minutes.

2. Stir in half-and-half and 2 cups milk, increase heat to medium-high, and bring to simmer. Cook uncovered, stirring often and adjusting heat as needed to maintain simmer, until rice is soft and pudding is thickened and clings nicely to spoon, 35 to 45 minutes.

3. Off heat, stir in maple syrup, vanilla, and cinnamon. Transfer pudding to large bowl and let cool completely, about 2 hours. If desired, cover cooled pudding and refrigerate until cold, about 2 hours. Just before serving, stir in remaining ½ cup milk.

BEFORE 32 grams sugar $\longrightarrow$ **AFTER** 19 grams sugar

maple flan

Serves 8

WHY THIS RECIPE WORKS Flan is a rich, custardy dessert with a deep toffee flavor and a uniformly silky texture; what sets it apart from other custards is its caramel layer, which bakes along with the custard and glazes the flan after baking. But most recipes we've tried are cloyingly sweet, the custard is heavy and dense, and there's an unappealing thick "skin" on the top after baking. For our naturally sweetened version, we started by cutting the sugar from a whopping 45 grams per serving to a more modest 22 grams by swapping the usual granulated sugar for a smaller amount of maple syrup. We loved the unique flavor that maple syrup brought to our flan, and we had no problem making a caramel out of the syrup: We simply cooked the syrup on the stovetop for 5 minutes to thicken it to a caramel-like consistency. To make the custard, many traditional recipes call for sweetened condensed milk—a nonstarter in our low-sugar recipe. Instead, we opted to make a custard using half-and-half, eggs and egg yolks, and a bit more maple syrup, a combination which produced a rich flavor while maintaining a silky smooth texture. To prevent an unsightly "skin," we baked the flan in a water bath so that it would cook gently, and we covered the pan with foil during baking to avoid exposing the custard to direct heat. While traditional flan is often baked in a round cake pan, we found that switching to a loaf pan produced a sturdier, more statuesque flan. For safety, be sure to use a tall-sided saucepan to cook the maple syrup in step 1. The test kitchen's preferred loaf pan measures 8½ by 4½ inches; if you use a 9 by 5-inch loaf pan, start checking for doneness 10 minutes earlier than advised in the recipe.

¾ cup maple syrup
3 large eggs plus 4 large yolks
3 cups half-and-half
1 tablespoon vanilla extract
½ teaspoon salt

1. Bring ½ cup maple syrup to simmer in small saucepan over medium heat. Once simmering, cook, stirring occasionally, until syrup reaches 260 degrees and smells slightly burnt, 5 to 8 minutes. Carefully pour syrup into 8½ by 4½-inch loaf pan and tilt pan to coat bottom evenly.

2. Adjust oven rack to middle position and heat oven to 300 degrees. Line bottom of 13 by 9-inch baking pan with dish towel and bring kettle of water to boil.

3. Whisk eggs and yolks and remaining ¼ cup maple syrup together in large bowl. Combine half-and-half, vanilla, and salt in medium saucepan and heat over medium heat until just steaming, about 6 minutes. Slowly whisk warmed half-and-half mixture into egg mixture until well combined. Strain through fine-mesh strainer directly into loaf pan with caramel.

4. Cover loaf pan tightly with aluminum foil, place in prepared baking pan, and transfer to oven. Carefully pour enough boiling water into baking pan to reach halfway up sides of pan. Bake until center of custard jiggles slightly when shaken and registers 180 degrees, about 1 hour.

5. Transfer pans to wire rack. Remove foil but leave custard in water bath until loaf pan has cooled completely, about 1 hour. Remove loaf pan from water bath, cover with plastic wrap, and refrigerate until chilled and firm, at least 30 minutes or up to 4 days.

6. To unmold, run paring knife around edges of pan. Invert serving platter on top of pan, then turn pan and platter over. When flan is released, remove loaf pan. Using rubber spatula, scrape residual caramel onto flan. Slice and serve.

BEFORE 45 grams sugar ⟶ **AFTER** 22 grams sugar

Sweetener Substitutions

COCONUT SUGAR	**6 tablespoons (1¾ ounces)** Mousse will have milder strawberry flavor.
GRANULATED SUGAR	**¼ cup (1¾ ounces)** Mousse will taste less sweet.

strawberry mousse

Serves 6

WHY THIS RECIPE WORKS We set out to create a naturally sweetened strawberry mousse with a beautifully light, fluffy texture and unmistakable strawberry flavor. We decided to swap the granulated sugar in our traditional recipe for a small amount of Sucanat, which gave the mousse a pleasant, rounded sweetness without masking the flavor of the berries. To further enhance the strawberries' natural sweetness, we macerated some of the berries with the Sucanat. This drew out some of the berries' juices; we didn't want to toss the juice (and the flavor) down the drain, but we knew the large amount of liquid would make the mousse too runny. The solution was to reduce some of the juice to a thick syrup, concentrating its flavor. We combined the remaining juice with a small amount of gelatin, which contributed to a more stable texture in the finished mousse. Whipped cream and cream cheese gave the mousse just enough richness and tang while also helping to ensure that the mousse set nicely. Garnishing the finished mousse with fresh diced strawberries was a perfect finishing touch. Be careful not to overprocess the berries in step 1.

2 pounds strawberries, hulled (6½ cups)

⅓ cup (1¾ ounces) Sucanat
Pinch salt

1¾ teaspoons unflavored gelatin

4 ounces cream cheese, cut into 8 pieces and softened

½ cup heavy cream

1. Dice enough strawberries into ¼-inch pieces to measure 1 cup; refrigerate until serving. Pulse remaining strawberries in food processor in 2 batches until most pieces are ¼ to ½ inch thick, 6 to 10 pulses. Combine processed strawberries, Sucanat, and salt in bowl. Cover and let strawberries sit, stirring occasionally, for 45 minutes (Do not clean processor.)

2. Drain processed strawberries in fine-mesh strainer set over bowl (you should have about ⅔ cup juice). Measure out 3 tablespoons juice into small bowl, sprinkle gelatin over top, and let sit until gelatin softens, about 5 minutes. Place remaining juice in small saucepan and cook over medium-high heat until reduced to 3 tablespoons, about 10 minutes. Remove pan from heat, add softened gelatin mixture, and whisk until dissolved. Add cream cheese and whisk until smooth. Transfer mixture to large bowl.

3. While juice is reducing, return drained strawberries to now-empty processor and process until smooth, 15 to 20 seconds. Strain puree through fine-mesh strainer into medium bowl, pressing on solids to remove seeds and pulp (you should have about 1⅔ cups puree). Discard remaining solids. Add strawberry puree to juice-gelatin mixture and whisk until incorporated.

4. Using stand mixer fitted with whisk attachment, whip cream on medium-low speed until foamy, about 1 minute. Increase speed to high and whip until stiff peaks form, 1 to 3 minutes. Add whipped cream to strawberry mixture and whisk until no white streaks remain. Portion into dessert dishes and chill for at least 4 hours or up to 2 days. (If chilled longer than 6 hours, let mousse sit at room temperature for 15 minutes before serving.) Garnish with reserved diced strawberries before serving.

BEFORE 25 grams sugar ⟶ **AFTER** 16 grams sugar

puddings, custards, and frozen treats

Sweetener Substitutions

COCONUT SUGAR	⅓ cup plus ¼ cup (2⅔ ounces) Semifreddo will taste similar; grind sugar as directed in step 2.
GRANULATED SUGAR	6 tablespoons (2⅔ ounces) Semifreddo will have mild chocolate flavor; do not grind sugar in step 2.

chocolate-hazelnut semifreddo

Serves 8

WHY THIS RECIPE WORKS A cross between mousse and ice cream, semifreddo is an elegant summer dessert. We wanted a rich chocolaty semifreddo studded with toasted hazelnuts, so we set our sights on a base that would be light and airy yet sturdy enough to support the chocolate and nuts. A cooked meringue, which calls for a warm sugar syrup to be poured into the egg whites as they are beaten, fit the bill perfectly; Sucanat stood in for the usual white sugar. You can use Dutch-processed or natural cocoa powder in this recipe; our favorite brand of Dutch-processed cocoa is Droste Cocoa and our favorite brand of natural cocoa is Hershey's Natural Unsweetened Cocoa. Do not skip grinding the Sucanat in step 2 or the semifreddo will be gritty.

1 cup heavy cream

½ cup (2⅔ ounces) Sucanat

7 tablespoons water

1 ounce semisweet chocolate, chopped

2 tablespoons unsweetened cocoa powder

3 large egg whites, room temperature
Pinch cream of tartar

1 teaspoon vanilla extract

½ cup plus 2 tablespoons hazelnuts, toasted, skinned, and chopped coarse

1. Using stand mixer fitted with whisk attachment, whip cream on medium-low speed until foamy, about 1 minute. Increase speed to high and whip until soft peaks form, 1 to 3 minutes. Cover bowl with plastic wrap and refrigerate until needed.

2. Working in 2 batches, grind Sucanat in spice grinder until fine and powdery, about 1 minute. Combine 6 tablespoons ground Sucanat and ¼ cup water in small saucepan and bring to boil over medium-high heat. Cook until slightly thickened and syrupy (mixture should register about 235 degrees), about 4 minutes. Remove syrup from heat and cover to keep warm.

3. Microwave chocolate, cocoa, and remaining 3 tablespoons water in bowl at 50 percent power, stirring occasionally, until melted and smooth, about 1 minute.

4. Using clean, dry mixer bowl and whisk attachment, whip egg whites and cream of tartar on medium-low speed until foamy, about 1 minute. Increase speed to medium-high and whip whites to soft, billowy mounds, about 1 minute. Gradually add remaining 2 tablespoons ground Sucanat and whip until glossy, stiff peaks form, 2 to 3 minutes.

5. Reduce speed to medium and slowly add warm syrup, avoiding whisk and sides of bowl. Increase speed to medium-high and continue to whip until the meringue has cooled slightly and is very thick and shiny, 2 to 5 minutes. Add warm melted chocolate and vanilla and continue to whip until incorporated, about 1 minute.

6. Gently fold one-third reserved whipped cream into meringue with rubber spatula. Fold in remaining whipped cream and ½ cup hazelnuts until just incorporated.

7. Divide mixture evenly between eight 6-ounce ramekins and gently tap ramekins on counter to settle batter. Wrap ramekins tightly with plastic wrap, making sure wrap doesn't touch semifreddo, and freeze until firm, at least 4 hours or up to 5 days. Before serving, let semifreddo soften at room temperature for 5 to 10 minutes, then sprinkle with remaining chopped hazelnuts.

BEFORE 19 grams sugar ⟶ **AFTER** 12 grams sugar

puddings, custards, and frozen treats

vanilla frozen yogurt

Makes 1 quart; serves 8

WHY THIS RECIPE WORKS We set the bar high with this recipe: We wanted a naturally sweetened, pleasantly tart vanilla frozen yogurt with the creamy, smooth texture of premium ice cream. We started with plain whole-milk yogurt; not wanting to mask the yogurt's tangy flavor, we immediately ruled out the additional dairy we saw in some other recipes. Next, we needed to choose a natural sweetener that wouldn't disrupt the clean flavor of the yogurt. Sucanat, coconut sugar, and honey proved to be overpowering, but maple syrup worked perfectly: It offered just the right amount of rounded sweetness without being distracting. To develop distinct, nuanced vanilla flavor, we used a whole vanilla bean along with a small amount of extract. With the yogurt's flavor down, we turned our attention to fine-tuning the texture. Usually, sugar helps to prevent ice crystals from forming in ice cream and frozen yogurt, but with the small amount we were using we needed to find a different way to avoid an icy texture. We wondered if the water in the yogurt was to blame. Draining the yogurt overnight and eliminating a measured amount of liquid resulted in a much better final texture, but the ultrasmooth creaminess we coveted was still proving elusive. We knew that store-bought frozen yogurts often rely on additives and stabilizers to achieve a smoother texture, and we wondered if we could re-create the effect at home by using gelatin. We tested yogurts made with various amounts of gelatin (blooming it in the strained yogurt liquid kept our recipe streamlined), and landed on 1 teaspoon. Finally, we prevented large ice crystals from forming by allowing the frozen yogurt base to cool to 40 degrees or lower before churning. You can increase the vanilla extract to 1 tablespoon if you don't have a vanilla bean, though the flavor will be duller. We prefer to use whole-milk yogurt in this recipe; the frozen yogurt will be less creamy if you substitute low-fat yogurt.

1 quart plain whole-milk yogurt
1 teaspoon unflavored gelatin
1 vanilla bean
½ cup maple syrup
1 teaspoon vanilla extract
⅛ teaspoon salt

1. Line colander or fine-mesh strainer with triple layer of cheesecloth and place over large bowl. Place yogurt in colander, cover with plastic wrap (wrap should not touch yogurt), and refrigerate until at least 1¼ cups liquid has drained from yogurt, at least 8 hours or up to 12 hours.

2. Discard ¾ cup of drained liquid and return remaining liquid to bowl. Sprinkle gelatin over liquid and let sit until softened, about 5 minutes. Microwave mixture until bubbling around edges and gelatin dissolves, about 30 seconds. Cut vanilla bean in half lengthwise. Using tip of paring knife, scrape out seeds; discard bean. Add seeds to warm gelatin mixture and let cool for 5 minutes.

3. In large bowl, whisk drained yogurt, maple syrup, vanilla extract, salt, and cooled gelatin mixture until well combined and smooth. Place bowl over ice bath, or cover and refrigerate, until yogurt mixture registers 40 degrees or lower.

4. Transfer mixture to ice cream machine and churn until mixture has consistency of thick soft-serve and registers about 21 degrees, 25 to 35 minutes. Transfer frozen yogurt to airtight container and freeze until firm, at least 2 hours or up to 5 days. Serve.

BEFORE 29 grams sugar $\longrightarrow$ **AFTER** 18 grams sugar

strawberry frozen yogurt

Omit vanilla bean (do not omit vanilla extract). Process 1½ cups hulled strawberries in food processor until smooth, about 1 minute. Add strawberry puree to drained yogurt with other ingredients in step 3.

BEFORE 30 grams sugar $\longrightarrow$ **AFTER** 19 grams sugar

peach frozen yogurt

Omit vanilla bean (do not omit vanilla extract). Reduce maple syrup to 6 tablespoons. Pulse 1 pound peaches, peeled, pitted and chopped, in food processor until mostly smooth, 7 or 8 pulses. Cook processed peaches in 12-inch skillet over medium heat until darkened in color and slightly thickened, 8 to 10 minutes. Add 3 tablespoons peach schnapps and cook until evaporated, about 1 minute. Let peach mixture cool to room temperature, about 15 minutes, then add to drained yogurt in step 3.

BEFORE 33 grams sugar $\longrightarrow$ **AFTER** 19 grams sugar

Making Frozen Yogurt

1 Line colander with triple layer of cheesecloth and place over large bowl. Place yogurt in colander and let drain in refrigerator for 8 to 12 hours.

2 Discard ¾ cup of drained liquid and place remaining liquid in bowl. Sprinkle gelatin over liquid and let sit until softened.

3 Whisk drained yogurt, maple syrup, vanilla extract, salt, and gelatin mixture until smooth. Place bowl over ice bath, or cover and refrigerate, until mixture registers 40 degrees or lower.

4 Churn in ice cream machine until mixture registers 21 degrees and is consistency of thick soft serve. Transfer to airtight container and freeze until firm.

raspberry sorbet

Makes 1 quart; serves 8

WHY THIS RECIPE WORKS We wanted to create a boldly flavored low-sugar raspberry sorbet that rivaled the smooth richness of its dairy-based cousins. But traditional recipes for sorbet rely heavily on the correct ratio of sugar and water to achieve the best texture, so we knew that reducing one of these key ingredients was going to be no small challenge. Usually, the sugar and water in sorbet work in tandem: Some of the water freezes, but because sugar (like salt) lowers the freezing point of water, the rest of the water remains liquid, giving the sorbet its hallmark delicately icy texture. We started our testing by replacing the granulated sugar and the corn syrup called for in our traditional recipe with Sucanat. We tested several ratios of water to Sucanat, and found that we got closest to the texture we were after with a cup of water for just over half a cup of Sucanat. But "closest" wasn't close enough—the texture still needed some work. The sorbet was a bit too icy and had a grainy, crumbly texture. Because of the decreased sugar content, more of the water was freezing into large, crunchy ice crystals. To create smaller crystals, we needed the base to freeze faster so that large crystals didn't have time to form. The solution was to freeze a small amount of the base before churning: The smaller volume froze quickly, forming small ice crystals. When we combined the frozen base with the remaining refrigerated base, the small crystals initiated a chain reaction, immediately causing more small crystals to form. This sorbet was almost perfect: fruit-forward, flavorful, and creamy-smooth. But tasters had one last complaint: the sorbet melted rapidly once it was served. Commercial brands stave off melting by incorporating additives like guar gum, but we hoped that more readily-available pectin (which could already be found naturally in the berries we were using) would work instead. A mere teaspoon of pectin was all it took to help slow the melting and maintain our sorbet's texture long enough to eat. For fruit pectin, we recommend both Sure–Jell for Less or No Sugar Needed Recipes and Ball RealFruit Low or No–Sugar Needed Pectin. Do not skip grinding the Sucanat in step 2, or the sorbet will be too icy.

1 cup water
1 teaspoon low- or no-sugar-needed fruit pectin
¼ teaspoon salt
½ cup plus 2 tablespoons (3½ ounces) Sucanat
1¼ pounds (4 cups) raspberries

1. Cook water, pectin, and salt in medium saucepan over medium-high heat, stirring occasionally, until pectin is fully dissolved, about 5 minutes. Remove saucepan from heat and let cool slightly, about 10 minutes.

2. Working in 2 batches, grind Sucanat in spice grinder until fine and powdery, about 1 minute. Process ground Sucanat, raspberries, and cooled water mixture in food processor until smooth, about 30 seconds. Strain puree through fine-mesh strainer into bowl, pressing on solids to remove seeds and pulp (you should have about 3 cups puree); discard solids.

3. Transfer 1 cup puree to small bowl and place remaining puree in large bowl. Cover both bowls with plastic wrap. Place large bowl in refrigerator and small bowl in freezer and let chill for at least 4 hours or up to 24 hours. (Small bowl will freeze solid.)

4. Remove puree from refrigerator and freezer. Using tines of fork, scrape frozen puree into large bowl with chilled puree. Stir occasionally until frozen puree has fully dissolved.

5. Churn mixture in ice cream machine until mixture resembles thick milkshake and lightens in color, 10 to 15 minutes. Transfer sorbet to airtight container and freeze until firm, at least 2 hours or up to 5 days. Serve.

BEFORE 26 grams sugar → **AFTER** 15 grams sugar

raspberry, ginger, and mint sorbet

Add 1 tablespoon grated fresh ginger and ¼ cup fresh mint leaves to water in step 1.

BEFORE 26 grams sugar ⟶ **AFTER** 15 grams sugar

mixed berry sorbet

Reduce amount of raspberries to 1¼ cups. Add 1¼ cups blackberries and 1¼ cups chopped hulled strawberries to food processor with raspberries in step 2.

BEFORE 26 grams sugar ⟶ **AFTER** 15 grams sugar

Making Raspberry Sorbet

1 Strain raspberry puree through fine-mesh strainer to remove seeds.
2 Transfer 1 cup puree to small bowl and place in freezer. Transfer remaining puree to large bowl and place in refrigerator.
3 Using tines of fork, scrape frozen puree into chilled puree and stir until frozen puree has fully dissolved.
4 Churn mixture until sorbet resembles thick milkshake, 10 to 15 minutes. Transfer to airtight container and freeze until firm.

Sweetener Substitutions

COCONUT SUGAR	¾ cup (3½ ounces) Sorbet will have subtle bitter flavor; grind sugar as directed in step 2.
GRANULATED SUGAR	½ cup (3½ ounces) Sorbet will taste less sweet; do not grind sugar in step 2.

puddings, custards, and frozen treats

Sweetener Substitutions

COCONUT SUGAR	½ cup plus 2 tablespoons (3 ounces) Sorbet will be have subtle nutty flavor; grind sugar as directed in step 2.
GRANULATED SUGAR	7 tablespoons (3 ounces) Sorbet will be bright yellow and have clean flavor; do not grind sugar in step 2.

pineapple sorbet

Makes 1 quart; serves 8

WHY THIS RECIPE WORKS For a great low-sugar pineapple sorbet, we started by pureeing the fibrous fruit and straining out any solids that might disrupt the sorbet's velvety consistency. To avoid an icy texture, we took a cue from our Raspberry Sorbet (page 274) and froze a small amount of the base before churning. We were surprised to discover that the churning time had a big impact on the final texture. Although sorbet churned for 30 minutes appeared promisingly thick and ice cream–like, the added air encouraged larger ice crystals to form and resulted in a crumbly texture and muted flavor. Reducing the churning time fixed the problem. For fruit pectin, we recommend both Sure-Jell for Less or No Sugar Needed Recipes and Ball RealFruit Low or No-Sugar Needed Pectin. Do not skip grinding the Sucanat in step 2, or the sorbet will be too icy.

1 cup water
1 teaspoon low- or no-sugar-needed fruit pectin
¼ teaspoon salt
⅓ cup plus ¼ cup (3 ounces) Sucanat
18 ounces (3 cups) chopped pineapple

1. Combine water, pectin, and salt in medium saucepan. Cook over medium-high heat, stirring occasionally, until pectin is fully dissolved, about 5 minutes. Remove saucepan from heat and let cool slightly, about 10 minutes.

2. Working in 2 batches, grind Sucanat in spice grinder until fine and powdery, about 1 minute. Process pineapple, ground Sucanat, and cooled water mixture in food processor until smooth, about 30 seconds. Strain puree through fine-mesh strainer into bowl, pressing on solids to remove pulp (you should have about 3½ cups puree); discard solids. Transfer 1 cup puree to small bowl and place remaining puree in large bowl. Cover both bowls with plastic wrap. Place large bowl in refrigerator and small bowl in freezer and cool completely, at least 4 hours or up to 24 hours. (Small bowl will freeze solid.)

3. Remove puree from refrigerator and freezer. Using tines of fork, scrape frozen puree into large bowl with chilled puree. Stir occasionally until frozen puree has fully dissolved.

4. Churn in ice cream machine until mixture resembles thick milkshake and lightens in color, 10 to 15 minutes. Transfer sorbet to airtight container and freeze until firm, at least 2 hours or up to 5 days. Serve.

BEFORE 33 grams sugar ⟶ **AFTER** 16 grams sugar

piña colada sorbet
Do not substitute low-fat coconut milk here or the sorbet will taste watery and have an icy texture.
Substitute canned coconut milk for water in step 1.
BEFORE 33 grams sugar ⟶ **AFTER** 16 grams sugar

fruit punch sorbet
Reduce amount of pineapple to 1 cup. Add 1 cup pitted sweet cherries and ½ cup orange juice to food processor with pineapple in step 2.
BEFORE 33 grams sugar ⟶ **AFTER** 16 grams sugar

puddings, custards, and frozen treats

no-fuss banana ice cream

Makes 1 quart; serves 8

WHY THIS RECIPE WORKS Traditional ice cream relies on sugar for its smooth, creamy texture, so we set out to create a low-sugar, naturally sweetened ice cream alternative that wouldn't feel like a compromise. While we were at it, we decided to ditch the ice cream machine and develop a recipe that could be made using only standard kitchen equipment. Bananas were a perfect choice for our "ice cream" base: Their high pectin content allows them to remain creamy when frozen and their natural sweetness meant that we didn't need to add any sugar. We started by simply freezing whole peeled bananas and then sliced them and processed them into a smooth puree. Letting the bananas come to room temperature for 15 minutes before slicing made them easier to cut through and kept the processing time at only 5 minutes. The end result had good banana flavor, but wasn't quite as creamy as tasters wanted. Hoping to intensify the flavor and rid the bananas of some excess liquid, we tried roasting the bananas (in their peels to avoid overbrowning the fruit) before freezing them. Although this approach successfully deepened the banana flavor, the liquid that leached out of the roasted bananas froze, resulting in a dessert that was far too icy. Instead, we opted for a different route and decided to try adding a little dairy to help achieve our desired creamy consistency. We tested ice creams made with both milk and heavy cream; the version made with heavy cream produced an unbeatable silky-smooth texture. A teaspoon of lemon juice and a bit of cinnamon gave our ice cream more dimension, while a tablespoon of vanilla rounded out the other flavors. Be sure to use very ripe, heavily speckled (or even black) bananas in this recipe. You can skip the freezing in step 3 and serve the ice cream immediately, but the texture will be softer.

6 very ripe bananas
½ cup heavy cream
1 tablespoon vanilla extract
1 teaspoon lemon juice
¼ teaspoon salt
¼ teaspoon ground cinnamon

1. Peel bananas, place in large zipper-lock bag, and press out excess air. Freeze bananas until solid, at least 8 hours.

2. Let bananas sit at room temperature to soften slightly, about 15 minutes. Slice into ½-inch-thick rounds and place in food processor. Add cream, vanilla, lemon juice, salt, and cinnamon and process until smooth, about 5 minutes, scraping down sides of bowl as needed.

3. Transfer mixture to airtight container and freeze until firm, at least 2 hours or up to 5 days. Serve.

BEFORE 30 grams sugar ⟶ **AFTER** 12 grams sugar

no-fuss peanut butter–banana ice cream
Reduce amount of heavy cream to ¼ cup. Add ¼ cup peanut butter to food processor with bananas in step 2.
BEFORE 30 grams sugar ⟶ **AFTER** 13 grams sugar

no-fuss chocolate-banana ice cream with walnuts
Add ½ cup unsweetened cocoa powder to food processor with bananas in step 2. Before removing ice cream from processor, add 1 cup walnuts, toasted and chopped, and pulse to combine, about 5 pulses.
BEFORE 30 grams sugar ⟶ **AFTER** 12 grams sugar

puddings, custards, and frozen treats

strawberry granita

Serves 6

WHY THIS RECIPE WORKS Granita is a simple, refreshing Italian dessert similar to shaved ice; it's typically made by freezing a puree of fruit and sugar and then scraping the mixture with a fork every 30 minutes for several hours to produce a crunchy, granular texture. Our traditional strawberry granita recipe called for ⅓ cup of sugar along with the fruit, but since we weren't trying to create a smooth, creamy texture, we wondered if the sugar was really necessary. A quick test revealed that granita made with only berries and water was a bit too dull. We tested adding small amounts of Sucanat, coconut sugar, maple syrup, and honey. Just 2 tablespoons of honey won tasters over—its floral notes complemented the strawberries' flavor perfectly. Satisfied with the granita's flavor, we turned next to streamlining the traditionally fussy method. The scraping technique posed two significant issues: It required hours of off-and-on attention, and it couldn't be prepared in advance because it needed to be served just as the crystals of freezing liquid hardened to the proper consistency. We wanted to create the same texture without the time constraints. We found our answer in a piece of basic kitchen equipment: ice cube trays. We froze our strained strawberry puree mixture in the ice cube trays and simply pulsed the cubes in the food processor just before serving. We found that the key to achieving the best texture—one that wasn't too slushy and didn't contain large ice chunks—was limiting the amount of frozen puree cubes in the food processor to what could fit comfortably in a single layer. This created an even, finely chopped granita. The frozen puree cubes can be stored in a zipper-lock bag for up to a week.

1 pound strawberries, hulled (3 cups)
2 tablespoons honey
⅛ teaspoon salt

1. Process strawberries, honey, and salt in food processor until smooth, about 30 seconds. Strain puree through fine-mesh strainer into bowl, pressing on solids to remove seeds and pulp (you should have about 2⅓ cups puree); discard solids.

2. Pour strawberry puree into ice cube trays and freeze until firm, at least 2 hours or up to 5 days. Place serving bowls in freezer to chill for 30 minutes before serving.

3. Working in batches, place single layer of frozen cubes in food processor and pulse until no large chunks of ice remain, 25 to 30 pulses. Transfer granita to chilled serving bowls and repeat with remaining puree cubes. Serve immediately.

BEFORE 19 grams sugar ⟶ **AFTER** 9 grams sugar

strawberry-lime granita
Add 3 tablespoons lime juice to food processor in step 1.
BEFORE 19 grams sugar ⟶ **AFTER** 9 grams sugar

strawberry-basil granita
Bring ½ cup water and ½ cup fresh basil leaves to simmer in small saucepan over medium heat and cook for 5 minutes. Add to food processor with strawberries in step 1.
BEFORE 19 grams sugar ⟶ **AFTER** 9 grams sugar

strawberry cream paletas

Makes 6 paletas

WHY THIS RECIPE WORKS A cousin of popsicles, *paletas* are Mexican-style frozen treats that usually rely on fresh fruit juice as their base and often have chunks of fresh fruit stirred in. We thought the idea was perfectly suited for a naturally sweet dessert, and chose to create strawberry paletas. We used the berries in two ways: First, we pureed half of them to a smooth consistency with a small amount of honey for sweetness. We pulsed the rest of the berries to a coarse chop to ensure bites of fresh fruit throughout our pops. For richness, we wanted to add some dairy to our paletas, and tested milk, half-and-half, and heavy cream. Pops made with milk and half-and-half were too icy, but heavy cream provided just the right velvety texture. This recipe was developed using 3-ounce popsicle molds. We prefer the flavor of fresh strawberries in this recipe; however, you can substitute 1 pound frozen strawberries, thawed and drained on paper towels to dry.

1 pound strawberries, hulled (3 cups)
½ cup heavy cream
¼ cup honey
1 teaspoon lemon juice
⅛ teaspoon salt

1. Process 1½ cups strawberries, cream, honey, lemon juice, and salt in food processor until smooth, about 30 seconds, scraping down sides of bowl as needed. Add remaining 1½ cups strawberries and pulse until coarsely chopped, about 5 pulses. Transfer mixture to large liquid measuring cup.

2. Divide strawberry mixture evenly among six 3-ounce molds. Insert popsicle stick in center of each mold, cover, and freeze until firm, at least 6 hours or up to 5 days. To serve, hold mold under warm running water for 30 seconds to thaw.

BEFORE 26 grams sugar ⟶ **AFTER** 15 grams sugar

coconut paletas

Makes 6 paletas

WHY THIS RECIPE WORKS We wanted a rich, creamy, and decadent frozen treat that was big on flavor but not on sugar. Using richly flavored coconut milk as our base, we added a small amount of honey for sweetness, vanilla extract for deeply nuanced undertones, and salt for balance. But tasters wanted even bolder coconut flavor. We immediately ruled out sweetened coconut, which is loaded with unnecessary sugar, and settled instead on unsweetened flaked coconut, which not only provided great coconut flavor but also gave our paletas a bit of textural contrast that tasters enjoyed. This recipe was developed using 3-ounce popsicle molds. Our favorite brand of coconut milk is Chaokoh; other brands may contain different amounts of sugar and fat, which will affect the overall flavor and texture of the paletas. Do not substitute low-fat coconut milk or the paletas will taste watery and have an icy texture.

2 cups canned coconut milk
3 tablespoons honey
1 tablespoon vanilla extract
¼ teaspoon salt
3 tablespoons unsweetened flaked coconut

1. Whisk coconut milk, honey, vanilla and salt together in large liquid measuring cup to dissolve honey and salt. Stir in flaked coconut.

2. Divide coconut mixture evenly among six 3-ounce molds. Insert popsicle stick in center of each mold, cover, and freeze until firm, at least 6 hours or up to 5 days. To serve, hold mold under warm running water for 30 seconds to thaw.

BEFORE 28 grams sugar ⟶ **AFTER** 10 grams sugar

horchata paletas

Add ½ teaspoon ground cinnamon and ⅛ teaspoon ground cloves to coconut mixture in step 1. Substitute 3 tablespoons toasted sliced almonds for flaked coconut.

BEFORE 28 grams sugar ⟶ **AFTER** 10 grams sugar

coconut, lime, and cardamom paletas

Add 2 teaspoons grated lime zest, 1 tablespoon lime juice, and ½ teaspoon cardamom to coconut mixture in step 1.

BEFORE 28 grams sugar ⟶ **AFTER** 11 grams sugar

striped fruit popsicles

Makes 6 popsicles

WHY THIS RECIPE WORKS Multicolored popsicles are fun and festive, but store-bought versions are loaded with sugar, corn syrup, and artificial colorings—and their lackluster flavor leaves something to be desired. To make an ultraflavorful, naturally sweetened version that would please kids and adults alike, we started with two kinds of berries. We settled on honey as our sweetener since it tasted great paired with the berries and wouldn't mar the bright colors we were after. We made a vibrant red raspberry puree for one layer; a blueberry puree made for a beautifully contrasting purple layer. For the middle layer, we aimed for a clean-looking white to make the red and purple stand out. We tested several bases, including buttermilk, cream, and lemon. Tasters felt the buttermilk's tang distracted from the clean fruit flavors of the other layers, while lemon alone was too tart even when tempered by the honey. In the end, using a little bit of cream along with the lemon juice created the perfect balance of flavor and texture. A small amount of water in each layer ensured that the popsicles froze solid. For clean, well-defined stripes, be sure to let each layer freeze completely before adding the next layer, and be careful not to spill the mixture onto the sides of the popsicle molds when pouring. This recipe was developed using 3-ounce popsicle molds.

raspberry layer

- 4 ounces raspberries (¾ cup)
- ¼ cup water
- 1 tablespoon honey
- Pinch salt

lemon layer

- ¼ cup water
- 3 tablespoons heavy cream
- 4 teaspoons honey
- 1 tablespoon lemon juice
- Pinch salt

blueberry layer

- 4 ounces blueberries (¾ cup)
- ¼ cup water
- 1 tablespoon honey
- Pinch salt

1. FOR THE RASPBERRY LAYER Process all ingredients in food processor until smooth, about 1 minute. Using 1-tablespoon measuring spoon, carefully pour 2 tablespoons of raspberry mixture evenly into six 3-ounce popsicle molds, being careful to keep walls of molds free from drips. Cover molds and freeze until firm, about 4 hours.

2. FOR THE LEMON LAYER Whisk all ingredients together in bowl. Using 1-tablespoon measuring spoon, carefully pour 2 tablespoons lemon mixture into each popsicle mold. Cover molds tightly with double layer of aluminum foil. Push popsicle stick through foil into center of each mold until tip hits frozen raspberry mixture. Freeze until firm, about 4 hours.

3. FOR THE BLUEBERRY LAYER Process all ingredients in food processor until smooth, about 1 minute. Using 1-tablespoon measuring spoon, carefully pour 2 tablespoons blueberry mixture into each popsicle mold. Cover molds with foil and freeze until solid, at least 6 hours or up to 5 days. To serve, hold mold under warm running water for 30 seconds to thaw.

BEFORE 18 grams sugar ⟶ **AFTER** 12 grams sugar

NUTRITIONAL INFORMATION FOR OUR RECIPES

Analyzing recipes for their nutritional values is a tricky business, and we did our best to be as realistic and accurate as possible throughout this book. We were absolutely strict about measuring when cooking and never resorted to guessing or estimating. And we never made the portion sizes unreasonably small to make the nutritional numbers appear lower. We also didn't play games when analyzing the recipes in the nutritional program to make the numbers look better. To calculate the nutritional values of our recipes per serving, we used The Food Processor SQL by ESHA Research. When using this program, we entered all the ingredients, including optional ones, using weights for important ingredients such as flour and sweetener(s). We also used all of our preferred brands in these analyses.

Note: Unless otherwise indicated, information applies to a single serving.

	Cal	Fat	Sat Fat	Sodium	Carbs	Fiber	Sugar	Protein
MUFFINS, QUICK BREADS, AND BREAKFAST TREATS								
Blueberry Muffins	240	9g	6g	320mg	33g	1g	11g	4g
Anise–Poppy Seed Muffins	240	10g	6g	300mg	32g	1g	11g	5g
Coconut-Cashew Muffins	400	24g	14g	310mg	42g	3g	16g	7g
Bran Muffins	210	7g	4g	240mg	32g	4g	13g	5g
Harvest Muffins	280	13g	4.5g	260mg	37g	3g	12g	5g
Cherry-Almond Muffins	290	13g	5g	300mg	36g	3g	11g	7g
Banana–Trail Mix Muffins	280	15g	7g	330mg	32g	3g	8g	4g
Blueberry Scones	360	23g	14g	410mg	32g	1g	9g	5g
Chai Oat Scones	380	24g	15g	250mg	33g	2g	5g	6g
Banana Bread	280	12g	5g	230mg	37g	2g	12g	6g
Date-Nut Bread	360	18g	7g	270mg	42g	3g	18g	7g
Pumpkin Bread	290	16g	2.5g	350mg	31g	2g	11g	6g
Cardamom-Spiced Zucchini Bread	310	13g	1.5g	350mg	41g	3g	13g	8g
Crumb Cake	340	16g	10g	170mg	42g	1g	13g	6g
Honey-Almond Coffee Cake	460	24g	12g	440mg	52g	3g	23g	9g
Monkey Bread	400	11g	7g	320mg	68g	2g	25g	7g
Cinnamon Buns	390	14g	9g	470mg	59g	2g	22g	8g
Honey Buns	400	21g	9g	135mg	46g	2g	21g	6g
Apple-Cinnamon Danish	110	4g	1.5g	135mg	21g	2g	14g	1g
Granola with Almonds, Apples, and Cherries	290	16g	1.5g	95mg	31g	5g	11g	7g
Granola with Coconut, Blueberries, and Macadamia Nuts	320	21g	4g	70mg	30g	5g	10g	4g

	Cal	Fat	Sat Fat	Sodium	Carbs	Fiber	Sugar	Protein
COOKIES AND BARS								
Chocolate Chip Cookies	210	10g	6g	170mg	28g	1g	15g	3g
Oatmeal-Raisin Cookies	200	9g	5g	70mg	27g	2g	13g	3g
Peanut Butter Cookies	130	7g	2g	160mg	14g	1g	8g	4g
Fudgy Chocolate Cookies	120	5g	3g	115mg	16g	1g	9g	2g
Molasses Spice Cookies	210	9g	5g	125mg	29g	1g	14g	3g
Lemon–Poppy Seed Cookies	70	3.5g	2g	55mg	9g	0g	5g	1g
Coconut Washboards	80	4.5g	3g	35mg	9g	1g	3g	1g
Almond-Cardamom Thins	70	4g	2g	25mg	7g	0g	2g	1g
Pecan Shortbread Cookies	80	4g	1.5g	35mg	9g	0g	3g	1g
Spiced Shortbread	170	10g	6g	75mg	16g	1g	3g	2g
Holiday Cookies	100	5g	3.5g	20mg	12g	0g	5g	1g
Graham Crackers	70	2.5g	1.5g	65mg	9g	1g	2g	1g
Almond Biscotti	100	4.5g	1.5g	55mg	11g	1g	3g	3g
Hazelnut-Orange Biscotti	100	5g	1.5g	55mg	10g	1g	3g	2g
Pistachio-Spice Biscotti	90	4.5g	1.5g	55mg	11g	1g	4g	3g
Granola Bars	180	12g	2.5g	50mg	13g	2g	5g	4g
Pomegranate and Nut Chocolate Clusters	80	6g	2g	0mg	6g	1g	4g	1g
Mango and Nut Chocolate Clusters	80	6g	2.5g	0mg	7g	1g	4g	2g
Cherry and Nut Chocolate Clusters	80	6g	2g	0mg	7g	1g	4g	2g
Honey Blondies	200	12g	6g	90mg	23g	1g	13g	3g
Maple Pecan Bars	210	16g	6g	120mg	14g	1g	6g	2g
Fig Bars	130	7g	3.5g	80mg	15g	2g	6g	2g
Honey-Lemon Squares	170	11g	6g	70mg	17g	0g	9g	3g
Strawberry-Chamomile Streusel Bars	180	10g	5g	75mg	20g	1g	7g	2g
CAKES								
Chocolate Layer Cake	680	48g	22g	410mg	63g	5g	39g	8g
Chocolate Sheet Cake	510	36g	16g	310mg	47g	4g	29g	6g
Chocolate Cupcakes	340	24g	11g	210mg	31g	3g	19g	4g
Maple Layer Cake	530	35g	12g	310mg	49g	0g	28g	6g
Maple Sheet Cake	400	26g	9g	230mg	37g	0g	21g	4g
Carrot-Honey Layer Cake	480	33g	12g	420mg	41g	2g	23g	6g
Carrot-Honey Sheet Cake	360	25g	9g	320mg	31g	1g	17g	5g
Red Velvet Cupcakes	240	15g	9g	170mg	21g	1g	11g	4g
Strawberry Cupcakes	240	15g	9g	250mg	23g	1g	13g	3g
Pumpkin Cupcakes	270	19g	6g	260mg	22g	1g	12g	4g
Easy Vanilla Frosting	270	23g	15g	60mg	14g	0g	14g	0g
Half-Batch Easy Vanilla Frosting	270	23g	15g	60mg	14g	0g	14g	0g
Easy Coffee Frosting	270	23g	15g	60mg	14g	0g	14g	0g
Easy Almond Frosting	270	23g	15g	60mg	14g	0g	14g	0g
Easy Coconut Frosting	270	23g	15g	60mg	14g	0g	14g	0g
Creamy Chocolate Frosting	250	21g	13g	35mg	17g	1g	14g	2g
Half-Batch Creamy Chocolate Frosting	250	21g	13g	35mg	17g	1g	14g	2g

	Cal	Fat	Sat Fat	Sodium	Carbs	Fiber	Sugar	Protein
Honey Cream Cheese Frosting	200	17g	11g	115mg	10g	0g	9g	2g
Half-Batch Honey Cream Cheese Frosting	200	17g	11g	115mg	10g	0g	9g	2g
Maple Cream Cheese Frosting	200	17g	11g	115mg	8g	0g	7g	2g
Maple Whipped Cream	120	11g	7g	30mg	4g	0g	4g	1g
Half-Batch Maple Whipped Cream	120	11g	7g	30mg	4g	0g	4g	1g
Chocolate Pound Cake	370	23g	14g	260mg	37g	3g	19g	6g
Chai-Spiced Pound Cake	400	19g	11g	270mg	48g	1g	18g	7g
Summer Peach Cake	290	15g	9g	280mg	30g	1g	16g	4g
Berry Snack Cake	250	11g	7g	230mg	32g	1g	13g	4g
Apple Cake	340	17g	11g	320mg	42g	3g	18g	4g
Pear Upside-Down Cake	310	20g	6g	140mg	29g	3g	19g	5g
Honey-Rosemary Polenta Cake with Clementines	340	16g	10g	260mg	44g	3g	15g	6g
Chocolate Cherry Almond Torte	310	25g	11g	100mg	23g	4g	15g	6g
Honey-Oat Bundt Cake	310	10g	6g	350mg	51g	1g	25g	6g
Spiced-Citrus Bundt Cake	400	17g	10g	320mg	53g	1g	25g	6g
Chocolate Pudding Cake	380	21g	13g	360mg	45g	4g	23g	7g
Mocha-Mascarpone Jelly Roll Cake	370	27g	15g	170mg	27g	1g	17g	7g
Blueberry Cheesecake	360	29g	17g	290mg	19g	1g	16g	7g
PIES AND TARTS								
Apple-Pear Pie	530	21g	13g	380mg	79g	9g	34g	6g
Peach Pie	430	21g	13g	370mg	55g	4g	19g	7g
Blueberry Pie	440	23g	15g	340mg	53g	4g	13g	6g
Roasted Sweet Potato Pie	430	23g	14g	390mg	46g	4g	16g	7g
Summer Berry Pie	300	15g	8g	170mg	42g	5g	24g	3g
Dark Chocolate Cream Pie	640	54g	31g	250mg	39g	3g	24g	8g
Lemon Cream Pie	510	38g	22g	220mg	37g	1g	26g	6g
Banana Cream Pie	510	34g	20g	250mg	44g	2g	24g	7g
Coconut-Lime Cream Pie	520	42g	28g	240mg	31g	1g	18g	6g
Blueberry–Lemon Curd Tart	420	23g	13g	150mg	49g	2g	27g	6g
Pear and Almond Tart	450	27g	11g	190mg	48g	5g	25g	7g
Caramel-Nut Tart	560	38g	15g	290mg	48g	3g	26g	9g
Fresh Fruit Tart with Mascarpone and Honey	380	24g	15g	90mg	36g	2g	16g	4g
Apple, Goat Cheese, and Honey Tart	400	23g	15g	210mg	39g	2g	20g	9g
Fig, Cherry, and Walnut Tart	470	26g	12g	105mg	46g	5g	23g	6g
Peach-Blackberry Free-Form Tart	350	19g	12g	210mg	40g	3g	12g	5g
Pear-Ginger Free-Form Tart	420	19g	12g	260mg	57g	6g	23g	5g
FRUIT DESSERTS								
Apple Crisp	410	16g	8g	110mg	66g	8g	41g	5g
Cherry-Hazelnut Crisp	450	27g	9g	250mg	46g	6g	28g	6g
Peach-Raspberry Crumble	390	18g	8g	150mg	53g	8g	28g	6g
Peach Cobbler	370	15g	9g	370mg	55g	5g	30g	6g
Strawberry Shortcakes	620	38g	23g	510mg	61g	4g	22g	8g

	Cal	Fat	Sat Fat	Sodium	Carbs	Fiber	Sugar	Protein
Blueberry-Walnut Buckles	320	20g	9g	220mg	31g	2g	15g	6g
Raspberry-Pistachio Buckles	320	19g	9g	220mg	32g	5g	12g	7g
Blackberry-Hazelnut Buckles	330	22g	9g	220mg	29g	4g	12g	6g
Pear Strudel	350	15g	6g	290mg	47g	5g	19g	5g
Apple Turnovers	100	3g	1g	100mg	18g	1g	13g	1g
Blueberry Turnovers	120	3g	1g	95mg	22g	2g	13g	2g
Cherry Clafouti	290	16g	9g	135mg	31g	2g	21g	6g
Summer Berry Gratin	120	4.5g	2.5g	105mg	21g	3g	16g	2g
Pineapple-Mango Fools	460	32g	17g	100mg	43g	4g	29g	3g
Chilled Maple-Glazed Oranges	170	6g	1.5g	100mg	31g	3g	26g	2g
Maple-Caramel Apples with Cinnamon Cream	230	14g	7g	100mg	26g	3g	21g	2g
Roasted Pears with Cider-Caramel Sauce	130	6g	2.5g	40mg	21g	3g	14g	1g

PUDDINGS, CUSTARDS, AND FROZEN TREATS

	Cal	Fat	Sat Fat	Sodium	Carbs	Fiber	Sugar	Protein
Dark Chocolate Pudding	370	29g	17g	160mg	27g	2g	20g	6g
Toasted Coconut–Banana Pudding	360	25g	17g	150mg	29g	2g	21g	5g
Maple Rice Pudding	280	11g	7g	210mg	38g	0g	19g	6g
Maple Flan	250	14g	8g	220mg	25g	0g	22g	6g
Strawberry Mousse	220	14g	8g	110mg	21g	3g	16g	3g
Chocolate-Hazelnut Semifreddo	240	19g	8g	40mg	15g	2g	12g	4g
Vanilla Frozen Yogurt	130	4g	2.5g	95mg	19g	0g	18g	5g
Strawberry Frozen Yogurt	140	4g	2.5g	95mg	21g	1g	19g	5g
Peach Frozen Yogurt	150	4g	2.5g	95mg	21g	1g	19g	5g
Raspberry Sorbet	90	0g	0g	85mg	20g	5g	15g	1g
Raspberry, Ginger, and Mint Sorbet	90	0g	0g	90mg	21g	5g	15g	1g
Mixed Berry Sorbet	80	0g	0g	85mg	19g	3g	15g	1g
Pineapple Sorbet	70	0g	0g	85mg	19g	1g	16g	0g
Piña Colada Sorbet	130	6g	5g	90mg	19g	1g	16g	1g
Fruit Punch Sorbet	70	0g	0g	85mg	18g	1g	16g	1g
No-Fuss Banana Ice Cream	140	6g	3.5g	80mg	22g	2g	12g	1g
No-Fuss Peanut Butter–Banana Ice Cream	160	7g	2.5g	110mg	24g	3g	13g	3g
No-Fuss Chocolate-Banana Ice Cream with Walnuts	250	16g	5g	80mg	26g	5g	12g	4g
Strawberry Granita	45	0g	0g	50mg	11g	2g	9g	1g
Strawberry-Lime Granita	45	0g	0g	50mg	12g	2g	9g	1g
Strawberry-Basil Granita	45	0g	0g	50mg	12g	2g	9g	1g
Strawberry Cream Paletas	140	8g	4.5g	55mg	18g	2g	15g	1g
Coconut Paletas	180	13g	12g	125mg	11g	0g	10g	1g
Horchata Paletas	180	13g	10g	125mg	12g	0g	10g	2g
Coconut, Lime, and Cardamom Paletas	180	13g	12g	125mg	12g	0g	11g	1g
Fruit Striped Popsicles	80	3g	1.5g	75mg	15g	2g	12g	1g

CONVERSIONS AND EQUIVALENTS

Some say cooking is a science and an art. We would say that geography has a hand in it, too. Flours and sugars manufactured in the United Kingdom and elsewhere will feel and taste different from those manufactured in the United States. So we cannot promise that the pie crust you bake in Canada or England will taste the same as a pie crust baked in the States, but we can offer guidelines for converting weights and measures. We also recommend that you rely on your instincts when making our recipes. Refer to the visual cues provided. If the pie dough hasn't "come together," as described, you may need to add more water—even if the recipe doesn't tell you to. You be the judge.

The recipes in this book were developed using standard U.S. measures following U.S. government guidelines. The charts below offer equivalents for U.S. and metric measures. All conversions are approximate and have been rounded up or down to the nearest whole number.

EXAMPLE

1 teaspoon = 4.9292 milliliters, rounded up to 5 milliliters

1 ounce = 28.3495 grams, rounded down to 28 grams

VOLUME CONVERSIONS

U.S.	METRIC
1 teaspoon	5 milliliters
2 teaspoons	10 milliliters
1 tablespoon	15 milliliters
2 tablespoons	30 milliliters
¼ cup	59 milliliters
⅓ cup	79 milliliters
½ cup	118 milliliters
¾ cup	177 milliliters
1 cup	237 milliliters
1¼ cups	296 milliliters
1½ cups	355 milliliters
2 cups (1 pint)	473 milliliters
2½ cups	591 milliliters
3 cups	710 milliliters
4 cups (1 quart)	0.946 liter
1.06 quarts	1 liter
4 quarts (1 gallon)	3.8 liters

WEIGHT CONVERSIONS

OUNCES	GRAMS
½	14
¾	21
1	28
1½	43
2	57
2½	71
3	85
3½	99
4	113
4½	128
5	142
6	170
7	198
8	227
9	255
10	283
12	340
16 (1 pound)	454

CONVERSION FOR COMMON BAKING INGREDIENTS

Baking is an exacting science. Because measuring by weight is far more accurate than measuring by volume, and thus more likely to produce reliable results, in our recipes we provide ounce measures in addition to cup measures for many ingredients. Refer to the chart below to convert these measures into grams.

INGREDIENT	OUNCES	GRAMS
Flour		
1 cup all-purpose flour*	5	142
1 cup cake flour	4	113
1 cup whole-wheat flour	5½	156
Sugar		
1 cup granulated (white) sugar	7	198
1 cup packed brown sugar (light or dark)	7	198
1 cup confectioners' sugar	4	113
1 cup Sucanat	5⅓	151
1 cup coconut sugar	4⅔	132
1 cup date sugar	6	170
Cocoa Powder		
1 cup cocoa powder	3	85
Butter†		
4 tablespoons (½ stick, or ¼ cup)	2	57
8 tablespoons (1 stick, or ½ cup)	4	113
16 tablespoons (2 sticks, or 1 cup)	8	227

* U.S. all-purpose flour, the most frequently used flour in this book, does not contain leaveners, as some European flours do. These leavened flours are called self-rising or self-raising. If you are using self-rising flour, take this into consideration before adding leavening to a recipe.

† In the United States, butter is sold both salted and unsalted. We generally recommend unsalted butter. If you are using salted butter, take this into consideration before adding salt to a recipe.

OVEN TEMPERATURES

FAHRENHEIT	CELSIUS	GAS MARK
225	105	¼
250	120	½
275	135	1
300	150	2
325	165	3
350	180	4
375	190	5
400	200	6
425	220	7
450	230	8
475	245	9

CONVERTING TEMPERATURES FROM AN INSTANT-READ THERMOMETER

We include doneness temperatures in a few of the recipes in this book. We recommend an instant-read thermometer for the job. Refer to the above table to convert Fahrenheit degrees to Celsius. Or, for temperatures not represented in the chart, use this simple formula:

Subtract 32 degrees from the Fahrenheit reading, then divide the result by 1.8 to find the Celsius reading.

EXAMPLE

"Cook caramel until it registers 160 degrees." To convert:

160°F − 32 = 128°
128° ÷ 1.8 = 71.11°C, rounded down to 71°C

INDEX

Note: Page references in *italics* indicate photographs.

d

e

f

g

h

n

t

u

V

Vanilla

Frosting, Easy, *138, 139*

Frosting, Easy, Half-Batch, 139

Frozen Yogurt, 270, *272*

W

Walnut(s)

Banana Bread, *48*, 49

Banana–Trail Mix Muffins, 40, *41*

-Blueberry Buckles, *234*, 235

Caramel-Nut Tart, 200, *201*

Cherry and Nut Chocolate Clusters, 108

Date-Nut Bread, 50, *51*

Fig, and Cherry Tart, *206*, 207

No-Fuss Chocolate-Banana Ice Cream with, 279

Pear Strudel, 236–37, 238

Pear Upside-Down Cake, 154, *155*

Pumpkin Bread, 52, *53*

Whipped Cream

Cinnamon Cream, 252, 253

Maple, 143

Maple, Half-Batch, 143

White chocolate

about, 20

favorite brand, 20

Honey Blondies, *110*, 111

Y

Yogurt, Frozen

Peach, 271

Strawberry, 271

Vanilla, 270, *272*

Z

Zucchini

Bread, Cardamom-Spiced, 54, 55

shredded, removing moisture from, 55